RETIRE ON YOUR OWN TIMELINE

The Essential Guide to Building the Life and Wealth That Put You in Control of When You Retire

Finch Monroe

Retire on Your Own Timeline reflects the author's personal experiences, opinions, and editorial judgment. The book is informed by the author's academic background in psychology, independent study, including Financial Markets through Yale University and retirement planning through The American College of Financial Services. It also draws on established research, widely accepted retirement principles, and contemporary tools and resources. The author retained full creative and editorial control throughout the development of this work

This book is provided for educational and informational purposes only. It is intended to help readers understand financial and retirement planning concepts and identify topics they may wish to discuss with a qualified professional. It does not constitute legal, tax, financial, investment, or retirement planning advice and does not recommend the purchase or sale of any security or investment product.

Personal experiences, examples, opinions, and observations are included for illustrative purposes and should not be relied upon as a substitute for professional guidance based on a reader's individual circumstances.

Discussions of financial markets, securities, investments, retirement strategies, and historical performance do not predict or guarantee future results. All investing involves risk, including the possible loss of principal.

The information in this book reflects the author's understanding as of the date of publication. Laws, regulations, financial systems, tax rules, and retirement programs may change over time. Readers should consult qualified legal, tax, financial, investment, or retirement professionals before making decisions. Neither the author nor the publisher assumes liability for any loss, damage, or adverse consequence resulting from reliance on the information presented in this book.

Contents

Introduction

The transition from work to retirement is the single biggest pivot point of our lives. Yet because we're consumed by the demands of our careers and families, few of us give it the kind of focus it should receive if we want to be ready for the 30 to 40 years of retirement we'll fund without an employer paycheck. The truth is we'll spend hours planning a one-week vacation and yet avoid thinking about the decades we'll spend in retirement. A trip feels fun and urgent and easy to picture, so it grabs our attention. Retirement feels distant and complicated, so we push it aside, even though it matters far more. Because it doesn't feel immediate, we convince ourselves there's always time. Then one day we look up and realize the future is no longer something we can ignore.

My own journey began in the middle of a massive shift. I entered the workforce at a shaky moment in financial and retirement planning history, right as guaranteed pensions were evaporating and self-directed 401(k)s were taking their place. My generation became the test subject. We were handed the keys to our own retirement future while the instruction manual was still hot off the press and evolving in real time. I remember reviewing those early 401(k) enrollment forms trying to make sense of a system I'd never seen before. We'd call the benefits department for help, but it was hard to know what to ask because the whole thing was so new. And the internet was just beginning to appear in offices and homes, so even if helpful retirement information was out there, we didn't necessarily know how to find it. In many ways, we were on our own, doing the best we could with little guidance and limited information.

Like many of my peers, I navigated this complex new world with primitive tools, saving what I could and hoping that if I just put enough money away, the math would somehow work out. But over time, I realized hope wasn't a strategy. It was a gamble. I saw the writing on the wall. My company's role ended with offering the plan. Making it work was my responsibility.

That realization forced me to take a closer look at how retirement systems actually work in everyday life, not just how they're described in theory. I wanted to understand how the choices we make play out over time, so I immersed myself in retirement planning, building knowledge and practical experience to make more confident decisions. And as tools and technology improved, I used them to better understand possible outcomes.

Along the way, my focus widened beyond money alone. I came to see how financial stress, habits, and pressure can shape the choices we make. That changed how I thought about retirement. It became less about exact numbers and more about what would actually hold up in real life, which is why I focused on what was practical and realistic over the long-term.

I didn't come at this as an insider or a professional planner. I came at it as someone trying to make sense of the same uncertainty many of us are facing. This book brings those lessons together so you have a clearer path than I, and many in my generation, had. The focus is on something practical you can use, not abstract instruction or theory.

As I put these ideas into practice, I started to feel less uncertain. I paid less attention to the short-term noise of the stock market and more attention to whether my approach was resilient enough to hold up over time. I worried less about abstract what-ifs and more about whether my choices supported the life I actually wanted to live now and in retirement. It didn't happen overnight, but gradually the constant sense of doubt began to recede, and I felt more grounded and in control.

That sense of control is what *Retire on Your Own Timeline* is all about. It rejects the default plan where you're a passenger in your own life, working until a specific age or until you're forced to stop due to health issues or layoffs. Instead, you methodically build the structure that makes work optional, and execute on it. That way, your retirement isn't decided by a birthday or a pink slip. It's on your terms.

Retiring on your own timeline in the lifestyle you prefer comes down to being intentional. The pages ahead lay out how to do that, one decision at a time.

What you build from here is yours. Let's get to it.

How This Book Works

This book is meant to be used, not just read. Mark it up. Dog-ear the pages. Keep it on your nightstand next to a glass of water if that helps. Do whatever you need to do to put this book, and yourself, to work.

Each chapter ends with a list of actions because reading rarely changes much unless you actually do something. Those actions will walk you from defining the retirement life you want and the timeline you're working toward, all the way through retirement readiness and more.

The chapters build on each other in a deliberate order, so you'll likely get the most out of the book by reading it from start to finish. But hey, if you feel well versed on a topic in the book, you can skip it. No one's watching except for your bank account.

Here's the roadmap for what's covered as you enthusiastically move along from mapping your journey to getting ready for retirement.

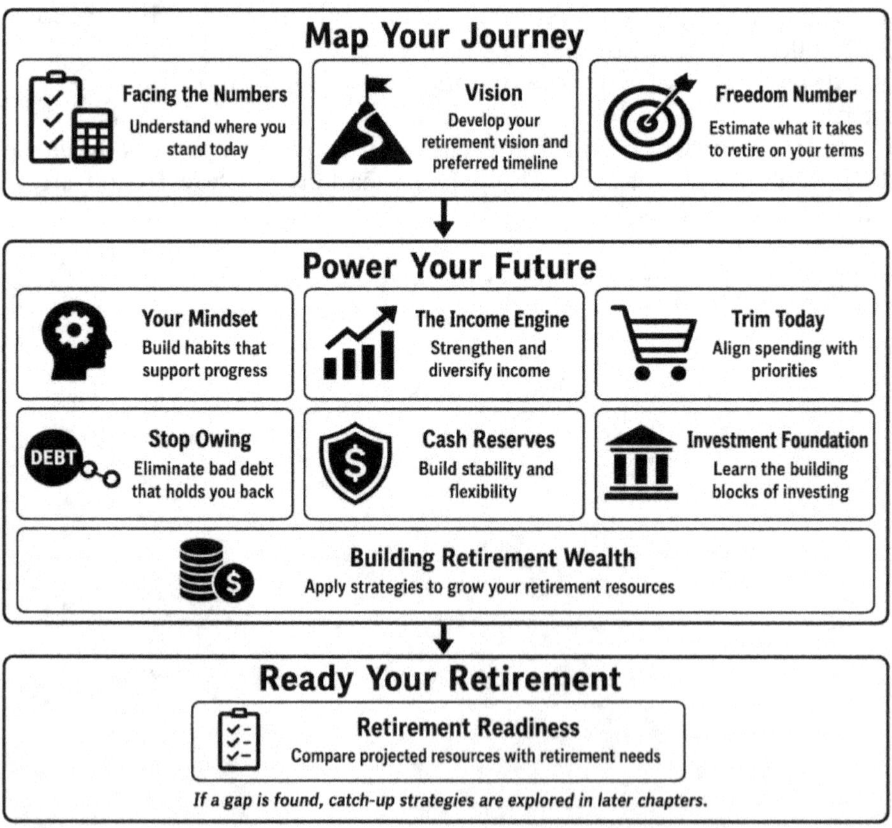

So as you can see, the first part of the book starts with where you are today and works its way toward retirement readiness. By then, you'll have taken a real look at your finances and built a clearer picture of the amazing retirement you want. You'll see which parts of your financial life are helping, which ones need work, and what you can do to strengthen them. And you'll check whether your projected resources can support the retirement you want.

The second part of the book starts with retirement income, because being ready is one thing, but knowing how the money will actually show up in your checking account once you retire is another. We'll look at how to turn your savings into a paycheck that comes from you, not from an overbearing boss.

Then we'll look at the alternate paths that may apply based on who you are and what your life looks like. There's also a landmines chapter, and it's a real reality check. It looks at the ugly things that can be lurking around the corner, just waiting to make life miserable, and how to avoid them. As we close, we'll look at how to protect what you've built so you can protect the people you love.

Nothing in this book replaces professional advice, and I'll annoyingly echo that throughout. The goal here is to help you understand retirement as a whole so you can ask better questions, make better decisions, and take the right actions at the right time. But you don't have to do that alone. The right professional team can make a real difference. If you don't have that team yet, this book will help you start building one.

Retirement on your own terms starts with the turn of the page.

1
Facing the Numbers

We can't map a route if we don't know where we're starting.

I know it's tempting to jump right into designing your ideal retirement, but that instinct skips a step. Before we get into goals, lifestyles, or timelines, we've got to understand the numbers. And looking at your own savings, income, and projections alone isn't enough, because retirement doesn't happen in a vacuum. Your choices matter, sure, but they're not the whole story. Retirement is also shaped by the economy, policy decisions, the benefits employers offer, and the fact that we're living longer than ever. Though some days, "living longer" can feel less like good news and more like a long-term test of our sanity.

As I mentioned in the introduction, the rules of retirement have changed dramatically over the past few decades. Traditional retirement planning was built around stable pensions, predictable career paths, rising real wages, and fewer years spent in retirement. Many of those foundations have disappeared. Healthcare costs have outpaced inflation for years, while more of the responsibility for retirement has shifted to the individual. Add higher debt and a system that assumes more financial know-how than most of us have time to build, and the gap creates real risk.

This chapter provides the context. We're taking an honest look at what retirement really looks like in the U.S. today. You'll see the economic pressures and broader shifts that have made preparing for retirement more difficult than it was for earlier generations. You'll also see why the approaches that may have worked for your parents or grandparents often don't work as well today, even when you're doing many things right.

You'll also see why retirement feels out of reach for so many today. The financial demands of modern life simply exceed what most households can absorb. Healthcare inflation, uneven wage growth, rising housing costs, and the slow erosion of employer benefits put constant pressure on long-term savings. And these aren't personal failings. They're systemic. Even the most responsible savers feel the squeeze and I've certainly experienced it.

Here's the good news. Once you see those pressures for what they are, you can make decisions with more context and plan with greater clarity. With a realistic view of where you're starting, you can begin building a retirement path that takes today's realities into account while still moving you toward security and peace of mind.

What the Numbers Show

I've got a lot of data and research coming your way, so you may want to stretch and hydrate before we get started.

Okay. Here we go ...

The retirement picture in the U.S. isn't as rosy as most of us would like to believe. A lot of households feel like they're on track, but when the numbers come into focus, the story gets a lot less comfortable. The gap between confidence and reality keeps getting wider.

The Federal Reserve's 2024 SHED report makes that uncertainty hard to ignore. Only about 33% of non-retired adults believe they're on track with their retirement savings. The rest either know they're behind or aren't sure where they stand. And while many of us have access to an employer-sponsored plan like a 401(k), access isn't the same as readiness. Some don't participate. Others contribute, but not enough for compounding to do the heavy lifting over a retirement that could last 30 years or more.

The account balances make the problem even clearer. According to Federal Reserve data, households ages 45 to 54 have a median retirement balance of about $115,000. For households ages 55 to 64, the median is roughly $185,000.

At first, $185,000 can sound like real money. And it is. But once you start asking what it can actually provide, the picture changes fast. Using the 4% Rule, a commonly cited withdrawal guideline we'll look at later in the book, that balance produces roughly $7,400 a year in income. That's less than $620 a month. After housing, transportation, groceries, healthcare, and the rest of real life show up, it's clear that amount doesn't come close to covering what most retirees need, even with Social Security serving as the floor for essential expenses.

That shortfall becomes even more serious when you factor in longevity. A long life is a gift, but it's also expensive. One in three Americans who reach age 65 today will live past 90, and one in seven will live past 95. That can mean decades of bills after the paychecks stop. And the national data makes one thing painfully clear. Most retirement portfolios aren't built for that kind of timeline.

Shifting Income Landscape

Before we look at the specific costs you'll face, we need to get clear on what actually pays for retirement.

For decades, retirement planning leaned on the famous three-legged stool: Social Security, employer pensions, and personal savings. But in today's economy, two of those legs have been weakened or sawed off almost entirely.

Social Security was designed as a safety net. It provides a base level of income protection, not a full retirement paycheck. Think of it as an inflation-adjusted annuity backed by the government. As of 2026, the average monthly benefit for a retired worker was just over $2,070. That baseline matters, but it's rarely enough to maintain a comfortable standard of living in most U.S. cities. For average earners, Social Security replaces roughly 40% of pre-retirement income, which leaves a pretty wide gap for other sources to fill.

In the past, pensions helped fill that gap. A worker could spend decades with an employer and retire with the promise of a monthly check for life, while the employer carried the investment risk. As I mentioned earlier, that model has mostly disappeared from the private sector. Recent data shows that only about 14% to 15% of private industry workers have access to a defined benefit pension. The burden has shifted to defined contribution plans, such as 401(k)s.

Because Social Security covers only the basics, if that, and pensions have largely faded, personal savings has gone from a helpful supplement to a financial necessity. That's why the median retirement savings figure of $185,000 is so concerning. With no pension helping close the gap between a roughly $2,070 Social Security check and, for example, a $6,000 monthly lifestyle, personal savings may need to generate the remaining $3,930 per month.

That shift is what makes the chapters ahead so important. You're not just saving for extra money. You're building the paycheck that pensions once provided in retirement.

Hidden Costs of Retirement

Retirement planning often focuses on replacing your *current* paycheck. However, retirement expenses aren't just a continuation of your working expenses because they evolve. There are five specific costs that tend to explode as we age, which serve as silent budget killers if we don't plan for them. They are:

Healthcare Inflation

This is often one of the largest hidden costs in retirement. While general inflation often runs around 2% to 3% over time, medical costs have historically risen faster. That means the cost of staying healthy can increase more quickly than the cost of many everyday necessities. Even with Medicare, healthcare can remain a major expense in retirement. Fidelity estimates that a 65-year-old couple may need roughly $345,000 to cover healthcare expenses throughout retirement. That estimate includes Medicare premiums and out-of-pocket medical and prescription costs, but *excludes* long-term care, dental care, vision care, and over-the-counter medications. Remember that long-term test of your sanity? This is one of the reasons why.

Long-Term Care

Most of us will need some level of assistance at some point, including help with bathing, dressing, getting in and out of bed, or other daily activities. Since Medicare doesn't cover long-term custodial care, we are responsible for planning and paying for those costs. And here's the shocker. Private-pay home care or assisted living can easily run $60,000 to $120,000 a year, depending on where you live. And these aren't always end-of-life expenses. They can show up suddenly after a stroke, a fall, or one bad day you didn't see coming. Without a plan, a single health event can drain your savings fast.

The point of laying out these costs isn't to scare you. It's to replace vague assumptions with a more realistic picture of what retirement may require. Retirement isn't a permanent vacation. It's a long phase of life, and over time, that life can bring changing needs, new challenges, and rising expenses.

Inflation Over Time

Inflation is the force that quietly reduces purchasing power over time. Even modest inflation has a significant long-term impact, especially over 30 to 40 years of retirement. A useful way to visualize this is the Rule of 72, which estimates how long it takes for prices to double by dividing 72 by the inflation rate. Hang with me here. I know this can feel a bit dry.

If inflation averages 3.5% (72 ÷ 3.5), prices will double in roughly 20 years. If you're 65 today, a lifestyle that costs $60,000 could cost about $120,000 by the time you're 85.

To understand why you need growth in your retirement portfolio, which we'll explore later in the book, look at what happens to $100,000 of purchasing power over time if it sits in an account that doesn't keep pace with inflation.

THE SHRINKING DOLLAR

What $100,000 in cash is worth over time, adjusted for inflation

Years in Retirement	At 3% Inflation	At 5% Inflation
Year 1	$100,000	$100,000
Year 10	$74,400	$61,300
Year 20	$55,300	$37,600
Year 30	$41,100	$23,100

Starting value: $100,000 held in cash with no investment growth

The numbers tell a clear story. Keeping your savings in an account that doesn't outpace inflation isn't playing it safe. It's guaranteeing a loss. In 20 years, that money will buy roughly half the groceries, gas, and medicine it buys today.

Social Security Tax Surprise

Many retirees assume their Social Security check is entirely tax-free. Often, it isn't. Once your income crosses certain IRS thresholds, part of your benefit can become taxable under federal income tax rules, and in some cases, up to 85% of your Social Security benefits may be included in taxable income. The calculation generally looks at your modified adjusted gross income, tax exempt interest, and half of your Social Security benefits. That can surprise new retirees who budget around the full benefit amount without realizing that taxes may reduce what they actually keep.

Housing Friction

Housing costs may drop once the mortgage is paid off, but homeownership still comes with ongoing expenses. Property taxes and insurance will likely remain part of your budget for the rest of your life, and both can rise over time. Lumpy expenses, which we'll talk about later in the book, can also be expensive.

Systems and structures still have to be maintained, repaired, and replaced. For example, HVAC systems and roofs wear out eventually. Some expenses show up all at once. Others are more predictable. If you retire at 60 and live to 90, there's a good chance you'll replace every major system in your house at least once during retirement, along with a hip or two.

Why So Many Fall Behind

Falling behind on retirement savings often reflects the reality that many families are carrying significant financial responsibilities that take priority, along with obstacles that make it harder to save consistently even when the intention is there.

One of the biggest pressures comes from being part of the sandwich generation, being squeezed between the needs of two generations at once. Many adults are helping aging parents financially or providing care while also raising children or helping pay for college. AARP estimates that family caregivers spend an average of $7,200 a year out of pocket on caregiving expenses, and that doesn't include the lost income that can come from cutting back hours or stepping away from work to help someone they love. Those are real financial tradeoffs, and they often come at the exact stage of life when retirement savings should be gaining momentum.

At the same time, wages haven't always kept pace with the rising cost of living. Real wage growth between mid-2024 and mid-2025 was only about 1% after inflation. When housing, education, and healthcare costs rise faster than paychecks, the margin for saving gets squeezed. Over the course of a working life, that squeeze can quietly turn into hundreds of thousands of dollars that never make it into a 401(k) or another long-term investment account. And I find that one particularly annoying.

Debt adds yet another layer of strain. Student loans and consumer debt have reshaped the financial lives of many households. Some borrowers carry student loan balances well into their 40s and 50s, with average balances for those ages 50 to 61 hovering around $45,000. Credit card debt reached nearly $1.3 trillion in 2025, and with interest rates often above 20%, even a modest balance can become difficult to escape. When debt payments compete with retirement contributions, saving for the future becomes hard even for those who are doing their best to be disciplined and responsible.

There's also the fundamental issue of the financial education many of us never received because formal schooling provided little or no training on how to handle money. That was certainly my experience. Thankfully, things are beginning to improve.

According to the Council for Economic Education's 2026 Survey of the States, 39 states now require students to take a personal finance course to graduate. But for previous generations, that number was effectively zero. Because we weren't taught the basics, we had to wing it. We learned through trial and error, and we often mimicked what our parents did even if their strategies no longer applied to our generation's economic reality.

Today, the problem has flipped. We've moved from having limited access to information to having too much information. The tools and data are finally available, but the sheer volume is overwhelming. If you search for "retirement investing" today, you're hit with thousands of conflicting articles and videos. Instead of finding answers, you often end up more confused than when you started. Faced with this complexity, many get stuck. We want to make the right choice, but without a clear path, doing nothing can feel safer than doing the wrong thing. In retirement planning, though, avoidance is expensive because financial mistakes made in our 30s and 40s are mathematically difficult to fix in our 50s. We can't get the time back.

When all of these financial pressures come together, saving becomes difficult for many of us. But when we see those obstacles clearly, we can stop viewing them as personal failings and start treating them as practical problems that can be solved.

Facing Your Own Numbers

If you want to retire on your own timeline, the single most important step you can take right now is to understand exactly where you stand. Everything that follows depends on your willingness to see the truth of your financial life with clarity.

Numbers aren't emotional, but the meaning we attach to them often is. That's why many of us delay this step for years. We guess. We hope. We avoid. But avoidance never leads to progress, while awareness does. It's time to look at reality. Even if you think you know where you stand, I encourage you to run these specific calculations again. Fresh data often reveals new insights.

Net Worth vs. Investable Assets

To create clarity, we'll focus on two numbers:

Net Worth: This is your total financial health score, which is assets minus liabilities. This includes your home and cars. It's good for seeing the big picture.

Investable Assets: This is your retirement engine. This number usually excludes your primary home because you can't sell your kitchen to buy groceries. This is the liquid capital that will generate income.

To calculate these accurately, you'll need a full audit. Don't guess. Log into every portal and pull the exact numbers. To get started, gather these details:

Retirement Account Balances: Check all accounts you hold, including 401(k), 403(b), 457, IRAs, Roth IRAs, and teacher or public-sector retirement systems.

Yearly Contributions: Note exactly how much you contribute to each account annually, both as a dollar amount and as a percentage of income.

Employer Match Details: Find the specific formula. How much does your employer contribute, and what percentage must *you* contribute to receive the full match?

Gross Income: List your total yearly income, including secondary sources or side work if it contributes meaningfully to your financial picture.

Savings Rate: Calculate the percentage of your gross income you consistently save or invest. For example, if you earn $70,000 and save $14,000, then your rate is 20%.

Pensions: Find the projected monthly payments for guaranteed income sources like defined benefit plans.

Social Security Estimate: Download your latest statement from SSA.gov to see your projected benefit at ages 62, 67, and 70. Crucially, review your earnings record for any zeros or missing years that could be corrected to increase your benefit.

Nonretirement Assets: List balances for brokerage accounts, high-yield savings, CDs, cash reserves, crypto holdings, etc.

Debts: List every liability, including mortgages, HELOCs, credit cards, student loans, medical debt, and car loans. You need the current balance and the interest rate for each.

From Here, Forward

When you step back and look at the documents and numbers together, the patterns start to show themselves. You'll see what you've built so far, where things are working, and where the pressure points are. And don't be surprised if your stomach has an opinion. Maybe you feel settled because things look better than expected. Or maybe you get queasy and want to crawl in bed. I get it. But hang in there. This could be one of those moments where a little discomfort is exactly the right medicine. Let it keep you going.

Now that you've gathered the facts, you're ready for the next step. Let's move into shaping your retirement vision and timeline so your numbers can start connecting to the life you're actually trying to build. Before we jump in, complete the actions for this chapter to get the ball rolling.

Chapter One Actions

Calculations (Complete this week)

[ ] **Calculate Total Net Worth:** Add up all your assets such as savings, investments, home equity, etc. Subtract all your liabilities such as debts. The result is your Total Net Worth.

[ ] **Calculate Investable Assets:** Add up *only* your liquid assets including retirement accounts, brokerage, and cash savings. This is the number that will generate your retirement income.

Analysis: What to Flag (Complete this week)

[ ] **Retirement Savings Rate:** If your savings rate is less than 15% of gross income, flag it. If it's under 10%, flag it as a high priority.

[ ] **Employer Match:** If you're contributing less than the amount required to receive the full employer match, flag it for immediate action.

[ ] **Yearly Contributions:** If your yearly contributions are inconsistent, lower than expected, or have not increased in several years, flag that.

[ ] **Pension and Social Security Income:** If your projected guaranteed income looks too low to support your retirement needs, flag it.

[ ] **Social Security Earnings Record:** If your earnings record shows missing years, zeros, or inaccurate income, flag it.

[ ] **Nonretirement Assets:** If too much of your money is sitting in cash or low growth accounts without a clear purpose, flag it.

[ ] **High Interest Debt:** If any debt carries an interest rate above 7%, flag it. If any revolving credit card balance carries a double digit rate, flag it as urgent.

2

Your Retirement Vision and Timeline

After looking at the numbers in Chapter 1 and understanding where you stand, the next step is to design a retirement vision and timeline that reflects the life you want to live. For many of us, this is the part we've never been encouraged to think about. We know what we want to retire *from* but not what we want to retire *to*.

A clear vision gives you something to aim for. It takes retirement from a fuzzy idea about "someday" and turns it into a life you can imagine and build toward. When you can picture what your ideal day looks like, what matters most to you, and the pace you want to live, the financial side becomes much easier to understand. You're no longer saving for an unknown future. You're creating a life with intention and purpose.

Along with the vision you have for your future, there's another very important element in creating your plan, and that's *your preferred timeline*.

Your timeline doesn't have to be dictated by a standard age, a government schedule, or anyone else's expectations. You can define it on your own terms, based on your values, your health, and your financial situation.

Three Seasons of Retirement

One of the biggest mistakes you can make is assuming retirement is a single, 30-to-40 year block of time where you spend the same amount of money every year. Retirement researcher David Blanchett described a pattern known as the Retirement Spending Smile. This concept suggests that retirement spending isn't a straight line. It starts high, dips in the middle, and curves back up at the end. Understanding these three distinct phases will help you build a more accurate vision and budget.

Active Years (Go-Go Phase)

This generally covers the first decade of your post-work life. It's the period where you finally have the time to pursue the interests you put on hold while building your career. Whether that involves travel, volunteering, or simply spending more time with family, this is typically the most active season of your retirement. Because of that activity, your discretionary spending often spikes as you explore your new freedom.

Routine Years (Slow-Go Phase)

Eventually, the novelty of travel wears off or energy levels dip. Retirees still enjoy life but settle into a comfortable routine. They might trade international trips for domestic road trips or trade expensive dinners for potlucks with friends. This is the bottom of the smile where spending typically drops and portfolios have a chance to recover.

Supported Years (No-Go Phase)

In the final phase, health becomes the primary focus. Mobility may be limited and spending shifts dramatically from lifestyle costs to care costs. While you spend less, or nothing, on travel, you spend more on medical services and assistance.

When you design your vision, ask yourself what you want to do in your active years while you have the energy to do them. Don't push your biggest dreams to age 80.

Retirement Archetypes

It can be hard to build a vision from scratch. To help you clarify what you want, consider these five common retirement archetypes. Most successful retirees align with one, or a hybrid, of these profiles.

Explorer (Traveler)

Your goal is to see the world. You want to spend 3 to 6 months a year in different countries or traveling by RV. This lifestyle requires a high discretionary budget during the Go-Go years and may involve meaningful trade-offs, such as downsizing a primary home to fund extended travel.

Creator (Artist/Maker)

You finally have time to paint, write, build furniture, or garden. You don't want to leave home. You want to go deeper into your craft. Your daily costs are low, but you may need a studio budget for supplies or a workshop renovation.

Ambassador (Volunteer)

You want to serve. You spend your days mentoring at-risk youth, helping care for newborns at a hospital, or sitting on nonprofit boards.

This is a low-cost, high-fulfillment path. However, you need to budget for giving if you plan to support these causes financially.

Entrepreneur (Encore Career)

You aren't tired of working. You're tired of corporate bureaucracy. You want to start a small business, consult, or turn a hobby into a profit center. You might not need to draw from your portfolio for several years. Your work funds your life, allowing your nest egg to compound longer.

Anchor (Family Pillar)

Your life revolves around grandchildren and family events. You want to be the hosting house for holidays and the available grandparent for childcare. You might need a larger home to host and a budget for family travel or contributions to grandchildren's education.

Impact of Your Home

As we'll explore more closely later in the book, your home plays a central role in how your retirement actually functions day to day. It affects how much time, flexibility, and energy you have, often in ways that aren't obvious at first. For many, the family home is a storehouse of memories, from cozy Thanksgiving dinners to those younger years when the kids routinely terrorized the dog. It can also be a source of ongoing costs and obligations. As mentioned, maintenance, property taxes, insurance, and physical upkeep don't disappear when work stops, and they can shape how freely you're able to use your time and resources.

If you chose the Explorer archetype but own a large, high-maintenance property, much of your time and energy may go toward upkeep rather than travel and new experiences. If you chose the Anchor, keeping a larger home may make sense because it supports your goal of hosting family, maintaining traditions, and staying rooted in one place. At a basic level, your home should make your chosen retirement easier to live, not harder.

Tuesday Morning Test

Research on retirement satisfaction points to something simple. Happiness in retirement usually has less to do with the big highlight moments, like travel, celebrations, or bucket list plans, and more to do with the quality of ordinary days. U.S. research on retirees' time use has found that active parts of daily life, such as socializing, walking, exercising, working, or volunteering, tend to bring more happiness than more passive routines like staying home or watching television. Other research using the American Time Use Survey shows that retirees spend much of their added time on ordinary activities like reading, relaxing, household tasks, meals, errands, and television. That helps explain why the rhythm of everyday retirement matters so much. And that's where the Tuesday Morning Test comes in. Picture a regular Tuesday, six months after you retire. Not a vacation day. Not a holiday. Not the first week when everything still feels shiny and new. Just a normal Tuesday.

What time do you wake up?

Who is the first person you speak to?

What is the "work" of your day?

How do you connect with others?

If your answer is *I'll figure it out*, you might not be quite ready. Before you hand in your notice, start building the routines, relationships, and support system that will help your retirement feel steady once work is no longer structuring your days.

Replacing Dopamine

Work fuels a critical biological reward system. It provides a steady stream of dopamine, the brain chemical associated with motivation, reward, and the satisfaction of making progress.

Think of it as your brain's way of saying, "good job." For decades, your career provided these small chemical rewards most days. You finished a project, you solved a problem, or you simply cleared your inbox. Each small win gave you a sense of competence and momentum. When you retire, that feedback loop diminishes.

For many, this sudden silence feels like a crash. Without those daily wins to signal that we're making progress, it's easy to feel listless, unanchored, or even slip into a situational depression. We might wake up feeling like we have no reason to get out of bed because there's no problem waiting for us to solve. That's why purpose needs to be part of your design. Consider having a goal to replace work with new challenges that keep that sense of satisfaction alive.

Research suggests that creating meaningful new roles, such as mentoring, can help replace some of what work once provided. Those roles can preserve purpose, structure, and social connection from the day you stop working through the years that follow.

Real-World Example

Conni, a former Boeing manufacturing engineer, retired in 2016 after decades with the company. Once the initial relief wore off, though, boredom started to creep in. She briefly returned to work part-time before realizing she didn't need more income as much as she needed more meaning.

Conni now volunteers with TAPS, the Tragedy Assistance Program for Survivors, a national nonprofit that supports families grieving the loss of a service member. In Oklahoma City, she started a local TAPS care group and serves as a peer mentor. The role restored her sense of purpose, and her experience was later featured in a 2020 Next Avenue article.

Partner Sync

A common challenge in retirement planning is the partner gap. For example, one partner may be ready to stop working at 62 and start traveling, while the other wants to keep working until 70 because they still love their career. When one person retires and the other doesn't, friction can build quickly. The retired partner may feel lonely or stuck, while the working partner may feel guilty or pulled in two directions. Over time, that mismatch can harden into resentment.

That's why it's so important to have a synchronization conversation early. The goal isn't to force the same retirement date. It's to understand each other's ideal timeline and plan intentionally for any gap between them.

Start with a simple, low-pressure question: "If money weren't an issue, when would you ideally want to stop working? And if our timelines are different, how do we want to design our days so we both feel fulfilled?" That question creates space for an honest conversation and helps you build a shared plan, even if your retirement dates don't line up perfectly.

Your Retirement Timeline Range

This step is central to designing a retirement that truly fits your life. You aren't locking yourself into a specific age. Instead, you're creating a flexible range that supports your vision. Your timeline consists of three ages.

Earliest Viable Age: The soonest you could walk away if you were laid off or had a health issue. This is your safety net.

Ideal Age: The age that feels aligned with your goals and energy. This is your target.

Latest Comfortable Age: The boundary where working longer would start to degrade your health or quality of life.

Visualize a triangle with your Ideal Age at the top, your Earliest Age in the bottom left, and your Latest Age in the bottom right. If the triangle is narrow (e.g., 64, 65, 66), your plan is rigid. You have very little room for error. If the triangle is wide (e.g., 55, 62, 68), you've built a resilient plan. You have options.

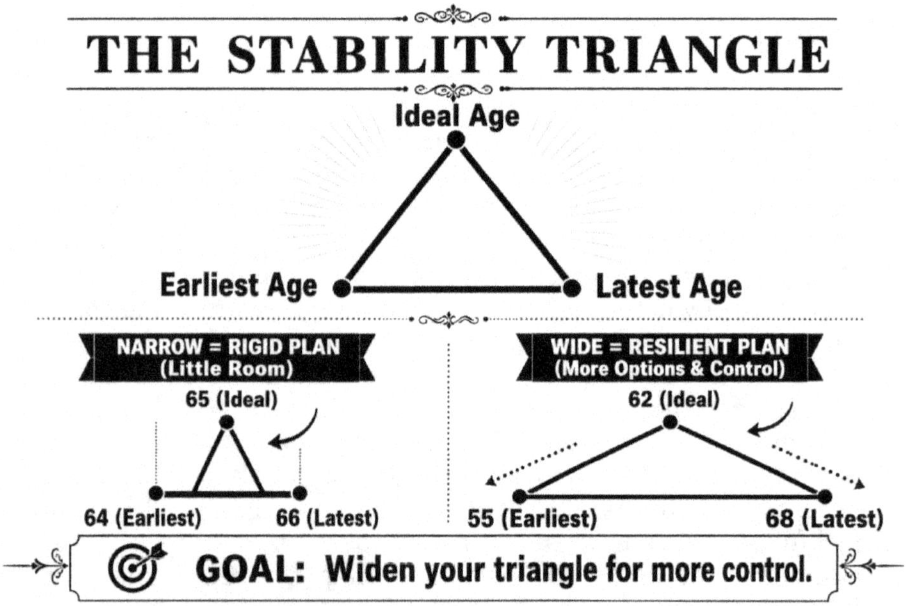

Three-Lane Roadmap

You can also view this as a highway with three lanes.

Fast Lane: This is your Earliest Viable Age. It requires aggressive saving and potential lifestyle cuts. It's for those who value freedom over luxury.

Cruising Lane: This is your Ideal Age. It balances saving with living well today.

Scenic Lane: This is your Latest Age. It allows you to spend more today because you're willing to work longer.

You can change lanes as your life changes. If you get a promotion, you might move into the Fast Lane. If you decide to pay for a child's wedding, you might shift to the Scenic Lane.

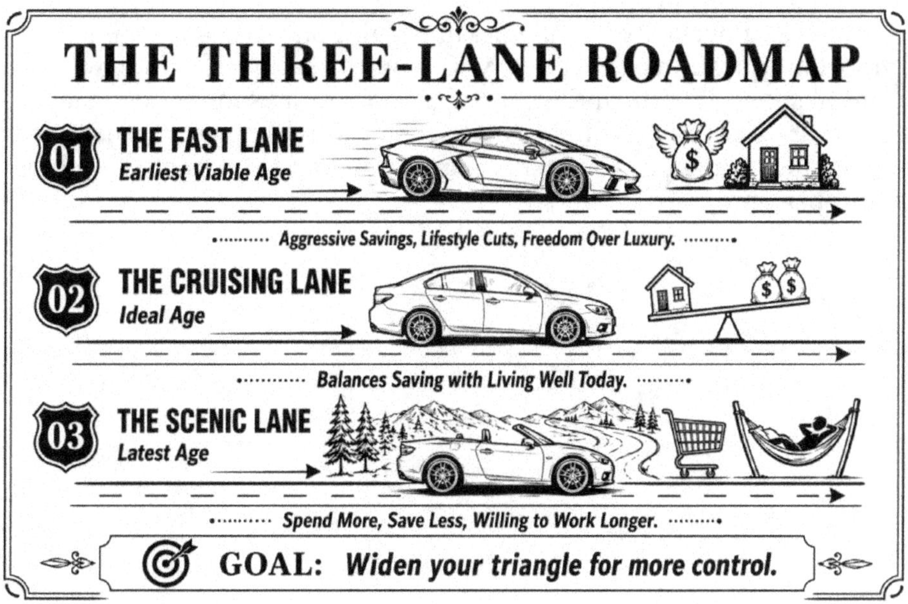

Defining Your Vision Statement

When you're ready, combine your vision and your timeline into a single statement. This will be your guiding compass moving forward. Here's an example:

I want a retirement centered around family and creative projects (the Anchor/Creator). I want my active years to include international travel while I am healthy. My ideal retirement age is 62, but I have a viable option at 58 if I downsize my home. My latest comfortable age is around 70. I will replace my work identity by serving on the board of the local food bank.

Now write yours, even if it's rough around the edges. You can refine it as you go.

Intention Over Chance

Retirement shaped by intention rather than chance starts exactly the way you've just approached it.

How you save, how you invest, and how you live your daily life will all connect back to the future you've defined here. The decisions you make from this point forward carry more weight because they're made with context and purpose.

That kind of clarity is quite meaningful. You've explored the important questions about how you want to spend your time, who you want to spend it with, and what will give your days meaning once you've freed yourself from the daily grind. Now the focus turns to what it will take financially to make it real. So in the next chapter, we'll put a number on it.

Chapter Two Actions

Vision Check (Complete this week)

[ ] **Pick Your Archetype:** Review the 5 Archetypes. Which one resonates with you? Write it down. This tells you where to allocate your budget.

[ ] **Environment Check:** Look at your current home. Does it support your Archetype? If it doesn't, make note of what you may want to change.

[ ] **Draft your Tuesday Morning:** Write down three specific activities you'll do on a random Tuesday morning in retirement. If you can't think of any, consider this an area that needs more thought before you move forward.

[ ] **Define Your Identity Bridge:** Identify at least one activity (hobby, volunteering, consulting) that will replace the sense of purpose and satisfaction you currently get from work.

Alignment and Timeline (Complete this month)

[ ] **Partner Sync:** If you're married/partnered, discuss your dates. If they are more than 2 years apart, brainstorm a plan for the gap.

[ ] **Define Your Seasons:** List major goals for your Active (Go-Go) years (e.g., Trip to Italy). Estimate the cost. This ensures you budget for the fun stuff.

[ ] **Draw Your Triangle:** Write down your Earliest, Ideal, and Latest ages.

[ ] **Practice Run:** Plan a 3-day weekend where you do none of your normal leisure activities (no TV, no shopping). Practice your Tuesday Morning routine to see if it feels fulfilling or boring.

Vision Statement (Complete this month)

[ ] **Vision Statement:** Combine your retirement vision and timeline to create your guiding compass.

3
Your Freedom Number

You've taken a snapshot of where you currently stand financially, and you've defined your vision of the retirement lifestyle and preferred timeline that are uniquely yours. Now it's time to bring those two things together and answer the question that sits at the center of every retirement plan. How much money will it take to fund the retirement you want?

That's where your freedom number comes in. It's the annual income you'll need to fund your preferred retirement. We'll walk through several ways to arrive at that estimate, from quick shortcuts to more detailed approaches, and we'll also talk about why a financial cushion should be part of your freedom number. We'll also do an initial readiness estimate so you can see where you stand today relative to the number you establish here.

Once you have your freedom number, the next step is learning how to reach it, strengthen it, and protect it. Whether you're just getting started or already well on your way, the work of growing and protecting what you've saved and invested never really stops.

From there, the Retirement Readiness chapter will take you through a deeper estimate that reflects the progress you've made. It will also give you a clearer picture of where you stand as retirement gets closer and as retirement itself unfolds.

One note before we get started. You'll notice this chapter doesn't include an action plan at the end, unlike the rest. That's because we've integrated the work directly into the chapter itself. So grab a pen or your laptop. You've got some fun and super exciting work to do here.

Retirement Spending Estimate

You can estimate your retirement spending using tools such as the AARP Retirement Calculator, Fidelity's Retirement Score, and Vanguard's Retirement Nest Egg Calculator, to name a few, which can factor in variables like inflation and longevity. I'll be referencing these and other tools as we go. You can also estimate manually, and we'll walk through several approaches so you can choose what works best for your situation. Each method has its own level of depth and precision, so wherever you are in the planning process, there's an approach that fits. We'll start with the most thorough of the bunch, the zero-based budget.

Zero-Based Retirement Budget

Although I leverage all of the methods we cover here and use various tools, this particular method is the one I lean on the most when calculating manually. I also use the information it produces to input into tools.

With this approach, you're starting from zero and building your retirement budget up from scratch, category by category, based on the life you actually plan to live and the expenses you anticipate you'll need to cover. Go through each one, assign a realistic number, and add them up. What you end up with is a retirement budget built around your specific life rather than a formula someone else designed.

This method takes more time than the others, but it produces an honest and personalized estimate. Financial experts tend to view it as the most thorough approach, particularly for those who want maximum clarity or whose retirement lifestyle will look significantly different from their life today. To help you get started, here's a comprehensive list of spending categories you can use as your guide:

Housing	Mortgage or rent, property taxes, maintenance, repairs, HOA fees
Food and groceries	Groceries, dining out, and everyday household staples
Utilities, phone, and internet	Electricity, gas, water, trash, mobile service, internet, streaming
Transportation	Car payments, gas, maintenance, insurance, public transit, rideshares
Healthcare	Medicare premiums, supplemental insurance, deductibles, prescriptions, dental, vision, and possible long-term care
Insurance other than health	Homeowners, renters, auto, umbrella, and life if still needed
Debt payments	Credit cards, personal loans, student loans, or any remaining balances
Travel and leisure	Vacations, hobbies, entertainment, clubs, and experiences
Gifts, donations, and family support	Charitable giving, gifts, helping children or grandchildren, and family assistance
Miscellaneous Spending	Clothing, grooming, subscriptions, small indulgences, and everyday extras
Lumpy Expenses	Irregular but important costs
Emergency reserve	Cash buffer for surprises and unplanned expenses
Taxes	Federal, state, and local taxes, depending on your situation

80% Rule

A common shortcut is the 80% Rule. Instead of building a budget from scratch, this method assumes you'll need roughly 80% of your pre-retirement income to maintain your lifestyle. The idea is that several expenses disappear in retirement, such as payroll taxes, retirement contributions, and work-related costs. It's a helpful starting point, but it can't capture personal lifestyle changes or healthcare needs that can skyrocket as you age, and it doesn't account for the fact that some retirees actually spend more in the early years of retirement, not less.

If you want a quick estimate without a lot of detail, apply the percentage to your current income and use that as your annual spending baseline. It won't be precise, but it'll get you in the ballpark fast.

Here's how it looks in practice:

Single earner making $75,000 a year: Applying 80% suggests an annual retirement spending target of roughly $60,000, or about $5,000 a month.

Married household earning $250,000 a year: Applying 80% suggests an annual retirement spending target of roughly $200,000, or about $16,667 a month.

These are simply starting point estimates. Your actual number will depend on your lifestyle, where you live, your health, and how you plan to spend your time in retirement.

Paycheck Replacement Method

This one's similar to the 80% Rule, but I find it more intuitive because it starts with your take-home pay rather than your gross income. After all, your take-home pay is what you actually live on. Your gross income is just a number on paper before taxes and benefits take their share.

Here's how it works. Start with your current monthly take-home pay and subtract the expenses that'll disappear when you stop working. Things like commuting costs, work-related clothing, and any debt payments you expect to have paid off by then. What's left is a pretty honest picture of your actual lifestyle cost and a solid starting point for your freedom number.

Here's how it looks in practice:

Single earner with a $75,000 gross income: After federal and state taxes and other deductions, take-home pay might be roughly $4,800 a month. Subtract $300 in commuting and work-related costs and you're looking at a retirement spending estimate of about $4,500 a month, or roughly $54,000 a year.

Married household with $250,000 in gross income: Take-home pay might be roughly $13,500 a month after taxes and deductions. Subtract $600 in work-related costs and you're looking at a retirement spending estimate of about $12,900 a month, or roughly $154,800 a year.

Income Replacement Ratio

While the Paycheck Replacement Method starts with your take-home pay, the Income Replacement Ratio works backward from your gross income, explicitly subtracting payroll taxes, retirement contributions, and work-related expenses one by one. The result is the same destination but a more transparent view of exactly what drops away when you stop working, which some find more clarifying. It's especially useful if you're within about ten years of retirement and want a more personalized estimate without building a full budget from scratch. This method won't account for lifestyle changes or healthcare cost increases in retirement, but it gives you a more personalized and grounded estimate than relying on a percentage alone.

Here's how it works. Take your gross income and subtract your retirement contributions, payroll taxes, and work-related expenses. What remains is a clearer picture of your true lifestyle cost.

Here's how it looks in practice:

Single earner making $75,000 a year: Subtract 10% in retirement contributions ($7,500), 7.65% in payroll taxes ($5,738), and $3,000 in work-related expenses. That brings the actual lifestyle cost down to roughly $58,762 a year, or about $4,897 a month.

Married household with one earner making $250,000 a year: Subtract 10% in retirement contributions, or $25,000, payroll taxes of approximately $15,064 based on the 2026 Social Security wage base limit of $184,500, and $8,000 in work-related expenses. That brings the actual lifestyle cost down to roughly $201,936 a year, or about $16,828 a month.

Your Annual Spending Estimate

Once you've selected your preferred estimation approach, whether that's the Zero-Based Budget, the 80% Rule, the Paycheck Replacement Method, or the Income Replacement Ratio, calculate your spending estimate and record it.

My annual retirement spending estimate: $___________

Lumpy Expenses

Now that you have a baseline spending estimate, there's one more layer to add before your annual number is complete. Many retirement methods assume smooth, predictable monthly spending, but real life doesn't work that way. Alongside your regular monthly expenses, there are larger, irregular costs that don't show up on a consistent schedule. They come in lumps, which is exactly why they're called lumpy expenses. If you leave them out, your estimate will fall short of what retirement actually costs.

Here's a list of common lumpy expenses to get you started. It's not exhaustive, and your list may look different depending on your lifestyle and circumstances, so think carefully about what applies to your specific situation.

Home Ownership

- **Roof** — It'll likely need replacing every 15–20 years ($15,000+).
- **HVAC Systems** — Furnaces and AC units fail every 10–15 years ($8,000+).
- **Appliances** — Washer, dryer, fridge, and dishwasher will all fail eventually ($4,000+).
- **Special Assessments** — If you live in a condo or HOA, you may be hit with a surprise bill for shared repairs ranging from a few hundred to thousands of dollars.

Technology

- **Hardware** — Laptops, tablets, and phones become obsolete every 4–6 years. Technology doesn't stop in retirement, and neither does the cost of staying current.

Transportation

- **Vehicle Replacement** — Even with a paid-off car today, you'll likely need to buy 2–3 more vehicles during a 30-year retirement, depending on how much you drive.
- **Major Repairs** — Transmission failures, battery replacements for hybrids and EVs, and other significant repairs can add up quickly.

Family & Lifestyle

- **Wedding Contributions** — Do you plan to contribute to a child's or grandchild's wedding? This is one of the most common unplanned expenses retirees face.
- **Once-in-a-Lifetime Trips** — That anniversary cruise or European tour isn't in your monthly grocery budget. Plan for it intentionally.
- **Pet Emergencies** — A single surgery for a dog or cat can cost $3,000 or more, often with little warning.

Health Maintenance Gap (Not Covered by Medicare)

- **Dental Work** — Implants, crowns, and root canals are expensive and generally not covered by Medicare ($3,000+).
- **Hearing Aids** — A quality pair costs $2,000–$6,000 and typically needs replacing every 5–7 years.
- **Vision** — Glasses, contacts, and cataract surgery copays are ongoing costs that add up over time.

Once you've identified the lumpy expenses that apply to your situation, the next step is putting a number on them.

Lumpy expenses don't all follow the same timeline, so one of the most accurate way to estimate them is to use a blended approach that accounts for both near-term and longer-term costs.

Start by listing the large expenses you can reasonably expect in the next ten years, such as a roof, HVAC system, major appliance replacements, vehicle replacement, or technology upgrades. Add those estimated costs together and divide by 120 months. That gives you a monthly amount for expenses most likely to arrive sooner. Then separately estimate the longer term expenses likely to occur over your full retirement, such as replacing vehicles multiple times, future home repairs, major out of pocket medical costs, or accessibility upgrades. Add those up and divide by the number of months in your expected retirement horizon, whether that's 30 or 40 years. Add both monthly figures together and multiply by 12. That's the annual amount to add to your retirement income target.

Here's how it looks in practice:

If you expect $30,000 in near-term expenses over the next ten years, such as a new roof, an HVAC replacement, and technology upgrades, dividing by 120 gives you $250 a month. If you estimate another $72,000 in longer-term expenses over a 30-year retirement, such as vehicle replacements, future home repairs, and major out-of-pocket medical costs, dividing by 360 gives you $200 a month. Together that's $450 a month, or $5,400 a year to add to your freedom number.

Your Annual Lumpy Expense Total

Once you've worked through your lumpy expense calculation using the blended approach outlined above, record your annual total.

My annual lumpy expense total: $___________

Healthcare Costs

Healthcare is one of the most important numbers to get right in your freedom number calculation, and one of the easiest to underestimate. As we covered earlier, healthcare inflation has historically risen significantly faster than general inflation, which means these costs can grow much more quickly than the rest of your retirement budget over time. I experienced this firsthand as my copays increased more than 275% in just the past few years. It's frightening to see how quickly those costs are increasing. I suspect you've experienced similar increases as well.

On top of that, what you'll pay depends heavily on when you retire and how your income is structured, making it one of the more complex variables in the entire estimate. At a minimum, your estimate should account for the cost of coverage before Medicare begins, what Medicare itself will actually cost you once you're eligible, and how your income in retirement may affect both. Premiums, deductibles, out-of-pocket maximums, and supplemental coverage all factor in, and they can add up quickly. The right number will vary based on your age, location, health status, and how your retirement income is structured.

Here are a few ways you can go about estimating:

- Visit healthcare.gov to price ACA plans based on your projected retirement income and location. This gives you a real-world estimate of what pre-Medicare coverage might actually cost.

-Visit medicare.gov to estimate Part B and Part D premiums, and research the cost of supplemental coverage like Medigap or Medicare Advantage plans in your area.

-Use a benefits calculator such as the Kaiser Family Foundation Health Insurance Marketplace Calculator, which can help estimate ACA premiums and subsidies based on your income and household size.

-Work with a health insurance broker who specializes in retirement coverage. A good broker can compare options across carriers and help you understand how your income choices in retirement affect your premiums.

-Ask your financial planner to incorporate healthcare costs into your broader retirement plan. This is especially important for understanding how income decisions affect both ACA subsidies and Medicare surcharges.

We'll cover a few healthcare hacks later, but for now, the goal is simply to make sure your freedom number includes a realistic healthcare estimate. And while you're estimating those costs, don't forget long-term care.

Your Additional Annual Healthcare Costs

Once you've estimated your additional retirement healthcare costs, including any pre-Medicare coverage and Medicare related expenses not already captured in your spending estimate, record your annual total.

My additional annual retirement healthcare costs: $___________

25x Rule and Adjustments

A common method that many financial professionals support for manually calculating an estimate is the 25x Rule, which is derived from the Trinity Study. The study suggests that a retiree with a diversified portfolio can withdraw 4% of their starting balance in the first year of retirement and adjust for inflation each year after that, with a high probability of the money lasting 30 years. The 25x Rule works backward from that. If you can safely withdraw 4% of a portfolio each year, then you need 25 times your estimated annual retirement expenses to make it work.

It's not a one-size-fits-all approach. Depending on your situation, you may need to adjust the multiplier upward for various reasons.

Retiring Early or Planning for a Longer Retirement: If you're planning to retire before full retirement age, or if you want to plan all the way to age 100, your money may need to last 40 or even 50 years. A 4% withdrawal rate that works well over 30 years becomes riskier the longer retirement stretches. Dropping to 3.3% or 3.5% improves the odds considerably, but it also pushes the multiplier from 25 toward 30 or even 33. On $60,000 in annual expenses, that's the difference between a $1,500,000 freedom number and roughly $1,700,000 to $1,800,000. Keep in mind that these figures assume your portfolio is funding retirement entirely on its own. If you have guaranteed income sources like Social Security or a pension and choose to factor them in, they can meaningfully reduce what your portfolio needs to cover.

Your Investment Mix: If you prefer a more conservative investment mix, your portfolio may generate lower long-term returns and may not reliably support a 4% withdrawal rate. In that case your multiplier may need to move closer to 30x, 40x, or higher. Risk tolerance isn't just an emotional decision. It has a direct impact on how much you'll need to save.

Taxes on Withdrawals: If most of your savings are in pre-tax accounts like a Traditional 401(k) or IRA, a portion of every withdrawal will go to the IRS, meaning the balance you see isn't entirely yours to spend. Many planners account for this by increasing the multiplier from 25x to closer to 30x. If your savings are primarily in Roth accounts, the original 25x Rule works more cleanly since qualified withdrawals are tax-free.

Freedom Cushion

A common recommendation in the financial planning community is to apply a cushion of 10 to 15% on top of your freedom number once you've calculated it. Think of it as the margin that turns a technically correct number into a practically resilient one. Costs may surprise you even when you've done all the right things to anticipate them, so having extra wiggle room built in from the start is always better than discovering you need it later.

Freedom Number

Now it's time to bring it all together into one number. Walk through the steps below in order. Each one builds on the last, and by the time you reach the end, you'll have your freedom number.

Step 1: Annual Retirement Spending Record your annual retirement spending estimate from the estimation method you selected earlier.

My annual retirement spending estimate: $____________

Step 2: Lumpy Expenses Record your annual lumpy expense total from the calculation you completed earlier.

My annual lumpy expense total: $____________

Step 3: Additional Healthcare Costs Record your additional annual retirement healthcare costs from the estimate you completed earlier.

My additional annual healthcare costs: $____________

Step 4: Your Total Annual Retirement Income Target Add Steps 1-3 together. This is the total annual income you'll need in retirement.

My total annual retirement income target: $___________

Step 5: Apply the 25x Rule Multiply your total annual retirement income target from step 4 by 25. This is your baseline freedom number.

My baseline Freedom Number: $___________

Step 6: Apply Any Adjustments Review the three factors that can raise your number. Apply whichever are relevant to your situation.

If you're planning to retire early, consider multiplying by 30 or 33 instead of 25.

If you plan to invest conservatively, consider moving your multiplier toward 30x, 40x, or higher.

If most of your savings are in pre-tax accounts, consider increasing your baseline by roughly 20%.

My adjusted Freedom Number: $___________

Step 7: Add Your Freedom Cushion Add 10 to 15% to your adjusted freedom number to build in the margin that protects against the unexpected.

My Freedom Number with cushion: $___________

There it is. Whether you arrived at this number by working through each step manually or by running it through a planning tool, what you're looking at is your estimated freedom number. It's your North Star as we move forward.

Initial Readiness Check

Now that you have your estimated freedom number, let's see how your current financial picture stacks up against it. To run your initial readiness check, you'll need two things. First, your current retirement and investment account balances from the financial audit you completed in Chapter 1, which includes your 401(k), IRA, Roth IRA, brokerage accounts, and cash savings.

My current retirement and investment account balances:
$___________

Second, if you plan to include guaranteed income in your calculation, add together your estimated annual Social Security benefit, based on your preferred retirement date, and any other dependable annual cash flow you expect, such as a pension, income annuity, rental income, or business income, for example. Calculate the total twice, once including Social Security and once without it. The second figure shows how much of your annual retirement income target can be supported independently if Social Security benefits are reduced.

My total guaranteed annual income, including Social Security and other dependable sources, if applicable: $__________

My total guaranteed annual income, excluding Social Security: $__________

With that information, there are three ways you'll run this check. Choose the one that best reflects your situation and philosophy.

Scenario 1: Guaranteed Income Only

Compare the guaranteed annual income figure you want to test, including or excluding Social Security, directly to your annual freedom number.

My annual freedom number: $__________

My Scenario 1 result: $__________

A positive number means your guaranteed income meets or exceeds your freedom number. A negative number shows how much other resources, such as your investment portfolio, may need to contribute.

Scenario 2: Portfolio Only

This scenario looks at how your current retirement and investment account balances stack up against your freedom number on their own, without factoring in guaranteed income. Any guaranteed income you receive in retirement then becomes a buffer on top of an already self-sufficient plan.

My current retirement and investment account balances: $__________

My freedom number: $__________

My Scenario 2 result: $__________

A positive number means your current retirement and investment account balances already meet or exceed your freedom number. A negative number shows how much ground your portfolio still has to cover.

Scenario 3: The Full Picture

This scenario shows how close you are after counting both the guaranteed income figure you want to test and your current savings. First, subtract that figure from your annual freedom number. This shows how much your portfolio needs to provide each year. Then multiply that amount by 25 to estimate how large your portfolio needs to be. Finally, compare that target to what you already have saved.

For example, if your annual freedom number is $60,000 and you expect $24,000 a year from Social Security or a pension, your portfolio needs to cover $36,000 a year. Multiply $36,000 by 25, and your portfolio target is $900,000. If you already have $600,000 saved, you still need to build another $300,000.

My annual freedom number: $___________

Minus my total guaranteed annual income, including Social Security and pension if applicable: $___________

My annual gap: $___________

My annual gap multiplied by 25: $___________

My current retirement and investment account balances: $___________

My Scenario 3 result: $___________

A positive result means you're ahead of the target. A negative result means you still have a gap to close. Either way, now you know where you stand.

For some, this may be the first time your retirement wishes have been turned into an actual number. For others, it may confirm the target you already had or help refine the number you've been using. Either way, the value is the same. You now have a clear benchmark for the decisions ahead.

From here, we'll start strengthening your position with strategies designed to help you reach, or secure, your freedom number. First up is mindset, because it sits underneath every strategy that follows.

4
Your Mindset

Money decisions are rarely just about the numbers. The numbers matter, of course. They matter a lot. But there's a tempting little fantasy that once the numbers are clear, better decisions will naturally follow. Just show the numbers, make the spreadsheet look respectable, and surely everything will fall into place. If only.

If information alone were enough, we'd all be wealthy, debt-free, properly insured, and make excellent choices in the snack aisle. But that's not how it works. The challenge is to build a mindset and habits to actually do it.

Your mindset shapes every financial decision you make. It affects how you respond when life gets expensive, how you handle setbacks, and whether you believe lasting change is even possible. If your thinking is working against you, even the best strategy can fall apart. And if you don't trust yourself to follow the plan, the plan won't have much of a chance.

That's why this chapter starts with the aspect of finances that doesn't fit neatly in a spreadsheet. Before the numbers can work, your psychology has to be on board. Four levers help make that possible, and they are identity, safety, beliefs, and urgency. Think of them as the master switches for behavior. If one is stuck, progress slows. When all four are aligned, change becomes much more likely.

Lever 1: Identity

James Clear, author of *Atomic Habits*, argues that lasting behavior change begins with identity. In his view, real change doesn't come from focusing only on outcomes or even on habits in isolation. It begins at a deeper level with the way a person sees themselves. Someone who says, "I'm trying to save money," is treating change as a temporary act. Someone who says, "I'm a saver," is grounding that behavior in identity. That distinction matters because behavior is far more likely to stick when it feels consistent with who a person believes they are.

That same principle applies to retirement planning. Building a future becomes much harder when it's tied to an old self-concept. One helpful way to think about this shift is through the contrast between the consumer and the architect. It reflects a different way of seeing one's role in shaping the future.

Consumer vs. The Architect

A **Consumer** reacts to life. They spend what they have, hope for the best, and view money as something that disappears.

An **Architect** designs their life. They build structures (accounts, automations, plans) that support their vision. They view money as a raw material for construction.

There comes a point when growing retirement savings is no longer the only goal. The question becomes how those resources will support the life you actually want to live. That's where the identity shift comes into focus. The role is no longer consumer. It's architect. An architect gives money a job, directs it with intention, and uses it to support a life built on purpose.

Lever 2: Safety

Now that we know *who* we are, we should address *how we feel*. One of the top reasons some folks ignore their finances is fear.

Scarcity Mindset

Research by Princeton psychologist Eldar Shafir and Harvard economist Sendhil Mullainathan reveals the true cost of financial anxiety. Studies show that when we're preoccupied with money problems, our cognitive function drops significantly. That worry acts like a heavy background program running on a computer, consuming bandwidth we normally use for reasoning and decision-making. Psychologists call this the *scarcity mindset*. When our brains are focused on what we lack, our vision narrows. Long-term decisions feel impossible because our attention is pulled toward whatever feels most urgent in the moment. This is why intelligent, responsible folks sometimes leave mail unopened or avoid looking at their 401(k) statements. It's a psychological coping mechanism designed to conserve energy when we're overwhelmed.

Small Wins

Behavioral research shows that we can't take complex action when we feel unsafe. If you feel overwhelmed, your brain might freeze. The antidote to freezing is a small win. A small win is a micro-action that requires little effort but provides immediate feedback that you're in control. Simply logging into your bank account without fixing anything counts. You faced the situation and saw it clearly. Unsubscribing from one retail email list also counts. You made a small decision and reclaimed a bit of attention.

These tiny actions lower the threat level in your brain. They signal to your nervous system that you're safe and capable. Once your stress levels come down, your thinking clears, and you can handle the bigger tasks. But as we move from just getting started to actually building wealth, we run into a different kind of biological trap called *loss aversion*.

Loss Aversion

Research by Nobel laureate Daniel Kahneman and Amos Tversky (1979) found that the pain of losing $1,000 feels about twice as powerful as the pleasure of gaining $1,000. That response is rooted in survival instinct. For our ancestors, losing a week's worth of food could mean starvation, while finding an extra week's worth was simply a welcome bonus.

Our brains are still wired to respond that way today. This biological tendency is one of the main reasons retirement plans get abandoned. When the market drops 10%, the brain doesn't interpret it as a temporary correction. It interprets it as danger. The same fight-or-flight response that once helped us survive physical threats can now be triggered by financial losses. The sense of alarm we feel when our account balance falls is our biology reacting to a number on a screen as if it were a real physical threat.

When you understand loss aversion, you can look at a red screen that shows the market is dropping and recognize that your brain may be overreacting. It may tell you that you're in trouble, but market history suggests you're experiencing normal volatility. If you react to fear and sell, you can lock in losses. If you resist the impulse, you give your plan a chance to keep working.

Sunk Cost Fallacy

The final mental trap to manage is the sunk cost fallacy. It shows up when past investments of money, time, or effort start shaping decisions that should be based on the future. Once we've put something in, walking away can feel like admitting it was a mistake. But the money and time are gone. Staying on the same path won't bring either one back.

Think about an expensive club membership or a subscription you rarely use. You might hesitate to cancel because you're thinking about the initiation fee or the months of service you've already paid for. You tell yourself you need to keep going just to get your money's worth. But continuing doesn't earn the money back. That money is gone whether you use the service or not.

This glitch often shows up in situations that keep draining resources. You see it when someone holds on to a losing stock because they want to get back to even. You see it when someone keeps pouring money into a car that is clearly breaking down because they cannot let go of what they have already spent.

We've all been there. We stay in bad investments or keep repairing something that no longer makes sense because we're emotionally attached to what we've already sunk into it. But as architects, we don't focus on what was spent yesterday. We focus on what makes sense next. I had to practice thinking that way until it became a habit, and it made it much easier to let things go when they no longer served me.

A simple way to beat this fallacy is to ask one question: *"If I didn't already own this today, would I buy it right now?"* If the answer is no, then the fact that you bought it in the past is not a good reason to keep holding on. Cutting a loss doesn't mean you failed. It means you stopped the bleeding. Staying in a bad situation doesn't recover what was lost. It only puts more of your future at risk. Stepping away is often the strongest move you can make for your long-term plan.

Lever 3: Beliefs

We all operate on money scripts, which are unconscious beliefs about money usually formed in childhood. Psychologists like Dr. Brad Klontz have found that identifying yours is the first step to dismantling it.

Money Avoidance

Someone with a money avoidance script tends to believe that money is bad, that rich people are greedy, or that they don't deserve wealth. That belief often shows up in behavior such as ignoring financial statements, delaying planning, or even sabotaging success in order to remain "good" or uncorrupted. A healthier correction is to recognize that money is value neutral. It's simply a tool. Having it doesn't make a person greedy. It can make them more secure, more generous, and more capable of helping others.

Money Status

A money status script ties self-worth to net worth. When that belief takes hold, it often leads to overspending on cars, clothes, or home upgrades in order to signal success. The focus shifts from becoming financially strong to appearing financially impressive. The healthier alternative is to separate identity from assets and remember that true wealth is often invisible. It's found in what's in the bank, not in what's sitting in the driveway.

Money Vigilance

Someone with a money vigilance script tends to believe that disaster is always around the corner. That can lead to disciplined saving, but it can also create fear around spending or investing. Cash starts to feel safer than movement, even when inflation is quietly eating away at its value. The goal here isn't to eliminate caution, but to balance it. A cash reserve can help calm the anxiety, while the rest of the money can be given a clear job to do.

Money Worship

A money worship script is built on the belief that more money will solve everything and that there can never be enough. That belief can fuel workaholism, compulsive spending, or an endless chase for the next dopamine hit, all without producing real contentment. The correction is to remember that money buys options, not happiness. At some point, the question stops being how to get more money and starts becoming whether you can recognize when you already have enough.

Co-Architects

For those of us who are married or partnered, retirement is a shared project. Many relationships involve blending different styles such as a vigilant saver and a status spender. One wants to hoard every penny; the other wants to enjoy the fruits of their labor. The solution is a guilt-free allowance. Consider creating a budget where the household bills are paid from a joint account (ours), and each partner gets a separate account (yours and mine) with funds to spend however they like. The vigilant partner doesn't see the spending, and the status partner doesn't feel judged.

Hedonic Treadmill

To truly master your money scripts, you have to understand a psychological glitch called the *hedonic treadmill*. This shouldn't be confused with the hedonistic treadmill, which is exhausting for entirely different reasons. You've likely experienced the former. You buy a new car, and for the first few weeks, you feel like a million bucks. You love the smell of the leather and the shine of the paint. By month six, the newness has mostly vanished. You're still paying for the upgrade, but you're back to viewing it as just the car. The thrill has evaporated, yet the monthly payment remains.

The hedonic treadmill is our brain's built-in reset button. We're remarkably good at returning to a stable level of happiness regardless of what happens to us. Whether we get a massive raise or a flat tire, our brain eventually resets to its baseline state. While this is a powerful survival mechanism during hard times, it can be a disaster for our retirement plan if we're not paying attention. It creates a cycle where we're constantly chasing the next purchase for a temporary dopamine hit, only for the new normal to set in almost immediately.

You can see the treadmill at work when your internal dialogue starts focusing on the next thing you want. Thoughts like, "I'll finally be happy when the house is renovated," or "I'll finally be happy once I buy that luxury SUV," are signs the goalposts have started moving again.

Another major red flag is the upgrade itch. This happens when you have a perfectly functional item, but you start researching a newer version simply because it exists. Your brain has stopped caring about how well the object works and started craving novelty instead. If you don't catch this pattern, you'll spend your entire life trading future freedom for a series of temporary new car smells.

Recognizing the treadmill isn't enough; you'll need a system to interrupt the loop. As an architect, you don't rely on willpower to stop spending. You build structures that make it impossible for the treadmill to win. For example, when the urge to buy something non-essential hits, you're experiencing a chemical surge in your brain. Your logic is offline. To fight this, implement a mandatory 72-hour waiting period for any purchase over a specific amount, like $200. By the time the three days are up, the dopamine has faded. You're able to look at the item with your architect eyes and ask if it truly builds your vision or if it's just a distraction. Most of the time, you'll find you don't even want it anymore. It's the rule I personally follow, and it's proven far more reliable than willpower alone.

Another approach is the satisfaction audit. Once a month, look at your recurring expenses and ask if they still actually matter to you. If you're paying for a premium subscription, a club membership, or a high-end data plan that you haven't truly appreciated in months, you've adapted to it. That's the moment to cut the cost. Your happiness won't stay down for long because your brain is wired to reset to its baseline. Reclaiming that money provides a permanent increase in your long-term security instead of just feeding a habit you've already stopped noticing.

You can also introduce intentional friction. Modern marketing is designed to make spending as frictionless as possible. One-click ordering and saved credit card info are the treadmill's best friends. To avoid the trap, introduce friction. Remove your credit card info from retail websites and delete shopping apps from your phone. Making it harder to spend gives your logical brain the time it needs to realize you're about to make a status-based mistake.

Many things we buy are expensive and the satisfaction wears off fast. Once we see that, we're able to stop the waste. We aren't losing out when we step off the treadmill. We're just keeping our money where it actually works. Reclaiming that cash doesn't mean we're deprived. We've just realized the rush of a new purchase is temporary and we'd rather have the money.

Architects don't build for temporary thrills; we build for permanent security. By understanding the hedonic treadmill, we're able to look at a potential purchase and ask, "*Will I still care about this in six months?*" If the answer is no, you've just found a way to keep your money working for you. You're trading a temporary status spike for actual stability.

Lever 4: Urgency

Understanding money isn't the same as acting on it. We know we should save more, invest consistently, and plan for retirement, yet we often delay getting started or contribute less than we should. This isn't laziness but a quirk of how the human brain works.

Behavioral economists call it *hyperbolic discounting,* which is the brain's tendency to value immediate rewards much more than future rewards. To your primal brain, spending $100 on a nice dinner tonight feels real. Saving that $100 for 30 years from now feels abstract. It can feel like throwing money into a black hole. Because of this bias, starting tomorrow always feels easier than starting today, and saving a little less today feels easier than saving more. The problem is that these small delays quietly accumulate. Years pass, balances grow more slowly than expected, and eventually many of us realize we're further behind than we'd hoped. When that realization hits, the emotion that often appears is panic.

There's a critical difference between panic and urgency. Panic says, "I messed up, and it's too late." And while it may feel similar to what happens when you've had too many Diet Cokes and are stuck in traffic, financial panic is its own special little nightmare. It causes paralysis. It makes us avoid looking at our accounts or opening financial statements. Urgency says, "This matters, so let's go." Urgency focuses attention on the next small step. It turns worry into action. The goal is to create enough urgency that you start moving. The most effective way to do this is to make the first step small and automatic. Increase your retirement contribution by 1%. Set up an automatic transfer to your investment account every payday. Schedule a single hour this weekend to review your finances. You don't have to do it all at once. Take the first step and build from there.

A different kind of mindset hurdle can show up in retirement. After 30 or 40 years of teaching yourself that saving is good and spending is bad, it can be surprisingly hard to start withdrawing money, even when that was the goal all along. In retirement, the strategy changes. The plan is no longer just to save. It's to use what you built. Even so, some retirees feel real discomfort when they sell investments to pay for something like a vacation. They continue living far below their means despite having ample resources because they can't fully release the saver identity.

To move past this, it helps to reframe the role of money in retirement. Spending isn't the problem anymore. It's now the purpose. One practical way to make that shift is to automate a retirement paycheck. When money arrives in your checking account each month, it should feel like income, not a loss. The mindset shift is simple but powerful. This money isn't savings anymore; it's your salary.

We'll cover strategies for creating a retirement paycheck in Chapter 12.

Bridge to Action

The concepts in this chapter aren't meant to stay on the page. They're meant to influence how you think, decide, and act in real life.

I can say these concepts became far more real to me once I began incorporating them into my day-to-day life, and continue doing so. Using these concepts helped me slow down, respond with more intention, and make smart decisions. That sort of awareness can influence how money is handled, and how everyday choices are approached. It can interrupt old patterns and make room for a more mature and informed way of thinking.

Now it's time to put what you've learned into practice through awareness of your patterns and by looking for opportunities to incorporate a new way of thinking where it makes sense. Consider keeping adjustments small, practical, and consistent. Meaningful progress rarely happens all at once. It tends to happen through repeated action, one decision at a time, until the architect in you becomes the only version you know.

Chapter Four Actions

Audit (Complete this today)

[ ] **Claim Your Identity:** Write down the statement: *"I am the Architect of my financial life."* Put it somewhere you can see it.

[ ] **Identify the Block:** Write down the one emotion hindering you most. Is it shame ("I'm too far behind"), fear ("I'll lose it all"), or perfectionism ("I don't know the perfect plan")?

[ ] **Diagnose Your Script:** Which money script (Avoidance, Status, Vigilance, Worship) sounds like you? Identifying it helps you catch yourself when you start to self-sabotage.

Momentum (Complete this week)

[ ] **Money Date:** If you're married or partnered, sit down and ask: *"What is your earliest painful memory involving money?"* Use this as an icebreaker to start a dialogue about one another's money scripts and learn more about the experiences that shaped them.

[ ] **Take One Micro-Action:** Cancel one unused subscription, or move $100 or more to savings. Show yourself that movement is possible.

Maintenance (Complete this month)

[ ] **Curate Your Input:** If financial news makes you panic, unsubscribe. Stop watching cable money shows. Replace them with resources that focus on long-term strategy, not short-term fear.

[ ] **Practice Spending:** If you're a *super saver*, force yourself to spend $50 this month on something purely frivolous. Practice the feeling of drawing from your resources without guilt.

5
The Income Engine

You now have a deeper awareness of how your mindset can either support or stand in the way of your retirement goals. That awareness matters because the way you think about money shapes the choices you make, the risks you're willing to take, and the opportunities you allow yourself to pursue. But insight alone isn't enough. At some point, the plan needs fuel. The next step is learning how to put more power behind your plan so you can create greater momentum.

Much of the retirement advice out there focuses on playing defense. It urges us to cut back on everything from unused subscriptions to excessive coffee runs and treats frugality as the primary path to progress. That advice has value. Being intentional with spending creates discipline and clarity. But cutting back alone is rarely enough to build real wealth or reach retirement on your own terms. There's a limit to how much you can reduce. There isn't the same limit to how much you can earn.

A higher income gives you more to work with, which can make it easier to save consistently, invest more aggressively, and adjust when life doesn't go according to plan. It can also give you more flexibility, more resilience, and more choice in how you build toward retirement. Discipline and smart saving still matter, but without enough earning power, progress can remain frustratingly slow.

Many of us think of income as something fixed, provided by our employer as a non-negotiable. That was my mindset early in my career, but over time I learned that income isn't static when you're willing to push for more. With a solid strategy, it can be increased over time. You can earn more in your current role, make career moves that increase your value in the marketplace, and build additional streams of income outside your primary job. When you start to see income as something you can influence rather than something you simply receive, you empower yourself to build wealth and create the retirement life you want.

In the pages ahead, we'll focus on the income engine and how to make it stronger. You'll learn practical ways to increase your earning power and put your retirement plan on firmer ground. We'll begin with how to get more out of your current job, then explore strategic career pivots that can increase long-term earning potential, and finally look at side hustles and passive income streams that can add extra horsepower to your financial life.

Income Decision Framework

Before exploring ways to increase your income, it's important to understand which approach fits your life as it is right now. Not every option works for every season of life. Most income growth requires some combination of time, skill acquisition, and sacrifice, and often you'll need to lean more heavily on one than the others. Use this roadmap to decide where to focus first.

Path A: "I Need Cash Now" (Immediate Liquidity)
This path is best for anyone carrying high-interest debt or living without an emergency fund. The trade-off is high upfront sweat equity because you're trading hours directly for dollars. The focus is Strategy 3 below, service arbitrage. Driving for Uber, picking up jobs on TaskRabbit, or working overtime doesn't require new skills, just effort and consistency. It isn't especially scalable, but it can stop the bleeding and create breathing room fast.

Path B: "I Need a Career Correction" (Mid-Term Growth)
This path is best for anyone who feels stuck or capped in their current role. The trade-off is skill acquisition because you may have to learn before you earn. The focus is on Strategy 2, a strategic pivot. That may mean spending several months on certifications, trade school, or other targeted training, but the payoff can be a permanent jump in your baseline salary and a stronger long-term career trajectory.

Path C: "I Want Freedom" (Long-Term Wealth)
This path is best suited for those who have capital to invest and are ready to let their money work harder than they do. The focus is Strategy 4, passive or semi-passive income. The goal is to use existing resources to buy assets or build systems that generate income over time. The trade-off is patience. Returns tend to be lower in the early years but can compound significantly over a longer horizon, often making this one of the stronger long-term plays available.

Skills Audit

You can't choose the right income path without first understanding your raw materials. Before you ask for a raise, pursue a promotion, or start a business, take time to do a quick audit of your existing leverage. Start with a professional inventory. Identify the three tasks you do at work that earn you the most appreciation and give you the most satisfaction. These are often strong clues to your competence zones, the areas where your skills and value already overlap.

Next, do a market value check. Look up those same skills on sites like Upwork or LinkedIn Jobs and see whether people are willing to pay for them. This helps you separate personal interests from income producing strengths. Enjoying a skill doesn't automatically make it marketable, but when there is clear demand for it, you may have the foundation for a stronger income stream.

Finally, do a speed test. Ask yourself which of those skills could generate money within the next 30 days. Some skills are long-term plays that require additional education, credentials, or experience before they can pay off. Others can be put to work almost immediately with the tools you already have. If a skill only requires a laptop and initiative, it may be one of the fastest ways to start creating additional income.

Income Stack

It's important to understand that the four strategies we'll cover aren't separate paths. They work best as an interconnected system, with each one supporting and strengthening the others. In many cases, they build on each other in sequence. Your day job, for example, often provides the stability you need to cover your living expenses, pursue training for a new career path, or begin investing in income producing assets.

Side hustle income can also play an important role in funding your future. One of the smartest ways to use that extra money is to direct it into cash reserves and investments rather than folding it into everyday spending. In that sense, you're trading temporary effort for long-term equity. Some of these strategies can operate at the same time, but not all combinations are sustainable. It's often realistic to manage your primary job alongside a side hustle, but trying to launch a new career while also maintaining a side hustle can quickly lead to burnout. Becoming a burnt-out hustler is not the goal here.

With that in mind, let's walk through the strategies.

Strategy 1: Earn More Without Changing Jobs

Before you start looking for a new opportunity, consider maximizing the asset you already have, which is your current job. This is often the path of least resistance because you already understand the culture, the systems, and the key players. In many cases, the fastest way to increase your income is not by starting over somewhere new, but by becoming more valuable where you already are.

Before you negotiate for more, you need leverage. Earning more is rarely the result of asking alone. It comes from making your value undeniable. One way to do that is through skill stacking. It's difficult to be in the top 1% of one skill, but much more realistic to be in the top 20% of two complementary skills. That combination can make you far more distinctive in the marketplace. An accountant, for example, may be seen as interchangeable. But an accountant who is also a strong public speaker, strategic thinker, or relationship builder becomes much harder to overlook.

Another important factor is revenue proximity. The closer your work is to money coming into the business, the more valuable your role often becomes. If you're currently in a support function, look for opportunities to move closer to sales, client retention, product launches, or other areas tied directly to growth. Companies are often far more motivated to reward and retain those who help generate revenue.

Stretch assignments can create powerful leverage. Volunteer for the project no one else wants, especially when it addresses a problem leadership cares about. Early in my career, I made a point of taking on those kinds of assignments, and that became a key reason I was sought after for bigger opportunities later on. In many businesses, promotions and salary growth often follow the people who can step into complex problems, figure out what's going wrong, develop effective strategies to fix them, and then execute those strategies well. When you do that consistently, you become highly valuable and increasingly sought after. Just be careful not to take on too much. That's where I struggled, and without clear boundaries, burnout can become a real risk.

Salary Negotiation

We don't get what we deserve; we get what we leverage. Most of us are terrified of negotiation because we fear appearing greedy. But silence is expensive. An annual $5,000 raise isn't just $5,000. It raises your baseline for every future percentage-based raise and bonus. And if you invested that extra $5,000 every year at a 7% return, in 25 years you'd have more than $300,000 in additional retirement savings. It also might raise your lifetime earnings record, which can increase your monthly Social Security check for the rest of your life.

Building Your Case

You can't walk into your boss's office complaining about inflation and expect to get anywhere. That conversation has to be built on evidence.

One practical way to prepare is to create a simple document called a Wins Tracker. Every Friday, spend five minutes writing down one thing you solved, improved, or saved. Over time, this gives you a concrete record of your contributions and makes it much easier to build a credible case for higher compensation.

As you track those wins, focus less on effort and more on output. Companies don't pay for how hard something felt. They pay for revenue, efficiency, and savings. Saying, "I worked really hard on the project," is far less persuasive than saying, "I renegotiated the vendor contract, saving the department $12,000 annually." The stronger the metrics, the stronger the case.

Value Script

When it's time to make the ask, the framing matters. A raise request shouldn't be built around personal expenses like a mortgage or rising bills. Employers are focused on business value, not household budgets. A stronger opening is something like, "I've been tracking my performance over the last 12 months, specifically regarding Project X and Project Y." From there, the case can be tied to outcomes: "Through these initiatives, I helped the team save X hours and reduced errors by Y percent. Based on this return on investment and the current market rate for this role, I'd like to discuss adjusting my base salary to better reflect the value I'm delivering."

Handling No

If the answer is no, that doesn't mean the conversation is over. "No budget" often means no salary increase right now, not no flexibility at all. Compensation can also include a one-time performance bonus, additional paid time off, or a company-sponsored certification. It can also help to agree on a specific metric that, if achieved, would trigger a raise in six months. And putting that agreement in writing gives both sides a clear reference point for later discussion.

Income Boosters

Even when raises are frozen, income opportunities may still exist inside the organization. An internal transfer can trigger a salary review in a way that a routine annual review may not, especially in departments with larger budgets such as sales or engineering. For hourly workers, shift differentials for nights or weekends can sometimes increase pay by 10 to 15% immediately. Another option is to become the go-to expert on a specific piece of software, equipment, or machinery. When one person becomes uniquely valuable in solving a problem others can't, their leverage tends to grow with it.

Secret Accelerator: Networking

Income growth is 80% who you know and 20% what you do. The hidden job market is real. Many of the highest paying roles are never posted on job boards. They're filled through relationships, reputation, and referral long before the public ever sees them. I've experienced this personally throughout my career. I was never promoted because I applied for a posted role. Each time, someone reached out and invited me to step into the position. That's how much opportunity lives inside trusted relationships. To access it, you need a strategy.

Sociologists have found that the biggest career jumps usually come from weak ties, which are acquaintances, former colleagues, or friends of friends rather than your close circle. Your close friends know the same people and opportunities you do. Your weak ties open doors to new worlds.

Once a month, invite someone in a role you admire to grab coffee and share their career story. Use the conversation to learn how they made the move, what helped them succeed, and what advice they'd give someone starting out. Keep it brief, respectful, and focused on learning, not asking for a job. Professionals tend to enjoy sharing their experiences and offering guidance in a casual setting.

The real opportunity is often in the follow-up. After the meeting, send a brief thank you message. Then set a reminder for three months later to share a relevant article or a quick update on your progress. This simple habit can turn a one-time conversation into a real professional relationship. It shows you were listening and that you value their insight beyond a single conversation.

Strategy for Age 50+

There's a common belief that income growth stalls after age 50. It doesn't have to. The key is to lean into strengths like emotional intelligence and crisis management. These strengths are highly valuable, and they often grow stronger with experience.

One way to do that is by positioning yourself as a steady hand. Startups and chaotic companies are often full of energy but short on direction. Presenting yourself as a Project Manager or Operations Director who brings stability, structure, and calm can be a strong path to higher income. Another option is fractional leadership. If you have 20 years of experience in HR or finance, you may not need a full-time job to earn well. You can work as a fractional CFO or fractional HR Director for several small businesses at once. In some cases, that can mean fewer hours and a much higher hourly rate because you're selling deep expertise, not just time.

Consulting is another path worth considering. If you're retiring from a specific industry, stop giving your advice away for free and consider staying on as a consultant. You know how the business works, where the risks are, and what others may miss. Companies will often pay a premium to keep access to that kind of institutional knowledge.

Real-World Example

In a case study published on Behance, Thomas, a designer, described how he approached his performance review by demonstrating the value he was creating for the company. He highlighted the four new clients he helped bring in, shared before-and-after examples of his work, and explained how his contributions had both generated revenue and saved money. He also showed that his value extended beyond design alone.

The Behance case study explains that, as a former business owner, Thomas brought strategic experience the company had not fully tapped into. His preparation helped him secure a $10,000 raise, increasing his salary from $82,000 to $92,000. The company was so impressed that they asked him to help shape a future role that would make better use of his broader skills.

Strategy 2: Strategic Pivot

Sometimes the well is simply dry. If your industry is shrinking or your salary has hit its ceiling, avoid waiting it out and instead pivot. That pivot might mean leveraging your existing skills in a field that values them more highly, or it might mean developing an entirely new set of skills in a market that's hungry for them. Either way, you're not starting over from scratch. You're making a deliberate move toward higher ground.

It's the approach I took more than once throughout my career. As my skills and experience deepened, doors began to open, and I walked right through them and never looked back.

Option A: Skilled Trades Renaissance

While many of us rushed to get college degrees, a massive shortage developed in the skilled trades. These jobs are AI-resistant, can't be outsourced to overseas call centers, and often pay six figures without the student loan debt. A few examples:

Elevator Installers & Repairers: The hidden gem of the trades. These pros frequently earn over $100,000/year, often with strong union benefits.

Home Inspection: A perfect pivot for those with construction knowledge who want to save their backs. You get paid for your eyes and your expertise.

HVAC Technician: Climate control is a survival necessity. As infrastructure ages and temperatures rise, demand (and pay) for skilled techs is skyrocketing.

Electrician: The world is electrifying. From EV chargers to solar panels to data centers, we don't have enough electricians to wire the future. Experienced master electricians often out-earn corporate middle managers.

Option B: Corporate Pivot

If you've spent decades in an office, your soft skills, institutional knowledge, and professional maturity are more valuable than you may realize. A corporate pivot doesn't always mean leaving your company. Sometimes the highest leverage move is right where you already are, transitioning from a functional role into a leadership or executive position, or stepping into an emerging area like AI strategy or operations where your business experience is exactly what's needed. Companies are hungry for people who understand how the business actually works. A few examples of roles worth exploring:

Construction Management: You don't need to swing a hammer to build a skyscraper. The industry needs organized leaders to manage budgets and schedules. With a median pay over $107,000, it's a perfect way to leave the cubicle while keeping the white-collar paycheck.

Project Management: Project management is a smart pivot because every industry benefits from someone who can organize chaos and implement plans. You don't have to be an engineer to manage an engineering project. The real value comes from coordinating moving parts, keeping teams aligned, and driving work across the finish line. Earning a project management certification can help you pivot into a professional PM role and build credibility along the way.

Salesforce Administrator: This involves managing the customer database. It pays remarkably well, and certification takes months rather than years.

AI Prompt Engineer: Companies need professionals who can craft precise instructions for AI tools to produce optimal business outputs.

Jobs that require AI skills pay nearly 28% higher wages than their non-AI skilled counterparts. No coding required, just clear thinking and strong communication. Certifications are available and can be completed in a matter of months.

AI Strategy Consultant: Organizations pay premium rates for consultants who can develop AI implementation roadmaps, with salaries ranging from $160,000 to $300,000. Your industry expertise is the asset here, not technical skills. Companies need professionals who can bridge the gap between business needs and AI capabilities. Personally, I think most any play in AI is a smart move.

Job Search Attack Plan

If you decide to leave your current company to level up, approach the job search like a professional move, not a desperate one.

Start with your resume. Stop listing duties and start showing impact. No one cares that you were "responsible for sales." They care that you "increased sales by 22% year-over-year." Use numbers wherever you can. Metrics make your value easier to see and harder to ignore.

Your LinkedIn profile matters too. Recruiters use LinkedIn like a search engine, and if your profile doesn't include the right keywords, you may be invisible. Look at three job descriptions for the role you want and identify the words that show up again and again, such as Agile, P&L management, or Python. Then work those exact terms naturally into your headline and summary.

Your interview strategy should focus on solving problems, not just answering questions. When someone asks, "Tell me about a time you failed," structure your response using the STAR method: **S**ituation, **T**ask, **A**ction, and **R**esult. Describe the problem, explain your role, walk through what you did, and always end with the outcome. That final piece is what makes your answer memorable.

Strategy 3: Side Income Arsenal

If you want to accelerate or fortify your retirement timeline, a second income stream can help. It doesn't have to be huge. You're simply looking for a reliable stream of cash that fits your life.

Freelance Economy (Selling Skills)

If you have a professional skill, stop giving it away for free. Sell it directly. A few examples:

Upwork & Fiverr: The global marketplaces for writers, designers, and programmers.

Belay & Boldly: Specialized platforms for high-paid Virtual Assistants and bookkeepers.

Wyzant: Connects tutors with parents willing to pay premium rates for math or science help.

Service Arbitrage (Selling Labor)

These platforms connect you with local demand immediately. A few examples:

TaskRabbit: Great for those who are handy and can help with things such as furniture assembly.

Rover & Wag: The go-to platforms for pet sitting.

Uber/Lyft: Good for instant cash, but watch out for vehicle wear and tear.

Goods Economy (Selling Products)

If you can make, find, restore, or sell something people want, you can turn physical products into income. This includes handmade goods, custom items, vintage finds, clothing, collectibles, and everyday household items. Places to sell:

Etsy: The global marketplace for handmade goods.

Poshmark & Mercari: The best apps for flipping clothes and household items.

Real-World Example

According to *Business Insider*, Larry Lundstrom is a pastor in rural Arkansas who also does creative work on the side. In the article, he explains that while spending about 40 to 60 hours a week on his pastoral work, he also puts another 10 to 20 hours into side projects like PowerPoint pitch decks, logos, and websites. He said he uses AI tools like ChatGPT and Tome to help create pitch decks for businesses, and that the work has become a meaningful extra income stream. The article states he charges between $500 and $1,000 per deck, completes two to three decks a week, and can make up to $3,000 a week from that side hustle. He built a second income stream around a practical skill, packaged it in a way clients were willing to pay for, and did it without leaving his day job.

Strategy 4: Passive and Semi-Passive Income

There's no shortage of articles and videos online that list hundreds of passive income ideas. Many of them highlight the same well-known approaches, such as blogging, affiliate marketing, dropshipping, or selling digital downloads. Rather than cover those here, I'll focus on a few less commonly discussed examples that illustrate the broader principle behind passive income. I've explored many of these over the years and acknowledge there's a good bit of upfront work required, but real opportunity for higher income that the more commonly known ones don't always deliver according to my research.

In each case, the goal is the same, which is to create or acquire an asset that continues producing income after the initial work has been completed. Some of these streams can become largely passive over time, while others are better described as semi-passive and require occasional oversight. Either way, they help reduce dependence on trading a significant portion of your time for additional income.

Infrastructure Placement Assets

Some businesses make money simply by owning access points where transactions happen. As electric vehicles continue to grow in adoption, property owners are installing EV charging stations and collecting usage fees each time a driver plugs in. And no, I'm not referring to installing a station in your garage. Can you imagine? You'd purchase an appropriate lot zoned for such a station and ensure the infrastructure is available. All transactions happen automatically. ATM placement works similarly. You place a machine in a bar, convenience store, or event venue and collect a small fee each time someone makes a withdrawal, without being present for any of those transactions.

Equipment That Works While You Sleep

Certain types of equipment generate revenue automatically once placed in the right location. Automated car washes are a good example. Modern touchless systems can operate with minimal staffing, generating income during operating hours without requiring the owner to be present for every transaction. Ice vending machines follow a similar model. Outdoor automated machines sell bags of ice around the clock with minimal labor, turning a single investment into an ongoing revenue stream.

Intellectual Property Licensing

You create something once, and companies pay to use it repeatedly. Product design licensing works this way. A designer develops a product idea or prototype and licenses it to a manufacturer who handles production and distribution, while the designer receives royalties without managing operations. Educational licensing follows the same principle. Training programs or curriculum licensed to schools and organizations can generate recurring income long after the original content was created.

Revenue Share Investments

Instead of owning a full business, you provide capital and receive a portion of revenue. Franchise partnerships follow this model. You contribute the capital while an experienced operator runs the location, and you share in the returns without managing the day-to-day operation. Equipment financing deals work similarly. You purchase equipment for a business and receive a percentage of the revenue it generates, turning a capital investment into an ongoing income stream.

Placement and Access Businesses

These models earn money by controlling valuable locations. Specialty machine placement is one example. Photo booths, arcade machines, claw machines, or massage chairs placed in high-traffic locations generate revenue continuously, with the owner collecting proceeds from machines that work independently. And it's not just fixed locations. There's real opportunity in mobile placement as well. Photo booths, for example, are wildly popular at weddings and events. A family member was recently married and had a photo booth at the reception, and it was very popular with the guests. The owner dropped it off at the location for the contracted hours and picked it up when the event ended. Not a heavy lift in terms of time, but it does require capital and ongoing maintenance. Another option is storage space rentals. Platforms now allow homeowners to rent unused garages, driveways, or land for storage, turning underutilized space into a recurring income source.

None of these income streams are truly effortless. Every asset requires research, setup, and occasional management. But once established, the asset keeps working even when you're not. That's the core idea behind passive income. You stop trading a significant portion of your time for additional income.

Activating Your Income Engine

The four strategies are now on the table. Each one offers a different way to generate money, and none of them require permission. You can target one or more of the strategies that fit your skills, your risk tolerance, and your current season of life. For example, you can strategically pivot your career to a new industry leveraging your existing skills, or new ones, and at the right time build a passive income stream.

But none of that happens if you're stuck in a waiting mindset, and it's easy to get there. The conventional path (school, job, salary, retirement) is built around patience and compliance, not initiative. Most of us weren't taught to negotiate, build, or create. We were taught to show up to work, and then when it comes to a raise, we just wait. But waiting leaves our future in someone else's hands.

I learned that lesson firsthand when for personal reasons I had to relocate to a different state with significantly higher income taxes. I knew that if I did nothing, the company would do nothing, and my take-home pay would take a hit. And that was indeed the case when I got my first paycheck after the move, before I'd had the opportunity to address it. Fortunately, even though I was reactive about it rather than proactive, I was still able to address it to my benefit. I put my big boy pants on and went directly to my manager with a significant ask for an off-cycle raise to cover the increase in taxes. It was a long shot because off-cycle raises were notoriously difficult to get through, but he agreed and worked with HR to make it happen. Nobody was going to do that for me. I had to do it for myself and it worked.

That's exactly what the Income Engine is about. You take full control by recognizing that in the modern economy, income is not capped by a job title or a salary. It's only capped by an unwillingness to negotiate salary increases, develop new skills, and build assets. If that's been you, it doesn't have to stay that way.

Whether you negotiate a higher salary, train to become an electrician, pivot into the growing field of AI, or build a business that sells while you sleep, every dollar you generate is a soldier fighting for your freedom.

You now have the frameworks and the examples. The next step is action. It's time to turn the engine on.

Chapter Five Actions

Skill Audit (Complete this today)

[ ] **Inventory:** Write down your top 3 professional skills.

[ ] **Market Check:** Search Upwork or LinkedIn to see what those skills pay.

[ ] **Speed Test:** Identify which skill you could monetize within 30 days.

Career Audit (Complete this week)

[ ] **Market Rate Check:** Go to Glassdoor, Payscale, or Salary.com. Look up your job title in your city. Are you being paid at least the median rate?

[ ] **Start the Tracker:** Open a blank document on your phone or laptop. Name it Wins Tracker. Write down at least one win from this week (do this every week).

[ ] **Pivot Check:** Is there a blue-collar trade or a white-collar certification (like Project Management Professional certification) that could jump your salary by $10k+? Research the cost and time required this weekend.

Networking Attack (Complete this week)

[ ] **Identify Targets:** Find 3 people on LinkedIn or connect with acquaintances and co-workers who are in roles you're interested in.

[ ] **Send the Invite:** Use the approach from the Networking section to request a 15-minute chat.

[ ] **Update LinkedIn:** Add 3 keywords from job descriptions to your headline.

Side Hustle & Passive Test (Complete this month)

[ ] **Match the Platform:** Look at the Strategy 3 and Strategy 4 lists. Which platform fits your skill? Create a profile on Upwork, TaskRabbit, or Etsy if it's something you want to pursue.

[ ] **Asset Check:** Do you have a car, room, or equipment you aren't using? Check rental rates on Turo or Fat Llama.

Execute (Complete this month)

[ ] **First Launch:** Choose one specific action from the audits above and put it into motion. This might mean hitting send on your first Upwork proposal or officially applying for a certification program. The goal is to move from planning to participation.

[ ] **Weekly Pulse:** Schedule a 15-minute recurring appointment on your calendar for every Friday. Use this time to update your Wins Tracker and review your progress on your career pivot or side hustle.

[ ] **Adjustment:** At the end of each month, look at your results. If a specific outreach or platform isn't working, don't quit. Instead, tweak your script or your profile and try again. Consistency is the only way to ensure your plan actually reaches the finish line.

6
Trim Today, Gain Tomorrow

Our finances are often shaped less by big decisions and more by the spending choices we make every day. Habits have a way of sneaking in until we're just cruising through life on autopilot. When we slow down and look closely at our everyday spending, we often find that some expenses genuinely support the life we want, while others remain only because we've never questioned them. Once we notice that difference, choosing to redirect what no longer serves us becomes a practical decision rather than a sacrifice. The goal is to spend with intention so that money supports priorities instead of drifting away unnoticed.

Ramit Sethi, author of *I Will Teach You to Be Rich*, teaches a simple but effective philosophy that emphasizes spending generously on what matters most and cutting costs mercilessly on what isn't truly needed. If a monthly 90-minute massage is what keeps you sane, book it without a second thought if it fits your budget. But that kind of spending requires discipline everywhere else. It means canceling unused subscriptions, dropping the overpriced phone or internet plan, and cutting back on mindless takeout orders. Guilt-free spending is a reward, not a right. And as Sethi points out, it only comes after savings and investments have been automated.

Too often, money gets spread across a little bit of everything until nothing feels especially meaningful. Interest piles up on cars, clothes, and home decor just to maintain a lifestyle that was never fully questioned. The real cost isn't just the debt. It's the freedom being given up. Major goals, like retiring on a preferred timeline, get traded for interest payments and expenses that barely even register. Saving and investing become the leftovers instead of the priority. That's the script that needs to flip. It starts by cutting the filler.

In this chapter, we're going to use *expense flips* to turn monthly drains into monthly gains. These flips target the structural costs that quietly bleed your bank account, redirecting that cash toward goals that build real momentum like paying off debt, stacking cash, and investing. We're going after the recurring expenses that usually fly under the radar despite having the biggest impact on your wealth. By optimizing the big three (housing, transportation, and food) and untangling the complexity of insurance and debt, you'll have the cash to enjoy your life today while building a foundation for the future you want.

I recently reviewed my own expenses and cut hundreds of dollars from my monthly bills. My spouse was thrilled since I'm usually the one who spends more. Every cent I saved was flipped into our investments, monthly. It felt great to watch that money work for us instead of watching it vanish into autopilot expenses.

Before we get into the tactics of expense flips, let's look at a real-world example that shows exactly how these strategies can shift a financial life from just getting by to building substantial wealth.

The Martin Family

Mark (38) and Sarah (36) earn a combined household income of $115,000. Mark goes to the office four days a week, and Sarah works from home. Despite a good income, they felt constantly broke. They had $4,000 in credit card debt and little retirement savings outside of a small 401(k) match. So, they executed expense flips.

Their housing costs were bloated by unnecessary fees (PMI and missed exemption tax breaks), and their systems were inefficient. They were paying for internet speed they didn't need, carrying expensive cell phone contracts, and ignoring energy waste. They took the following actions to create substantial expense flip opportunities:

Mortgage & Taxes: They called their lender and removed their Private Mortgage Insurance (PMI) based on increased home value. They also filed their county Homestead Exemption.

Connectivity: They downgraded their internet speed to 300 mbps and switched both cell lines into a bundle with the internet provider.

Energy: They installed a smart thermostat and put their home entertainment center (TV, gaming console, soundbar, and streaming devices) on a smart plug to kill the phantom load.

Monthly Savings to Flip: $170 PMI + $50 Tax Savings + $45 Internet + $90 Cell Phones + $15 Energy. Total of **$370** to flip.

They had two cars. One was a paid-off sedan; the other was a large SUV with a $680 monthly payment that Sarah drove less than 6,000 miles a year to drop the kids at school and run errands. To enable an expense flip, they implemented a one-car strategy by selling the SUV. Mark drove the sedan to work after dropping off the kids, and Sarah used Uber/Lyft for the occasional conflict. They eliminated the payment, the full-coverage insurance, and the gas guzzling.

Monthly Savings to Flip: $680 Payment + $100 Insurance + $70 Gas/Maintenance. Total of **$850** to flip.

They were DoorDash dependent and ordered dinner delivery three times a week because they were tired. They also shopped at a premium grocery store without a list. To enable expense flips, they deleted delivery apps and switched to online pickup at a budget grocer (Walmart) and bought store brands.

Monthly Savings to Flip: Reduced dinner delivery/dining out by $350 + reduced grocery bill by $200. Total of **$550** to flip.

As a result of those actions, their total monthly savings reclaimed to flip came to **$1,770**, or **$21,240** per year. The Martin family didn't keep those savings in cash. Instead, they automated the process by investing the money into a total market index fund each month.

If they maintain that strategy for 20 years and earn an average annual return of 8%, they will contribute $424,800, earn roughly $619,000 in compound interest, and end up with a total account value of about **$1,043,000**.

By optimizing structural expenses and flipping that money into an investment vehicle, the Martin family can create a million dollar retirement portfolio without getting a raise, winning the lottery, or working a second job. They simply stopped paying for inefficiencies and started paying themselves.

Trim Today

Many of us are leaving money on the table without even knowing it. I've been guilty of it too. Income quietly slips out through expenses that were set up once and never questioned again. Housing, transportation, food, and insurance are where the real money hides.

The following strategies show exactly where to look and what to do about it. I've personally implemented every one of them with significant success, which is why I'm comfortable putting them in front of you.

Optimizing Housing Costs

Housing is the single largest expense in most household budgets, accounting for roughly a third of total spending according to the Bureau of Labor Statistics. Yet it's often treated as a fixed cost that can't be touched. Whether you own or rent, there are meaningful ways to lower those costs without packing a single box.

Homestead Exemption

In some cases, homeowners overpay property taxes simply because they never file for a homestead exemption on their primary residence, which reduces the home's taxable value. For example, a $400,000 home with a $50,000 exemption is taxed as $350,000. In states like Texas or Florida, this can save $500 to $1,000 per year. Some states also offer additional exemptions for homeowners age 62 and older, such as school tax reductions. Check your county appraiser's website to make sure you're receiving all eligible credits. That annual savings is your first expense flip. Put it to work.

Private Mortgage Insurance

If you put less than 20% down when you bought your home, you're likely paying Private Mortgage Insurance (PMI). Banks require this because they view low-equity borrowers as higher risk. This insurance protects the lender if you default, but it does absolutely nothing for you. Home values have risen historically fast in recent years. It's possible to already have 20% equity even without paying down much of the loan simply because the home has increased in value. Call the lender and ask for an appraisal. If the new value shows you own 20% of the home, they must remove this fee.

When that PMI charge disappears, don't let that money quietly get absorbed into your lifestyle. Make a note of the amount you used to pay each month. We'll cover investment options in Chapters 9 and 10, but for now, your job is simple. Treat that old PMI payment as money that still leaves your checking account, only next time it'll be going to your future instead of the bank.

Utility Audit

Some households treat utilities as fixed costs. They aren't. In fact, utilities are one of the most overlooked and negotiable categories in the entire household budget. We tend to obsess over shaving a few dollars off our electric bill while ignoring the far larger savings that come from choosing the right providers, negotiating rates, and eliminating silent drains. Finding real money here means shifting your thinking from consumer to household Chief Financial Officer. LEDs and smart thermostats are good, but they won't change your financial life. The following moves can, to a degree, if the expenses are flipped:

Internet and Cable Negotiation

This is a major opportunity that often gets missed. Your internet bill is one of the easiest and fastest recurring expenses to cut. Internet providers expect you to put your bill on autopay and forget about it. They quietly raise prices over time, especially for loyal customers. But keeping existing customers is far cheaper than acquiring new ones. And this gives you leverage.

Call your provider once a year and say something to the effect of: "I'm reviewing my monthly bills and I need to reduce my cost. I'm seeing lower offers from competitors. What promotions or loyalty discounts can you apply to my account today?" You don't have to threaten to cancel. The word "competitors" is enough.

Many households save $20 to $50 a month with a single 5-minute phone call. That's up to $600 a year for a conversation you can have while walking the dog. As soon as the monthly fee drops, redirect that amount every month as an expense flip.

Also consider downgrading your internet speed. There's a good chance your speed exceeds your need. A 1,000 mbps connection sounds impressive, but unless you're running a data center out of your living room, you'll never notice the difference between that and 200 or 300 mbps. The difference in price can be enormous.

That is exactly what I did. I contacted my provider and they immediately lowered my bill by $30 just for asking about available discounts. When I also reduced my internet speed, the price dropped even further, and I didn't notice any difference in service.

A word of caution though. Always review contract terms and check for early termination fees before switching providers to avoid unexpected penalties.

Phone Service Optimization

This is typically a fast win. It's easy to overpay for cell service when you assume the big carriers have the best deals. They don't. The big carriers own the networks. Smaller companies, called MVNOs, rent space on those same networks and resell it to you at half the cost. Mint Mobile, Visible, Cricket Wireless, and US Mobile run on Verizon, AT&T, and T-Mobile towers. You get the same coverage for a fraction of the price. A typical switch can save $40 to $80 per line every month. For a family of four, that's roughly $2,000 to $4,000 a year.

If you want to stay with a major carrier, at least remove the expensive add-ons like international roaming you never use or extra data you'll never consume. And a lower data tier may also save money, especially if Wi-Fi is used 90% of the time. For example, dropping from an unlimited plan to a lower tier could reduce the monthly bill by $20 to $40.

Electricity Provider Switch
In states like Texas, Ohio, Pennsylvania, and others with deregulated energy markets, electricity isn't a single fixed price. It's a product you can shop for and prices vary dramatically between providers. A 15-minute comparison can reduce your rate by 10–30%. If the electricity bill is $200 a month, a 15% reduction saves about $30 a month or $360 a year with no lifestyle change. The lights work the same. The power is the same. Only the bill changes.

Phantom Load Audit
This is the silent 12% you never see. Phantom loads are real and measurable sources of energy waste. It accounts for around 10–15% of the average electric bill coming from devices that are "off" but still drawing power. This includes cable boxes, streaming devices, game consoles, smart TVs, computers in sleep mode, and chargers left plugged in. Individually, each one is small. Together, they form a meaningful drain. The easiest fix is to plug these devices into switched power strips and turn them off when not in use. Or use smart plugs that automatically disable power when devices go inactive. This isn't nickel-and-diming. It's removing a structural inefficiency that bleeds money month-after-month.

Water Bill Strategy
Water bills have risen dramatically nationwide, especially in the West and Southwest. Small habit changes and small adjustments can produce large savings. You can fix toilet leaks (they add up to hundreds of dollars a year), run dishwashers and washing machines only when full, reduce lawn watering days, and install inexpensive low-flow showerheads if your area charges high water rates. Water is the quietest bill in the entire household budget, but it's also one of the most predictable to control. Even a $20 change in your water bill each month is $240 a year. That's money that can now be redirected somewhere meaningful.

Seasonal Thermostat Strategy
Smart thermostat savings come from temperature strategy, not technology. Every degree you raise the thermostat in summer or lower in winter can reduce your bill by 3%. If you raise your AC from 72°*F* to 76°*F*, that's a 12% reduction and it adds up. Most homes run their HVAC out of habit, not intention. Temperature strategy costs nothing and produces recurring monthly savings.

Optimizing Transportation

Cars are depreciating assets that we often treat like investments. The average car payment in America is now over $700, and that's a wealth destroying emergency. To fix this, you have to choose a philosophy that fits your goals.

20/3/8 Rule

One way to determine whether a car is truly affordable is to use the 20/3/8 Rule. Many experts rely on it to make sure a vehicle doesn't rob retirement.

20% Down: Put at least 20% down. This ensures you aren't underwater (i.e., owing more than the car is worth) the minute you drive off the lot.

3 Years: Be able to pay it off in 3 years. If you need a 7-year loan to afford the monthly payment, you can't afford the car.

8% of Income: The payment shouldn't exceed 8% of your gross monthly income. If you make $5,000 gross per month, your car payment should be no more than $400.

The 20/3/8 Rule serves as a shield protecting your future self from a very common form of self-sabotage. If you want to take it even further, look at the philosophy popularized by Dave Ramsey. While the 20/3/8 rule provides guardrails for a loan, Ramsey's approach is more radical because he believes you should never, ever have a car payment. Today, the average car loan lasts about 6 years, with interest rates around 7% for new vehicles. On a $40,000 car financed over 6 years at 7%, the borrower pays roughly *$9,000 in interest* by the time the loan is paid off. Ramsey views car loans as a massive wealth killer and suggests you should only buy used vehicles with 100% cash.

Dave also uses a 50% rule, which suggests keeping the total value of everything owned with a motor, including cars, boats, and motorcycles, at no more than half of annual gross income. If you make $60,000, you shouldn't have more than $30,000 sitting in your driveway. The goal is to ensure you aren't tying up too much of your net worth in things that are rapidly losing value.

One of Dave's suggestions for anyone stuck with a car payment is to sell the expensive car and buy a reliable used beater with cash to free up monthly income. Once debt-free, the following cycle can begin:

Ghost Payment: Instead of paying a bank $600 a month, you pay yourself. You put that monthly $600 into a dedicated account, such as a high-yield savings account.

Upgrade Cycle: Let's say you drive a $5,000 car. After 10 months of saving $600, you have $6,000 in cash. You sell your current car for $5,000, add your savings, and now you have $11,000 to buy a better used car with zero debt.

Lather, Rinse, Repeat: You continue this process every few years. Because you aren't paying interest to a lender, you're the one keeping the extra $10,000 to $15,000 that many waste on a typical loan.

You'll eventually reach a point where you're driving a very nice vehicle you own outright. The goal is to stop the bleeding of your wealth so your money is able to grow in investments rather than evaporating into a car loan.

Sidebar Tip: Always take a used car to a trusted, independent mechanic for a full inspection before you sign anything. This usually costs between $150 and $300, but it could save you thousands in hidden repairs. While you're at it, pull a vehicle history report like Carfax or AutoCheck to check for accidents or title issues. A clean bill of health from a pro is the only way to ensure your new-to-you car isn't a ticking financial time bomb. If a seller or dealer refuses to let you take the car to your own mechanic, that's a massive red flag and you should walk away.

Depreciation Hack
New cars lose value quickly. According to industry data from sources like Edmunds and Kelley Blue Book, the average vehicle loses about 40% to 45% of its value within the first three years. Some buyers accept this because they want a brand new car that no one else has owned and that they can maintain from the beginning. For everyone else, a smarter move may be to buy a three-year-old vehicle coming off a lease. The original owner absorbed the steepest part of the depreciation curve. You get a modern car for roughly 55% to 60% of the original price.

Maintenance Hack
Stop going to the dealership for routine maintenance after the warranty expires. Independent shops are often 20–30% cheaper for the exact same work. You aren't paying for magical dealer tools. You're paying for a fancy waiting room and a logo on the wall. Also, don't be afraid of the DIY basics. You can change your own cabin air

filter and windshield wipers in 20 minutes for $20. A dealership will charge you $80 or more for the same service. Watch a how-to video and keep the money for yourself.

One-Car Experiment

This is extreme but powerful. If you're a two-car household, ask yourself if you truly need the second one. Selling a second car saves the payment, the insurance, the gas, and the maintenance. That's easily thousands a year. You don't have to decide today. Park the second car for 30 days and pretend it doesn't exist. Rearrange schedules. Try carpooling. Use rideshare once in a while. If you survive sharing a vehicle with your partner, consider selling it. You'll execute an expense flip on one of the largest expenses in your budget.

Optimizing Food and Variable Costs

Food is the hardest category to control because it's the most frequent transaction we make. We make food decisions several times a day, often when we're tired, stressed, or hungry. That vulnerability is expensive.

Convenience Tax

If you want to see where your wealth is leaking, look at your DoorDash or Uber Eats history. These services are convenient, but they charge a massive premium for that convenience. Let's look at the math of a burrito. In the restaurant, it costs $12. On the app, the menu price is marked up to $15. Then add the $4 service fee, the $3 delivery fee, and the $5 tip. That $12 burrito now costs $27. You aren't paying for food; you're paying a 125% convenience tax. If you're truly exhausted and don't feel like cooking, bake a frozen pizza or scrambled some eggs. Save the delivery apps for genuine special occasions, or delete them from your phone entirely to remove the temptation.

Grocery Game Plan

Supermarkets are designed by psychologists to make you spend money. Stores often put the essentials in the back so you've to walk past the impulse buys. Here's how to beat them:

Shop Online for Pickup

This sounds counterintuitive because there's often a small fee/tip, but it can save money. When you shop online, you don't impulse buy. You see a running total of your cart, so you can delete items if you go over budget. You also avoid walking through the aisles that are loaded with candy and snacks.

Check Unit Prices

Never look at the sticker price. Look at the tiny number in the corner of the shelf tag that lists the price per ounce. A family-size box of cereal might cost more per ounce than the regular box. The only way to know which size is the better deal is to compare the unit prices.

Generic Swap

Many store brand products are made by the same manufacturers as name brands, often in the same facilities. In fact, research from Dartmouth College found that more than 70% of private-label suppliers at the grocery retailers they studied were also national brand manufacturers. These products are typically produced by third-party manufacturers and simply packaged under a retailer's label, and in some cases may be nearly identical aside from branding, though not always exactly the same.

Freezer & Pantry Challenge

Most of us have hundreds of dollars of food sitting in our freezers and pantries right now. We buy new groceries out of habit while the old food goes bad. Pick one week this month where you spend $0 on groceries. You eat only what's already in the house. Breakfast might be oatmeal you forgot you had. Dinner might be pasta with that jar of sauce hiding behind the canned beans. You'll get creative, you'll clear space, and you might save $200–$400 in a single week to flip.

Optimizing Insurance

We've now reviewed the strategies for optimizing the visible infrastructure of your life, which are your home and transportation. But, owning these assets creates a secondary layer of expense that often goes unexamined. Let's turn our attention to the premiums we pay to protect them. Insurance is essential for financial safety, but without a clear strategy, it becomes a silent leak in your financial foundation.

Insurance is boring to most, but optimizing it is one of the fastest ways to protect your net worth and lower your monthly burn. The trick is to cut the waste without cutting the protection you actually need.

Self-Insure Strategy

Insurance is designed to protect you from catastrophe, not inconvenience. If you raise your auto and home deductible from $500 to $1,000 or even $2,500, the premium often drops. You're essentially betting on yourself. You're saying, "I can handle the smaller stuff. I want protection against the big stuff." The right way to do this is to take the money you save on premiums and move it into an emergency fund. Over a period of time, the savings from lower premiums will likely exceed the cost of paying a single deductible. For example, if raising your deductible reduces your auto insurance premium by $30 per month, that adds up to $360 per year. If those savings are set aside in a high-yield savings account rather than absorbed into everyday spending, the difference compared to paying one deductible becomes even more substantial.

Paying Annually Instead of Monthly
Many insurance companies quietly charge more when you pay month-to-month. They build in extra cost for the administrative hassle and for the fact that monthly payers are more likely to cancel. If you switch to paying annually or semi-annually, you can often save 3–10% on your premium. For a $1,500 auto policy, that might be $150 a year. On home insurance, it might be even more. This doesn't mean you need to have a huge pile of cash lying around. It means you plan ahead. You can create a sinking fund where you set aside one twelfth of the annual premium each month in a savings account, and when the bill comes due, you pay it in full and keep the discount. The important part is to view the discount as structural savings, not a chance to spend a little extra somewhere else.

Bundle With Your Eyes Open
We've all seen the commercials that promise big discounts if you bundle your home and auto policies. Sometimes those bundles are a great deal. Sometimes they're a trap. Here's the move. Get a quote for the bundle from your current insurer. Then get separate quotes from at least two competitors for each policy *individually*. You may discover that your current company is cheap on home insurance but expensive on auto, or vice versa. Bundling is only a win if the total cost of the bundle is lower than the total cost of your best separate policies. Don't be loyal to a logo. Be loyal to your net worth.

Cut the Useless Add-Ons
Insurance companies make enormous profits on optional add-ons that sound comforting but rarely deliver real value. These can include rental car reimbursement, roadside assistance that you might already have through your credit card or car manufacturer, glass coverage, and gap insurance long after the car has lost value. For each add-on, ask one question: "If this weren't on my policy today, would I pay extra to add it?" If the answer is no, remove it. Trimming even $10 or $15 of add-ons per month is $120 to $180 a year to flip.

Shop Every Two Years

Insurance companies practice price optimization. They slowly raise rates on loyal customers because they believe you won't notice or will be too busy to shop around. You can fight back by getting fresh quotes every 18 to 24 months. You don't need to switch every time. The point is to know the market and to force your current company to compete for your business. If you discover that a competing company is offering you the same coverage for $200 less per year, you can either switch or ask your existing agent to match it. Either way, you win and you flip.

Hidden Discount for Low Mileage

If you drive fewer than 7,500 miles a year, you're the insurance company's dream client. You're on the road less, which means fewer chances for accidents. But if you never tell them this, they won't reward you for it. Some companies offer pay-per-mile or low-mileage policies that can cut premiums dramatically for remote workers and retirees who don't drive much. If you work from home and your car mostly sits in the driveway, call your insurer and ask if they offer a low-mileage plan. The savings can be hundreds of dollars a year for a phone call that takes 10 minutes.

Healthcare

Before turning to healthcare cost optimization, it's important to distinguish between trimming expenses and cost avoidance.

Trimming is what we've been doing so far. It means you already have an expense and you're finding a way to reduce it. You negotiate your rent down. You raise your deductible and lower your premium. You cut a subscription that you're already paying for. Cost avoidance is different. It means you prevent a bill from ever hitting your account in the first place. For example, instead of getting an MRI at the hospital for $2,500, you call an independent imaging center in advance and pay $350 cash.

Research published in *Health Affairs* and *JAMA Network Open* has found wide variation in what patients and insurers pay for the same medical service, even within the same hospital. Saving money here starts with understanding how the system works. In the U.S., there is often no single price for a medical procedure. A hospital may list a chargemaster price, a discounted cash price, and different rates negotiated with different insurers. The chargemaster is generally a list price, not necessarily the amount the hospital ultimately receives.

Research has also found that billing and insurance related work creates substantial administrative costs for healthcare providers.

Although that doesn't mean every provider will offer a discount, some hospitals and medical practices charge self-pay patients less than the rates negotiated with commercial insurers. For certain scheduled services, the cash price may even be lower than your insurance copay or the amount you would owe toward an unmet deductible. That's why it can pay to ask for both prices before scheduling care.

Imagine you need a sleep study to check for apnea. If you schedule this at a hospital sleep lab, the bill to your insurance could easily exceed $4,000. If you're on the hook for a large deductible, that's a massive hit. However, many independent clinics offer a home study kit for a cash price of roughly $300. By asking one question, you save over $3,700 for the exact same medical diagnosis. Before you schedule any non-emergency test or procedure, make two phone calls to compare the insurance price against the cash price. Those calls can be worth thousands of dollars per minute. I've done this myself and the savings were significant. A few phone calls saved me thousands of dollars with very little effort.

Prescriptions

The price of medication is often detached from reality due to middlemen known as Pharmacy Benefit Managers. These companies negotiate rebates that pad their pockets but keep prices high for us. You can bypass this system entirely using platforms like Mark Cuban's Cost Plus Drug Company. They operate on a transparent model where they charge the manufacturing cost of the drug, a 15% markup to keep the lights on, and a $3 pharmacy labor fee. That's it. The difference can be staggering. A cancer drug might retail for over $2,000 a month at a local pharmacy. At Cost Plus, it might cost $17. You can check prescriptions against their database. If the price is lower, simply ask your doctor to send the prescription there instead of to your usual pharmacy.

Hospital Bills

If you end up with a large hospital bill, you should never pay the first number you see. Studies show that a significant percentage of medical bills contain errors. These systems are automated, and computers frequently double-charge for medication or bill for time a doctor wasn't actually in the room. To fight this, you can call the billing department and ask for an itemized bill with CPT Codes. CPT codes are the universal language of medical billing. When you ask for this, you signal that you know how to audit them. Often, simply making this request causes the bill to drop because the billing department reviews it and removes the mistakes, like charging you $50 for a Tylenol you never took, before they send the detailed version. If the bill is accurate but high, you can apply for Charity Care or financial assistance if you qualify. Nonprofit hospitals are legally required to have these programs, and the income limits are often much higher than we think. You might qualify for a partial discount even with a middle-class income.

Medical bills are the number one trigger that pushes otherwise stable households into debt, not because people are reckless but because the system is engineered to overwhelm us at our most vulnerable moments. Once your bill moves from the mailbox to a payment plan or a credit card it stops being a healthcare issue and becomes something far more dangerous. It becomes debt, and debt changes everything, particularly when it carries high interest.

Gain Tomorrow

You've looked at every major spending category and identified flips across the board, from housing to healthcare. Each one you execute adds to a growing monthly total that can be redirected toward your future. On their own, each flip might not feel like much. Together, they can change everything if you drive up your savings rate. Take a look at what happens as that rate increases as compared to the number of years you'll need to work.

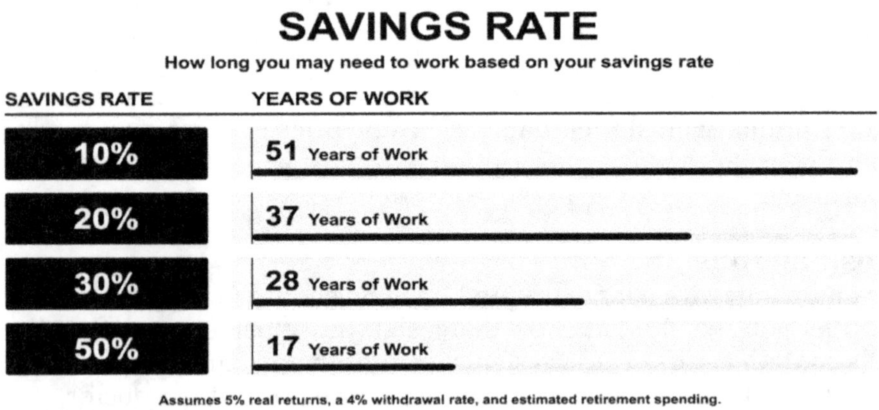

Every expense flip you execute is buying back your time. Every 1% you increase your savings rate through smarter spending can peel months off your prison sentence. I mean, your career.

Of course, none of that works if the savings quietly get absorbed back into your lifestyle. Warren Buffett said it best when he suggested we shouldn't save what's left after spending, but instead spend what's left after saving. With that in mind, your goal is to prioritize your savings rate and regularly look for opportunities to increase it. Every time you negotiate a bill, cut insurance costs, or lower your taxes, immediately update your automatic transfer. If you save $30 a month on car insurance, raise your savings or investing auto-transfer by $30 the same day. That's how you turn trimming into wealth.

Every dollar you reclaim by adopting the strategies we reviewed is a dollar snatched back from companies that are happy to take it. If you use your snatched cash to drive up your savings rate, you'll move faster toward the retirement you're targeting. That's the real return on every expense flip you execute. Not just a lower monthly bill. A shorter path to freedom.

Now that you've identified your expense flips and put a plan in place to redirect that cash, your progress must be protected. One bad month, one unexpected bill, or one emergency you didn't see coming can make that progress vanish faster than it was built if you're not prepared. After we tackle debt in Chapter 7, we'll turn to cash reserves in Chapter 8, because a solid reserve is critical to protecting what you've built, both now and over time.

Chapter Six Actions

Housing Audit (Complete this week)

[ ] **Check Your Exemption:** Verify that you're receiving homestead exemption on your primary residence. If not, file the exemption form right away.

[ ] **Check Your PMI:** If you purchased your home with less than 20% down, call your lender and ask what equity percentage they have on record. If it's near or above 20%, ask what's required to remove Private Mortgage Insurance (PMI) and whether an appraisal could qualify you.

Utility Optimization (Complete this week)

[ ] **Negotiate Your Internet:** Call your internet provider. Ask for loyalty discounts or match a competitor's price. If your speed is overkill, downgrade it.

[ ] **Optimize Cell Service:** Check if you're out of contract. Compare pricing with an MVNO like Mint or Visible. If you stay with your current provider, remove international and insurance add-ons.

[ ] **Phantom Load Check:** Walk through your house and look for devices that draw power when they're not in use. Put TVs, gaming systems, and similar electronics on switchable power strips, smart plugs, or auto-shutoff strips. Unplug old chargers and any other items that are not actively being used.

Transportation Tune-Up (Complete this week)

[ ] **20/3/8 Test:** Look at your current car payment. Does it pass the 20% down, 3-year payoff, and 8% of income test? If not, make a note. In the next 12 to 18 months, consider selling the car for a cheaper, reliable used model that fits the rule.

[ ] **One-Car Experiment:** If you have two cars, park one for 30 days. Treat it as if it doesn't exist. If you can manage schedules and commitments with one car, seriously consider selling the second.

Food and Digital Waste (Complete this month)

[ ] **Delivery App Audit:** Open your DoorDash, Uber Eats, or similar apps. Look at your last 10 orders and calculate what you spent versus what pickup would have cost. Decide on a new rule, such as delivery only once a month, or delete the apps.

[ ] **Pantry/Freezer Challenge:** Pick one week in the next month where you will spend $0 on groceries. Plan meals around what you already have in your pantry and freezer. Put the money you saved into your savings account.

[ ] **Subscription Audit:** Scan the last three months of bank and credit card statements. Highlight every recurring subscription. Cancel anything that you haven't used in the last 30 days or that you rarely use.

Insurance Optimization (Complete this month)

[ ] **Raise Deductibles Intentionally:** Call your auto and home insurer and get quotes for increasing your deductibles. Note the premium savings. If you decide to raise the deductibles, set up an automatic transfer for the exact amount saved into your emergency fund.

[ ] **Switch Billing Frequency:** Ask your insurer how much you'd save by paying annually or semi-annually instead of monthly. If it can be comfortably covered with current income, make the switch and direct the savings to your future.

[ ] **Bundle With Eyes Open:** Get a quote for bundling home and auto. Then get separate quotes from at least two competitors. Choose the combination that gives you the coverage you need at the lowest total cost.

[ ] **Cut Add-Ons:** Review your policies for rental reimbursement, duplicate roadside assistance, glass coverage, and outdated gap insurance. Remove any add-ons you wouldn't choose again today.

[ ] **Check Low Mileage Options:** If you drive fewer than 7,500 miles a year, ask about mileage-based policies and compare premiums.

Healthcare Cost Avoidance (As needed)

[ ] **Cash-Pay Check:** Before scheduling any non-emergency test or procedure, call at least two providers. Ask for the insurance price and the cash-pay price. Choose the option that makes sense for your situation.

[ ] **Prescription Price Check:** Look up your recurring medications on a transparent pricing platform such as Cost Plus. If the price is significantly lower, ask your doctor to send the prescription there.

[ ] **Itemized Bill Request:** For any large medical bill, request an itemized bill with CPT codes. Review it for duplicate charges or obvious errors. Ask about Charity Care or financial assistance if the bill is still unaffordable.

7
Stop Owing, Start Growing

Let's look at debt in two categories as a starting point. While all debt carries risk and should be handled carefully, some debt may be productive when it's used to add lasting value, such as a mortgage with affordable, fully amortizing terms, or help improve your financial future in some other meaningful way. On the flip side, there's counterproductive debt, such as high interest credit card debt, that can make reaching your freedom number take far longer than it should. That's why paying it off has to become a top priority, and that's what we'll focus on in this chapter.

This kind of debt has become a growing financial issue across America. By the end of the first quarter of 2026, total U.S. household debt had climbed to about $18.8 trillion, with credit card balances accounting for roughly $1.25 trillion of that. For accounts accruing interest, the average credit card APR was 21.52%, and among households carrying revolving credit card debt, the average balance was about $11,149.

The scale is hard to ignore. Even a common revolving balance can become a long term burden at rates like these. What feels manageable from month to month can quietly turn into years of payments, with a large share of every dollar going toward interest instead of progress.

That's where the real danger shows up. This kind of debt doesn't just strain your cash flow today. It steals from your future by choking off the money that could have been growing for you. Take a revolving credit card balance of $11,149 at a 21.52% interest rate. The first month's interest alone would be about $199.94. If a household made a fixed payment of about $200.72 per month, just slightly more than the interest due at the start, that debt could take about 26 years to pay off, with total interest costs reaching roughly $51,476 on that balance alone.

Now look at the other side of the equation. If that same $200.72 per month were invested instead and earned an average annual return of 8% over those same 26 years, it could grow to roughly $209,235. That's the real cost of bad debt. It's not just the interest you pay. It's the wealth you never get the chance to build. Over time, the difference between paying interest and earning interest can grow into tens or even hundreds of thousands of dollars.

In my early 20s, I gave very little thought to building future wealth, as many people that age do. For a short time, I carried bad debt and didn't fully appreciate how damaging it could become. Eventually, I had to take a hard look at my habits and course correct. I chose the avalanche strategy, and it worked very well for me. I got out of bad debt and stayed out of it. That experience taught me that the commitment to see it through is just as important as the strategy you choose, if not more so.

Whether the approach you choose is aggressive or methodical, the goal is the same: get out of bad debt, stay out of bad debt, and redirect that money toward building wealth instead.

Let's look at a few strategies you can consider to reach that goal.

Choosing Your Strategy

There are two primary strategies often used to pay off debt. Both work, but they work for different personality types. You'll want to choose the one that keeps you motivated because the best strategy is simply the one you stick to.

Debt Snowball Strategy

Popularized by Dave Ramsey, this method focuses on behavioral modification. You ignore the interest rates entirely and focus on the balance. You list debts from smallest balance to largest. You throw every extra dollar at the smallest debt until it's gone. It works because seeing progress helps with motivation. When you pay off that first $500 medical bill or $800 credit card, you feel a surge of accomplishment. That dopamine hit gives you the fuel to tackle the larger debts. It isn't mathematically optimal, but it's psychologically powerful.

Debt Avalanche Strategy

This method focuses on mathematical efficiency. It saves the most money and time, but it requires discipline because you might not see a win for a long time. You list debts from highest interest rate to lowest. You attack the debt with the highest rate first, which is often credit cards. By paying off the credit card balance with the highest interest rate, the total amount of interest paid over time goes down. It's a smart strategy, but if the highest interest debt is a massive $20,000 balance, for example, it might take a year or more to see it disappear. If you lose motivation during that year, the math doesn't matter.

In practice, the avalanche strategy usually saves the most money, while the snowball strategy often delivers faster psychological wins. The better choice is the one you can stick with long enough to finish.

Accelerate Freedom

Once you've committed to paying off debt, your tactics will shape the outcome. Here are five methods to accelerate your freedom:

0% Balance Transfer

Your goal is to stop the interest so your payments actually reduce principal. One way to do that is with a 0% APR balance transfer card. Paying a one-time fee of about 3% to 5% can be mathematically far better than paying 21% interest for years. On a $10,000 balance, that fee would typically cost $300 to $500 up front, which can still be far cheaper than carrying the same balance at a high APR.

Just remember, this is a bridge, not a hammock. The 0% rate usually expires after 12 to 18 months. And not all promotional offers work the same way. A true 0% APR offer is different from a deferred-interest offer. With deferred interest, if you don't pay off the full promotional balance by the deadline, you could be charged retroactive interest for the entire promotional period, not just on what remains. Read the fine print before applying.

A few additional things to know about balance transfers. According to my research, most credit card companies require a credit score of at least 670 to qualify, and the best offers typically go to those with scores above 720. The transferred balance also cannot exceed the new card's credit limit, and some issuers won't allow transfers between cards from the same bank. And making only minimum payments rarely gets the job done in time, so it helps to divide the total balance by the number of months in the promotional period and treat that as the monthly must-hit target.

APR Negotiation

We're customers, not hostages. Credit card companies spend vast sums acquiring new customers, and they don't want to lose you. So call the number on the back of your card and say something like, "I've been a customer in good standing, and I'd like you to lower my APR to better match the market. What can you do for me today?" If they say they can't lower the APR, ask whether you qualify for any promotional rate, hardship program, or retention offer. If the representative still can't help, ask to speak with a specialist or account manager who can review your account.

It won't work every time, but even a modest rate reduction can make a real difference. Dropping the APR by just a few percentage points can save a meaningful amount in interest and shorten your payoff timeline, especially if your payment stays the same. If you've been a solid customer, it's worth the call. And if the first attempt goes nowhere, try again later. Persistence can pay.

If you are seriously behind on payments, a direct hardship conversation with the creditor may be wise. Some creditors have internal hardship programs that aren't widely advertised. Missed payments, reduced income, or a temporary hardship can sometimes open the door to a reduced rate or a modified repayment arrangement.

Debt Consolidation Loan

For borrowers carrying multiple high-interest balances, a debt consolidation loan is worth considering. The concept is straightforward. You take out a single personal loan at a lower interest rate and use it to pay off several higher-rate debts, leaving one fixed monthly payment in their place.

The savings can be compelling. A borrower carrying $15,000 in credit card debt at a rate of 21% who qualifies for a personal loan at 11% could save thousands of dollars in interest and pay off the debt years sooner, assuming the monthly payment stays roughly the same or increases slightly.

There are a few things to keep in mind, however. Qualification depends on credit score, income, and existing debt load. Borrowers with strong credit, generally above 680, will have access to the best rates. Those with weaker credit may still qualify but at rates that narrow the advantage. It's also important not to run the credit cards back up after consolidating. That mistake turns one problem into two. Discipline is critical.

Home equity is another consolidation tool you may want to consider. A home equity loan or home equity line of credit, often called a HELOC, can offer interest rates far below those charged by most credit cards, sometimes in the 7% to 9% range depending on the market. But the trade-off is serious. Your home becomes collateral. If you miss payments, you could put your home at risk. This option deserves careful thought and is generally best reserved for those with stable income, strong financial discipline, and a clear plan not to run up new credit card debt after consolidating.

Early Mortgage Payoff (Bi-Weekly Payments)

For homeowners, a mortgage is likely the biggest liability on the books. To understand how to tackle it, you first have to understand how the bank makes money. When you sign a 30-year mortgage, the bank sets up an amortization schedule that's heavily front-loaded with interest. In the early years of the loan, nearly 70% to 80% of each monthly payment goes straight to interest, with only a small fraction touching the principal. This is why you can pay a mortgage for five years and barely see the balance move. The bi-weekly payment strategy is one way to work against that structure.

The concept is straightforward. Instead of making one full mortgage payment each month, you pay half the monthly amount every two weeks. Since there are 52 weeks in a year, that produces 26 half-payments, which equals 13 full payments annually rather than 12. That one extra payment each year goes directly toward principal, which is where the impact compounds. On a typical 30-year mortgage, this approach can shorten the payoff timeline by roughly five to seven years and save tens of thousands of dollars in interest.

The numbers make the case clearly. On a $400,000 mortgage at 6.5% over 30 years, the monthly payment is $2,528. Paying only the minimum for the full term results in roughly $510,000 in interest, bringing the total cost of the home to more than $910,000. Switching to a biweekly approach, paying $1,264 every two weeks, cuts the payoff timeline to just over 24 years and saves about $117,000 in interest.

Adding just $50 to each bi-weekly payment, bringing it from $1,264 to $1,314, pushes the savings further. The loan pays off in about 22 years, and total interest savings climb to roughly $157,000, about $40,000 more than the standard biweekly method alone. Small, consistent adjustments compound in your favor the same way interest compounds against you.

Before setting this up, a word of caution. Many banks will offer to manage a biweekly plan for you, but they'll often charge a setup or processing fee to do it. There's no need to pay that fee. You can achieve the same result on your own with a simple adjustment.

Take the monthly principal and interest payment only, not the escrow portion, and divide it by 12. Add that amount to your regular payment each month and direct it to principal. Over the course of a year, that adds up to one extra principal and interest payment, replicating the biweekly effect without the fees.

Debt Management Plan

A Debt Management Plan may be the intervention needed when debt has become unmanageable and bankruptcy is starting to feel unavoidable. These plans are offered through nonprofit credit counseling agencies accredited by the NFCC, the National Foundation for Credit Counseling, and they work very differently from debt settlement companies. Debt settlement companies are typically for-profit operations that make money by telling clients to stop paying their bills while they negotiate with creditors to accept less than the full balance owed. The damage to your credit score can be severe, and there's no guarantee creditors will agree. A nonprofit Debt Management Plan takes the opposite approach. The agency negotiates with creditors to lower interest rates, often to under 10%, with the goal of repaying the full balance under more manageable terms rather than settling for less.

In many plans, creditors waive fees and accept one consolidated monthly payment through the counseling agency. The enrolled accounts are usually closed while the plan is active, generally for three to five years, but for someone staring down bankruptcy, that may be a trade worth making.

A few things to know before enrolling. Not everyone qualifies. Creditors have to agree to participate, and not all debts are eligible. Student loans, mortgages, and other secured debts typically aren't included. Most plans cover unsecured debts like credit cards and personal loans. There's also a small cost involved. Nonprofit agencies typically charge a monthly fee in the range of $25 to $50, which is modest given what they're managing on your behalf.

Keep in mind a debt management plan will affect your credit score. The impact is real, but it's generally far less damaging than bankruptcy or the missed payments that often accompany debt settlement. For most in this situation, the credit hit is likely a worthwhile price for regaining control.

The approach is a last resort before bankruptcy, and for many people it's a far better outcome. If you think a debt management plan might be the right move, start at nfcc.org, where you can find accredited nonprofit counseling agencies and get a clear picture of your options before making any decisions.

Student Loan Strategies

Student loan debt sits in a category of its own. It's excluded from most debt management plans, it can't be discharged in bankruptcy under most circumstances, and it often carries terms and options that other forms of debt don't. For borrowers carrying federal student loans, a few key tools are important to know.

Income-driven repayment plans limit your monthly payment to a percentage of your discretionary income, typically between 5% and 20% depending on the plan. After 20 to 25 years of qualifying payments, any remaining balance is forgiven. For borrowers in lower income years or those with high balances relative to income, these plans can provide meaningful relief.

Public Service Loan Forgiveness, commonly known as PSLF, is available to borrowers who work full-time for a qualifying government or nonprofit employer and make 120 qualifying monthly payments under an eligible repayment plan. After meeting those requirements, the remaining federal loan balance is forgiven tax-free. It's a powerful benefit for those who qualify, but the eligibility rules are strict and should be verified at studentaid.gov.

Refinancing federal student loans into a private loan could potentially lower the interest rate for borrowers with strong credit and stable income, but it comes with a significant trade-off. Federal protections, including income-driven repayment options and forgiveness programs, are permanently lost. Refinancing makes the most sense for borrowers who are not eligible for forgiveness, have a stable income, and are focused purely on reducing their interest cost.

Private student loans offer none of the federal protections and require negotiating directly with the lender or refinancing through another private lender to improve terms. Borrowers with private loans in financial hardship should contact their servicer directly, as some offer temporary forbearance or modified repayment arrangements.

Staying Out of Debt

Getting out of debt is a major win. Once you're out of it, you have to stay out of it and that starts with understanding how debt found its way into your life in the first place. Debt usually comes from one of two places. It comes from known expenses that weren't quite planned well enough in terms of having money put aside to fund them, like holidays, major purchases, or lifestyle upgrades. And it comes from unplanned expenses like car trouble or medical bills, for example. Until you identify which pattern applies to you, it's easy to repeat it.

The first step to staying out of debt is to recognize your own debt triggers. What situations have caused you to borrow in the past, and what made spending easier to justify in those moments? The more specific the answer, the easier it is to build protection around it.

The next step is to create guardrails for those triggers before they show up again. If holidays have been a problem, set limits before the season begins. If emotional spending has been the issue, make a rule that purchases aren't made in moments of stress, anger, loneliness, or excitement. If social pressure has been the problem, decide in advance where you'll say no. And if income drops, adjust spending quickly instead of using debt to preserve a lifestyle the income no longer supports.

It's also important to recognize affordability traps. A purchase doesn't become affordable just because someone's willing to finance it. A lender's approval, a store's payment plan, or a manageable-looking monthly payment can make buying possible, but they don't make it financially wise. Just because you can pay for something by borrowing doesn't mean you should. That's the rule I had to adopt and the standard I hold. True affordability means the purchase fits your plan without pulling tomorrow's income into today's decision.

Finally, treat any return to debt as a warning light. A new balance shouldn't be ignored, normalized, or explained away as no big deal. It's a signal to pause and ask what happened. Was it a planning issue, a spending issue, an income issue, or a pressure issue? Catching the pattern early is what keeps a small slip from becoming another cycle. Your goal is to understand yourself well enough that debt no longer has an easy way back in.

Freedom from debt comes from two things working together. You'll need to aggressively attack existing balances and also build enough self-awareness to keep old patterns from returning. Breaking the cycle means cutting off credit cards, avoiding payment plans, and waiting to make purchases until the cash is actually there. Every balance paid down creates more breathing room, and every month without new debt is a month you're gaining ground toward financial freedom.

Attack the highest interest debt first and don't let up. When motivation starts to fade, clearing a smaller balance can remind you that progress is still happening. It's a long road for some and can be challenging. I can say that from experience.

It was a powerful feeling the day I closed out bad debt I'd taken on early, while I was still young and headed into my top earning years. There was a genuine sense of pride in knowing I'd done it, that I'd stayed the course and come out the other side. It felt like an albatross had been removed from around my neck. That feeling is available to anyone willing to see it through. Once the debt is gone, those same dollars finally get to work for you instead of against you.

The stop owing phase can be difficult, but it doesn't last forever. As debt falls away, more of your income becomes available to grow your retirement savings and bring your retirement vision closer to reality.

Chapter Seven Actions

Debt Attack (Complete this month)

[ ] **Map Your Triggers:** Write down the situations or emotions that have caused you to take on debt in the past. Identify your top two or three and decide in advance how you'll respond when they show up again.

[ ] **Choose Your Strategy:** List all your debts with their balances and interest rates. Decide whether the Snowball or Avalanche method fits your personality, write out your payoff order, and start executing the plan.

[ ] **Credit Card Rate:** Use the APR negotiation script and call every credit card company to request a rate reduction. If they can't lower the rate, ask about hardship programs, promotional rates, or retention offers.

[ ] **Balance Transfer:** Check your credit score and research 0% APR balance transfer offers. If you qualify, calculate whether the transfer fee is less than the interest you'd pay during the promotional period, and have a clear payoff plan in place before applying.

[ ] **Debt Consolidation:** If you're carrying multiple high-interest balances, compare personal loan rates from at least two or three lenders to see whether consolidating at a lower rate makes sense. Make sure not to run the cards back up after consolidating.

[ ] **Mortgage Paydown:** Contact your lender and confirm whether they charge a fee to set up a biweekly payment plan. If they do, skip it and DIY. Divide your monthly principal and interest payment by 12 and add that amount to each monthly payment, directing it specifically toward principal.

[ ] **Student Loans:** If you carry federal student loans, log in to studentaid.gov and confirm your repayment plan. If you need help, check whether you qualify for income-driven repayment or Public Service Loan Forgiveness before making any decisions about refinancing.

[ ] **Debt Counseling:** If debt feels unmanageable, visit nfcc.org to find an accredited nonprofit credit counseling agency and schedule a consultation.

8
Cash Reserves

A common source of financial stress is lack of breathing room in a household budget. When every dollar is needed for expenses and little or nothing is available for saving, common issues like a flat tire, a leaky roof, or any number of other inevitable surprises can feel like life-altering disasters and quickly lead to debt. The data shows just how widespread this is. According to a January 2026 U.S. News survey, 43% of Americans couldn't cover a $1,000 emergency expense from their savings, and more than 40% have no emergency savings at all. The good news is that progress starts with the very first dollar set aside as you build, or strengthen, a cash reserve to handle life's little emergencies. Even though it can be difficult, creating a cash reserve has to become a top priority, and the strategies we've covered are designed to help you get there. Bringing more money through the door, tightening up your spending, and getting and staying out of debt all create the room to carve out a surplus, a portion of which can be used for your cash reserves.

Before we look at ways to do that, it's important to watch out for two common hurdles that can seriously hinder your progress. The first is leaving the extra money in your checking account, where it looks available for everyday purchases. If it's sitting there staring at you, saying "spend me, spend me," guess what? You'll likely spend it. We want to avoid that by moving it into the proper account structure, automatically every month.

The second is the temptation to invest all of your surplus in the stock market. While you do want your money to grow, putting all of it into investments can make you vulnerable. If every dollar is tied up in a 401(k) or brokerage account, for example, a cash need can force you to sell an investment at a loss, turning a temporary emergency into a lasting financial setback. A better approach is typically to put a portion of the surplus into an account or investment vehicle appropriate for cash reserves, while the remainder can be directed toward a growth-oriented portfolio.

The first step is deciding where the cash reserve portion should live. Some of it needs to be immediately accessible, while other portions can be placed where they may earn more without taking on stock market risk. We'll start by looking at credit unions, which can be a good place for relatively quick access to your money and competitive rates on some savings vehicles appropriate for cash reserves.

Credit Union Advantage

Big banks like Chase or Wells Fargo are often the default choice because their names feel familiar and established. But for building cash reserves, big banks are often the enemy.

Banks are for-profit corporations with a legal obligation to serve their shareholders. That often shows up in higher fees and lower interest paid on deposits. Credit unions, on the other hand, are nonprofit cooperatives owned by their members and often pass value back through lower loan rates, higher savings rates, and fewer fees.

It's common to assume military service or union membership is required to join a credit union. That used to be true. Today, many top-tier credit unions have open charters. Here are some of the top ones:

Alliant Credit Union

A broadly accessible credit union often praised for strong savings rates and digital banking. If you don't qualify through an employer or another eligibility category, you can join the Alliant Credit Union Foundation during the application process, and Alliant covers the one-time nominal fee.

PenFed (Pentagon Federal Credit Union)

A broad-membership credit union with competitive auto loan and certificate offerings. Membership is open to everyone and can be established by opening a savings account with small deposit.

Navy Federal Credit Union

A well-regarded credit union, though membership is restricted to those tied to the military or eligible family or household relationships. Eligibility runs through military, veteran, DoD, or qualifying family or household status, with eligible family including parents, grandparents, siblings, spouses, children, grandchildren, and household members.

NASA Federal Credit Union

A credit union with broader access than its name suggests. If you don't qualify through NASA, a partner group, or family or household eligibility, you can select the National Space Society affiliated-membership option during application, which NASA Federal says is complimentary for one year.

Digital Federal Credit Union (DCU)

Known for its standout Primary Savings feature. Membership is available through participating organizations such as Reach Out for Schools, which DCU lists as a small one-time donation option.

High-Yield Online Savings Banks

If a credit union isn't the right fit, an online bank can be an excellent alternative. I'm a big fan because they often offer higher savings rates and fewer fees than traditional brick-and-mortar banks. Some commonly cited high-yield savings options include:

Ally Bank

A long-standing online bank known for no monthly maintenance fees, no minimum balance requirements, and a strong digital experience. Ally also offers a full range of banking products, including checking, CDs, and money market accounts, making it a solid all-in-one option.

Marcus by Goldman Sachs

Offers a simple high-yield online savings account with no fees and no minimum deposit. Backed by Goldman Sachs, Marcus keeps its lineup focused on savings and CDs rather than full-service banking, which appeals to those who want simplicity.

Capital One 360

Offers a competitive online savings account with no fees or minimums, along with a broad suite of banking products. Capital One also operates physical branches and cafés in select cities, offering a hybrid experience for those who occasionally want in-person access.

SoFi Bank

Known for a high savings APY for customers who meet certain requirements, such as eligible direct deposit or qualifying deposits, along with a broader financial platform that includes investing, lending, and credit card products.

Discover Bank

Offers online savings with no fees and no minimums. Discover is also known for its cashback debit account and strong customer service reputation, though its product lineup is narrower than some competitors.

Betterment

Best known as a robo-advisor, Betterment also offers a high-yield cash account through program banks. It's not itself a bank, so deposits are held at partner institutions, which can mean expanded FDIC coverage across multiple banks.

Keep in mind that interest rates change frequently, so the specific institution matters less than the overall structure. The key is to keep your cash in an account where it works for you instead of sitting idle at a traditional bank.

Tiered Emergency Fund Strategy

Keeping $50,000 in a checking account may feel safe, but it isn't efficient. As we covered, cash that sits idle loses purchasing power every year as inflation quietly erodes its value. Instead of keeping your entire emergency fund in one place, consider a tiered approach that balances access, growth, and protection.

This approach is widely accepted. Financial experts such as Suze Orman and Clark Howard have both recommended keeping some emergency cash immediately accessible while allowing additional reserves to earn more in higher-yield accounts or other conservative vehicles.

Think of your cash reserves as a layered defense system. Each layer has a different job. Some money should be available immediately. Some should earn a competitive yield while still being easy to access. Some can be set aside for true worst-case scenarios, where giving up a little liquidity may be worth the tradeoff for higher returns.

Tier 1: Immediate Cash (1 month)

Keep roughly 1 month of expenses in your checking account. This is your everyday buffer, designed to cover monthly bills and smaller surprises such as a flat tire, a broken phone, or an urgent home repair. This money should be available the moment you need it.

Tier 2: High-Yield Reserve (2 to 4 months)

Keep the next layer of your emergency fund in a high-yield savings account or money market account. This portion is meant for larger disruptions, such as a major car repair, or an unexpected home expense. The money is still relatively easy to access, even if transfers may take a day or two, and it can earn a competitive yield while it waits.

Tier 3: Deep Reserve (4 or more months)

Keep the deepest layer of your reserve in vehicles such as CD ladders, Treasury securities, or I Bonds. This is your long-term backstop for serious emergencies such as extended unemployment, a medical crisis, or a major life disruption. Because this money is less likely to be needed right away, it can be placed in options that may offer better returns in exchange for reduced liquidity. It isn't your first line of defense, but it's there when life happens.

CD Ladder

A certificate of deposit, or CD, is a contract with a bank in which you agree to leave your money untouched for a set period, such as one year, in exchange for a guaranteed interest rate that is typically higher than what a standard savings account pays. The tradeoff is liquidity. If you withdraw the money before the CD matures, you usually pay an early withdrawal penalty, often equal to about three months of interest.

A CD ladder is a simple way to manage that tradeoff. If you put all of your money into a single five-year CD, you may earn a higher rate, but you give up access to the cash. If you keep everything in a savings account, you preserve flexibility but may earn less. A ladder solves this by dividing your money into smaller CDs with staggered maturity dates. For example, instead of putting $25,000 into one large CD, you might split it into five $5,000 CDs. One year later, CD #1 matures and you receive your $5,000 plus interest. If you need the cash, you can use it. If you don't, you can reinvest it into a new five-year CD. As each CD matures, you repeat the process. Over time, this creates a system in which one CD comes due every year. Take a look at this flow that shows how a CD ladder works.

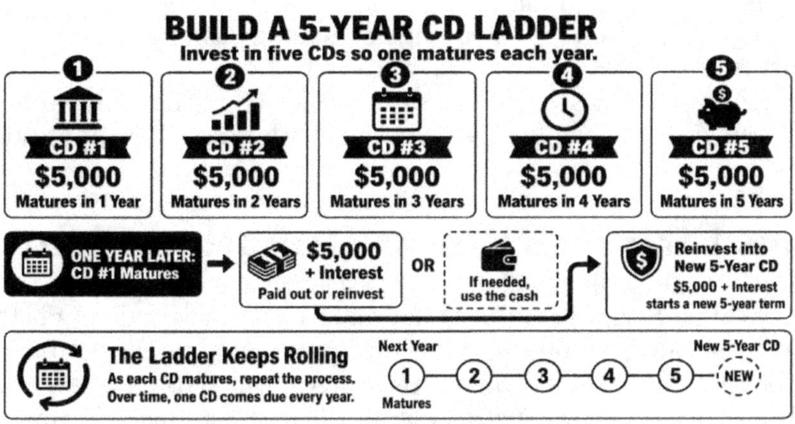

The benefit is that you can generally capture higher rates associated with longer-term CDs while still regaining access to part of your money at regular intervals. In other words, you get a balance of yield and flexibility rather than having to choose one or the other.

Major brokerages such as Fidelity and Vanguard offer tools that make CD ladders easier to build and manage. You enter the amount you want to invest, and the platform can help you purchase CDs from multiple banks with staggered maturity dates.

Treasuries

Treasuries are another savings vehicle to consider as part of your cash reserves. When you buy a Treasury bill or note, you're lending money to the U.S. government. Because they offer predictable maturity dates and have historically held up well during periods of economic stress, they can be a strong fit for the deeper layers of your reserves.

Treasuries can be a smart place to keep savings because they often yield more than standard savings accounts and some short-term CDs. They're also exempt from state and local income tax, which can make their after-tax return even more attractive. And because you can buy them in small increments, often starting at just $100, they're accessible for a wide range of savers.

The two main categories most relevant are Treasury bills and Treasury notes. Treasury bills, often called T-bills, mature in as little as 4 weeks and up to 52 weeks, which makes them especially useful for short-term savings and laddering. Treasury notes have longer maturities, ranging from 2 to 10 years, and may make sense if you want somewhat higher yields without locking money away for decades.

You can purchase Treasuries at TreasuryDirect.gov, directly from the government, or through major brokerages like Fidelity, Schwab, and Vanguard, which often make buying and selling easier than TreasuryDirect.

Compared with CDs, Treasuries often offer better liquidity and state tax advantages, while CDs sometimes offer higher promotional rates.

Series I Savings Bonds (Inflation Fighter)

Also, for Tier 3 of your reserves, there's a special asset from the U.S. Treasury called Series I Bonds. What makes I Bonds appealing is that their interest rate includes an inflation component, so if inflation rises, the rate adjusts too. That helps protect your purchasing power over time. They also come with a couple of tax advantages. You won't pay state or local income tax on the interest, and you can generally defer federal taxes until you cash the bond in or it reaches final maturity. There are a few rules to keep in mind, though. You can buy up to $10,000 per person per calendar year in electronic I Bonds, you have to hold them for at least one year, and if you cash them in before five years, you give up the last three months of interest.

Electronic I Bonds are purchased through TreasuryDirect.gov, although paper I Bonds can still be bought in limited amounts with a federal tax refund.

Cash Wedge

If you're within five years of retirement, your cash reserves may need to do more than cover emergencies. They may also need to support what's known as a cash wedge. A cash wedge is a pool of very safe, liquid assets set aside to cover several years of spending needs in retirement, so you don't have to sell stocks in the middle of a market decline.

This matters because one of the biggest risks in retirement is sequence of returns risk, a topic I explain in more detail later. When the market falls early in retirement, withdrawals can lock in losses at exactly the wrong time. That's where a cash wedge comes in. It gives you another source of spending money while the stock portion of your portfolio has time to recover.

In most cases, a cash wedge is built to cover about three to five years of your portfolio gap. Your portfolio gap is the amount your investments need to provide each year after other income sources, such as Social Security, are taken into account. So if you need $60,000 a year to live and Social Security covers $30,000, your portfolio gap is $30,000. In that case, a 3-to 5-year cash wedge would be about $90,000 to $150,000 in very safe assets.

That money can be held in places such as high-yield savings accounts, money market funds, short-term Treasury bills, CDs, or even a portion in I Bonds. The goal of a cash wedge is to create a buffer. When the market is up, withdrawals can come from investments, depending on your overall strategy, and the cash wedge can remain in place. When the market is down, spending can come from the cash wedge instead of forcing stock sales at depressed prices.

In that sense, the cash wedge acts as a stabilizer. It gives you a store of safe money to draw from during bad markets, which can make the rest of your retirement portfolio more resilient over time.

FDIC/NCUA Insurance

Before you decide where to keep your savings, it's important to understand what actually protects your money. For banks, that protection comes from the Federal Deposit Insurance Corporation, or FDIC. For credit unions, the equivalent protection comes from the National Credit Union Administration, or NCUA.

FDIC insurance means that if an insured bank fails, your deposits are protected up to certain limits. That protection generally applies to accounts such as checking, savings, money market deposit accounts, and certificates of deposit. It can also apply to cash management accounts at brokerages when your cash is swept into FDIC-insured partner banks.

The standard FDIC coverage limit is $250,000 per depositor, per bank, and per ownership category. In practice, that means you can increase your total coverage by spreading money across different banks, using different ownership categories such as individual, joint, trust, or retirement accounts, or choosing institutions that spread deposits across multiple partner banks.

It's just as important to know what FDIC insurance doesn't cover. It doesn't protect investments such as stocks, bonds, mutual funds, index funds, or ETFs. It also doesn't cover crypto assets or losses caused by fraud or identity theft, although those may be addressed separately through a bank's or brokerage's own policies.

What Doesn't Belong in Savings

Savings serves a very specific purpose. It's meant to be safe, liquid, and predictable. Because of that, some financial products, even popular ones, aren't a good fit for money that may be needed in the short term or during an emergency.

Stocks and stock funds, for example, may offer strong long-term growth, but they can also lose 30% to 50% of their value in a severe downturn. That kind of volatility may be acceptable in a long-term investment portfolio, but it's not appropriate for cash reserves that need to be there when they're needed.

Bond funds can also create problems for savings. Even though bonds are often seen as safer than stocks, bond funds still fluctuate in value, especially when interest rates rise. Long-term bond funds and many intermediate-term funds can lose money in exactly the kind of period when stability matters most. For savings, price stability matters more than yield.

Crypto is even less suitable. Its extreme volatility and the possibility of permanent loss make it inconsistent with the purpose of savings. I've had firsthand experience with crypto's wild swings and, fortunately, started with only a very small investment to get a feel for how volatile it can be. Even at that size, the swings can be unsettling. Whatever role crypto may play in speculative investing, it doesn't function well as a safety reserve.

Some insurance products are also presented as savings alternatives, including cash value life insurance, indexed universal life, and certain annuities. These products are often marketed around safety or guarantees, but they usually come with high fees, surrender charges, and complicated rules. That makes them very different from straightforward savings vehicles.

Illiquid investments of any kind can also undermine the purpose of a reserve fund. If money is difficult to access, tied up for long periods, or subject to penalties when withdrawn, it may not be available when an emergency actually happens.

Long-term CDs fall into a gray area. CDs can be useful for savings, but longer maturities can reduce flexibility. If the money is needed early, withdrawal penalties can eat into interest and make that portion of your reserves less useful.

Brokerage money market funds are a bit different. They aren't FDIC-insured bank deposits, and they charge management fees because they're investment products. At the same time, some advisors still use them for savings because they've generally been stable, liquid, and competitively priced. The distinction matters less in everyday use than in understanding that they aren't the same as insured cash at a bank.

The broader point is that savings isn't meant to maximize return. Its job is to be there when you need it, hold its value, and remain accessible. As Fidelity puts it, emergency savings belongs in "an account that pays some interest but preserves liquidity." Once a product starts to compromise one of those qualities, it starts to drift away from what savings is supposed to do.

Automation: Set It and Don't Forget It

Consistency is what makes saving work. Savings usually grows through steady habits repeated over time. That's why automation matters so much. It turns saving from something you have to remember and debate each month into something that simply happens in the background.

Automated savings works well because it aligns with basic principles of behavioral finance. One of those is *status quo bias*, which is the tendency to stick with whatever is already in motion. Once an automatic transfer is in place, saving becomes the default. It stops feeling like a fresh decision every payday and starts feeling like the normal order of things.

Another reason automation works is *loss aversion*, which we covered in Chapter 4. Most of us feel the pain of giving something up more strongly than the satisfaction of doing something beneficial. When money moves to savings automatically, it's removed before it gets folded into your everyday spending decisions. That small shift matters. Saving feels less like a sacrifice when the decision has already been made.

Automation also helps with decision fatigue. The more choices you have to make, the harder it becomes to make them well and consistently. Saving manually every pay period may sound simple, but in real life it competes with bills, distractions, impulses, and plain forgetfulness. Automation removes that repeated moment of choice and makes saving less dependent on willpower.

There are a couple of simple ways to put this into practice. One is the payroll split method. If your employer uses a payroll system such as ADP or Workday, you may be able to send part of every paycheck directly into a separate high-yield savings account. If 15% of each paycheck goes directly to savings, it's set aside before it ever reaches your checking account.

Another option is what you might think of as a day-two transfer. If splitting your paycheck isn't possible, you can set up an automatic bank transfer for the day after payday. So if you're paid on the 1st and 15th, you might schedule transfers for the 2nd and 16th. The effect is similar. The money moves out quickly, before it gets absorbed into everyday spending, and saving becomes part of the rhythm of your financial life.

That said, automation isn't the same as autopilot. Set it, but don't forget it. Check in every month or so to make sure the transfers actually went through, the right amount moved, and the balance is growing the way you expected. Banks change, employers switch payroll systems, and accounts get flagged. A quick look once a month is all it takes to catch a problem early instead of discovering six months later that nothing has been moving.

Strengthening Your Cash Reserves

The main goal of building cash reserves is to create a buffer you can count on when life gets expensive, unpredictable, or both, and we know that happens more often than we'd like.

One of the biggest challenges is balancing savings with high-interest debt repayment. Cash reserves protect you when life gets disrupted, but high-interest debt quietly weakens your finances in the background. A common approach is to build a starter emergency fund first, then pay down high-interest debt aggressively while continuing to add to savings. That way, a small setback doesn't send you straight back into borrowing, but expensive debt also doesn't keep draining your progress.

It also helps to separate true emergencies from predictable expenses. A job loss, a medical crisis, or a major unexpected repair belongs in an emergency fund. Routine car maintenance, annual insurance premiums, home upkeep, and deductibles usually don't. Those expenses may be frustrating, but they aren't surprises. They're better handled through sinking funds, which simply means setting money aside over time for known future costs. That keeps your emergency reserves available for the things you truly couldn't have planned for.

Another important principle is having a replenishment plan. Using your emergency fund doesn't mean the system failed. It means the system worked. But once that money has been used, rebuilding it needs to move back near the top of your priority list. A reserve fund is strongest when it's restored deliberately, not only when there happens to be extra money left over.

Cash reserves also need regular review. The right amount won't stay the same forever. Inflation changes the cost of everyday living. Income can rise or fall. Families grow. Housing, insurance, food, and transportation costs shift over time. A reserve target that felt adequate two years ago may not provide the same level of protection today. Reviewing your reserves at least once a year helps keep them tied to your actual life instead of an outdated snapshot.

It also helps to think in layers rather than absolutes. Savings should be the first line of defense, but it doesn't always stand alone. In some situations, a home equity line of credit, unused low-or-no interest credit card capacity, or another backup source of liquidity can provide additional flexibility in a true worst-case scenario. Those options aren't replacements for savings, and they come with their own risks, but they can still serve as last-resort backstops.

Finally, many emergency planners recommend keeping a small amount of physical cash at home, often a few hundred dollars in small bills. During storms, power outages, or temporary disruptions to card networks and ATMs, a modest amount of cash can help bridge the gap until normal systems return.

The broader lesson is that strong cash reserves don't come from a single account. They come from structure. A solid system includes emergency savings, sinking funds for predictable costs, a plan to replenish what gets used, and periodic adjustments as life changes. That kind of structure makes your reserves more durable and much more useful when you actually need them.

Putting It All Together

The following example graphic that brings the chapter's ideas together in one view. This model uses an eight-month emergency reserve, which aligns with Suze Orman's recommendation to keep at least eight months of living expenses in emergency savings. Each account in the structure has a clear job, which helps keep the overall system organized and manageable.

ASSUMPTION: ASSUME MONTHLY SPENDING IS $7,000.

1 EMERGENCY RESERVE – THREE TIERS (8 MONTHS OF EXPENSES = $56,000)

	ACCOUNT NUMBER	ACCOUNT / PURPOSE	ACCOUNT TYPE	AMOUNT	WHAT IT'S FOR
TIER 1 IMMEDIATE CASH	1	CHECKING ACCOUNT (IMMEDIATE ACCESS) PLUS $500 IN PHYSICAL CASH AT HOME	CHECKING	$7,000 (1 MONTH) +$500 CASH AT HOME	FIRST LINE OF DEFENSE FOR ONE MONTH OF EXPENSES, BILLS, CASH FLOW, AND SMALLER SURPRISES. SMALL BILLS FOR OUTAGES, PAYMENT DISRUPTIONS, OR WHEN CARDS/ATMS ARE UNAVAILABLE.
TIER 2 HIGH-YIELD RESERVE	2	HIGH-YIELD SAVINGS (CORE RESERVE)	HIGH-YIELD SAVINGS ACCOUNT	$21,000 (3 MONTHS)	COVERS THREE MONTHS OF EXPENSES AND SERVES AS THE CORE EMERGENCY RESERVE.
TIER 3 DEEP RESERVE	3	I BONDS	TREASURYDIRECT	$10,000 (~1.5 MONTHS)	LONGER-TERM, INFLATION-PROTECTED PORTION OF THE DEEP RESERVE.
	4	TREASURY BILL LADDER (4 T-BILLS)	BROKERAGE ACCOUNT	$10,000 (~1.5 MONTHS)	SPLIT INTO FOUR T-BILLS OF $2,500 WITH MATURITIES AT 3, 6, 9, AND 12 MONTHS.
	5	CD LADDER (4 CDS)	BANK OR BROKERAGE	$8,000 (~1 MONTH)	SPLIT INTO FOUR $2,000 CDS WITH MATURITIES AT 1, 2, 3, AND 4 YEARS.
TOTAL EMERGENCY RESERVE (ACCOUNTS 1–5)				$56,000	EQUALS EIGHT MONTHS OF EXPENSES

2 SINKING FUNDS – PREDICTABLE EXPENSES

ACCOUNT NUMBER	ACCOUNT / PURPOSE	ACCOUNT TYPE	AMOUNT	WHAT IT'S FOR
6	SINKING FUNDS (PREDICTABLE EXPENSES)	HIGH-YIELD SAVINGS ACCOUNT	$5,700	FOR PREDICTABLE EXPENSES SUCH AS CAR REPAIRS, HOME MAINTENANCE, INSURANCE PREMIUMS, AND MEDICAL DEDUCTIBLES.

3 CASH WEDGE – NEAR-TERM RETIREMENT INCOME (2–3 YEARS OF SPENDING)
BUILT OVER TIME FOR AN ACCOUNT OWNER NEARING RETIREMENT.

ACCOUNT NUMBER	ACCOUNT / PURPOSE	ACCOUNT TYPE	AMOUNT	WHAT IT'S FOR
7	CASH WEDGE – YEAR 1	HIGH-YIELD SAVINGS ACCOUNT OR MONEY MARKET FUND	$42,000 (YEAR 1)	HELD IN A HIGH-YIELD SAVINGS ACCOUNT OR MONEY MARKET FUND FOR YEAR ONE OF WITHDRAWALS.
8	CASH WEDGE – YEAR 2	TREASURY BILLS OR SHORT-TERM TREASURIES	$42,000 (YEAR 2)	HELD IN TREASURY BILLS OR SHORT-TERM TREASURIES FOR YEAR TWO.
9	CASH WEDGE – YEAR 3	CDS OR ADDITIONAL TREASURIES	$42,000 (YEAR 3)	HELD IN CDS OR ADDITIONAL TREASURIES FOR YEAR THREE.

TOTAL: 9 ACCOUNTS (NOT INCLUDING CASH AT HOME) | A CLEAR, ORGANIZED SYSTEM DESIGNED TO PROTECT AGAINST EMERGENCIES, COVER PREDICTABLE EXPENSES, AND SUPPORT A STABLE RETIREMENT.

NOTE: AMOUNTS ARE EXAMPLES ONLY. ADJUST BASED ON YOUR ACTUAL SPENDING AND GOALS.

As the account owner ages, a simpler structure with fewer accounts may become more practical. The goal is to preserve the purpose of each pool of money while reducing the number of accounts that must be monitored and maintained.

Building Financial Margin

Cash reserves give you financial margin. They put a buffer between your life and the next surprise. When there's no cushion, problems may feel bigger than they really are because there's no financial margin to handle life's inevitable emergencies. When there's a cushion, the pressure changes. You may still be dealing with something frustrating or expensive, but you're not dealing with it from a place of panic because you have the cash available to handle it.

Having the money is critical, but the way it's held can help it earn more while still staying accessible. Some cash needs to be available right away, while some can be held farther out as a deeper reserve, and if retirement is in your near future, some of your cash may need to serve a different role as a cash wedge to help prevent selling investments during a market decline. Each part has its own job, and that's what makes the whole system so powerful.

Cash reserves help keep short-term problems from interfering with long-term investing. Investments need time. They need room. They need to stay put when life gets messy. Without a cash foundation, even a temporary setback can force you to pull money from the wrong place at the wrong time. With a reserve in place, you're far less likely to have one bad moment spill into the rest of your life.

And that's really the point of this chapter. Cash reserves give you steadiness and control. It's easier to absorb the unpredictable without everything else falling apart. Once that foundation is in place, you're in a stronger position to put the rest of your surplus to work for the future.

Chapter Eight Actions

Quick Wins (Complete this week)

[ ] **Check Your Bank Setup:** Review your current checking and savings accounts. Compare them with credit unions and high-yield savings options to see whether you could earn more interest, pay fewer fees, or get better overall terms. If a switch makes sense, make it a priority.

[ ] **Confirm Deposit Protection:** Make sure the institutions holding your savings are protected by FDIC or NCUA insurance, and make sure your balances stay within the applicable limits for each ownership category.

[ ] **Keep a Small Amount of Cash at Home:** Set aside a modest amount of physical cash in small bills for storms, outages, or temporary payment disruptions.

Strategic Setup (Complete this week)

[ ] **Build Your Tiers:** Organize your cash into Tier 1, Tier 2, and Tier 3. Keep immediate cash in checking, hold the next layer in a high-yield savings or money market account, and place deeper reserves in vehicles such as CDs, Treasuries, or I Bonds. Don't let excess cash sit idle in checking.

[ ] **Separate Emergencies from Predictable Expenses:** Decide which expenses belong in your emergency fund and which belong in sinking funds. Job loss, medical crises, and major unexpected repairs belong in emergency reserves. Routine maintenance, annual premiums, and deductibles belong in sinking funds.

[ ] **Set Up a Sinking Fund:** Open or designate a separate savings bucket for predictable expenses.

[ ] **Ladder Check:** If you've built up a meaningful cash reserve, log into your brokerage account and look at its CD ladder tool. Try modeling a ladder so you understand how staggered maturities can improve yield while preserving access over time.

[ ] **Treasury Check:** Review Treasury bills and notes as possible Tier 3 options. Compare them with CDs for yield, liquidity, and tax treatment.

[ ] **I Bond Check:** Review current I Bond terms at TreasuryDirect and decide whether they fit part of your Tier 3 reserve, especially if inflation protection is important to you. Remember the one-year lockup and early redemption rules.

[ ] **Automate Everything:** Set up payroll split or automatic transfers so savings moves out before it gets absorbed into everyday spending.

Maintenance (Put this in place now)

[ ] **Create a Replenishment Plan:** Decide in advance how you'll rebuild reserves after using them. When emergency savings gets tapped, replenishing it should move back near the top of your priority list.

[ ] **Review Once a Year:** Revisit your reserve targets at least annually to adjust for inflation, income changes, and changing household needs.

[ ] **Know Your Last-Resort Backstops:** Identify backup liquidity sources, such as available credit, but keep them in the category of emergency backup rather than primary reserves.

Pre-Retirees (Within 5 years of retirement)

[ ] **Calculate Your Portfolio Gap:** Estimate how much annual spending will remain after Social Security or other reliable income sources are covered.

[ ] **Build Your Cash Wedge:** Gradually move about 3 to 5 years of that portfolio gap into very safe, liquid assets.

9
Investment Foundation

Cash reserves help protect your financial progress by giving you a buffer for the unexpected, while investing helps grow your long-term wealth. The two work together. As you continue strengthening your reserves, part of your income should also be going to work in assets suited for your long-term goals. To build or strengthen a retirement plan that may need to support you for 30 years or more, saving alone usually isn't enough. Before you can build a portfolio with confidence, though, it helps to understand the foundation underneath it.

That foundation matters because many people never get comfortable enough to invest in the first place. Gallup found that 38% of U.S. adults didn't own stock in 2025, and research from the Federal Reserve Bank of Philadelphia suggests limited financial knowledge and low confidence remain part of the problem. Research also suggests that investing is often perceived as complex enough to make investors and potential investors feel as though success requires predicting the future, analyzing balance sheets, and timing the market, which can lead some to stay on the sidelines. In reality, successful long-term investing is often much simpler than it's made to seem.

In practice, successful retirement investing is often boring, repetitive, and simple. You can build a diversified mix of investments, review them periodically, rebalance when needed, and avoid constant tinkering. Jack Bogle, the founder of Vanguard, championed this philosophy by promoting a simple, low-cost approach through broad index funds. He famously said, "Don't look for the needle in the haystack. Just buy the haystack!" In other words, you don't have to pick individual stocks or time the market. As you'll see ahead, something as simple as purchasing a single broad index fund can give you exposure to a large slice of the market.

That idea can sound almost too simple at first, and I understand why you might be skeptical. I felt the same way in my early days. Investing seemed like something that required constant research, market predictions, and the ability to spot opportunities before everyone else did. But after years of learning, investing, and seeing how markets actually behave, Bogle's point made more sense to me. Investing felt less intimidating, the decisions in front of me became clearer, and it became easier to stay focused when markets got noisy. That's the real value of learning the foundation. It can make investing feel less mysterious and much easier to stick with through the inevitable ups and downs. You don't need to become obsessed with investing to benefit from understanding it. You just need enough knowledge to know what questions to ask, what tradeoffs matter, and what mistakes to avoid.

In this chapter, you'll see how that simple philosophy fits into the bigger picture of investing. We'll start with the kinds of risk that shape every portfolio, including the difference between what you can afford to handle and what you can emotionally tolerate.

From there, we'll look at why markets can move sharply when uncertainty rises, how the right guidance can help you think through decisions more clearly, and why compounding and costs can have such an enormous impact over time. We'll also walk through the basic pieces most portfolios are built from, including stocks, bonds, and alternatives, along with the common ways investors hold them, such as mutual funds, index funds, and exchange-traded funds. Finally, we'll look at the accounts that serve as the containers for those investments, from retirement accounts to taxable accounts, so you can better understand not only what you own, but where it belongs.

Two Sides of Risk

Before you make any decisions about your investment portfolio, it's best to understand your own limitations. Many assume *risk* is a single idea, but it actually has two distinct components. If you don't recognize the difference, you might find yourself responding emotionally when the market swings.

Risk Capacity

This represents the mathematical side of the equation. It defines how much volatility you can afford to absorb based on your bank account and your calendar. A 30-year-old with a stable job and decades until retirement typically has high capacity. If the market drops 50% tomorrow, they have time to recover. Conversely, a 65-year-old retiring next year has low capacity because a market crash could devastate their plans.

Risk Tolerance

This represents the emotional side. It defines how much volatility you can actually stomach and lives entirely in your nervous system. You might have high capacity because you're young, but if you panic easily, you have low tolerance. On the flip side, you might be near retirement with low capacity, but because you've lived through many market cycles, your tolerance is high.

Financial mistakes can happen when these two forces are out of sync. You might take on too much risk because the math says you can, only to sell in a panic when your nerves fail you. The goal is to build a portfolio that honors the math while respecting your emotions. The framework in this chapter is designed to solve for both. You want to reach a state of smooth sailing where you remain content when the market rises and composed when it inevitably tumbles.

Volatility

Over the years, I've learned that the market reacts instantly to new information, and when that information creates uncertainty, the reaction can be swift and severe. If you're an investor, you've almost certainly experienced that yourself. When bad news hits, like a war, a pandemic, or political turmoil, the future suddenly looks cloudy. Investors rush to sell riskier assets to protect their cash, while buyers step back and wait. This imbalance forces prices down until they reach a level where it's worth taking the risk again. The good news is that the market isn't broken. It's simply adjusting to new information.

Keep in mind that if the market never tumbled, it would be perfectly safe. But if it were perfectly safe, it would pay the same lower interest rates as a savings account. You'd be lucky to just keep up with inflation. One reason stocks have historically delivered strong long-term returns is that investors have to endure volatility, drawdowns, and uncertainty along the way. Part of the return premium comes from being willing to stay invested through the scary times.

Hanging tight in a bad market is much easier if you have a proper investment framework. If you're investing without a plan, there's very little comfort to be found when the charts turn red. But when you trust the strategy you've built alongside your planner, you can stay the course while others panic.

Second Set of Eyes

Investing can be a solo pursuit, but it doesn't have to be. The financial landscape is full of risks, including tax traps and behavioral pitfalls, that can cost you dearly if you don't know how to spot them. Even highly confident DIY investors can benefit from working with a Certified Financial Planner™ who can challenge assumptions and help guard against costly investment mistakes and emotional decisions.

I work with a certified planner whose perspective I genuinely value. Over time, I've learned that going it alone can create blind spots I might not catch on my own. My planner acts as a second set of eyes on my investment decisions, stress tests my retirement plan, helps me think through complex scenarios, and keeps me grounded when markets get volatile. I come to each meeting prepared, I set the agenda, and I stay in control of the decisions.

I sleep better knowing a professional has challenged my assumptions, checked my calculations, and helped me see what I might have missed. That value has proven itself again and again over the years.

Where to Start Looking

The financial planning world is crowded, and finding a quality planner can be challenging. It can help to have a simple, thoughtful way to approach the search. Rather than relying solely on a general online search, you can start with trusted resources that help connect people with vetted professionals, such as these:

CFP Board (cfp.net)

The CFP Board offers a searchable database of all Certified Financial Planners. It's especially useful for verifying that a planner is actually certified and has a clean disciplinary history.

National Association of Personal Financial Advisors (napfa.org)

NAPFA offers a directory of fee-only fiduciary planners who are prohibited from earning commissions on product sales. It's especially useful for those who want to reduce conflicts of interest.

Garrett Planning Network (garrettplanningnetwork.com)

Garrett Planning Network offers access to planners who work on an hourly basis rather than requiring ongoing asset management. It's especially useful for those who want a periodic checkup or validation of their plan.

XY Planning Network (xyplanningnetwork.com)

XY Planning Network offers access to planners who often specialize in Gen X and Gen Y clients and may work on a monthly subscription or flat-fee model. It's especially useful for younger investors or those with high income but lower accumulated assets.

Planner Credentials

A planner's credentials can offer helpful clues about their training and approach. Here are a few of the most common designations you're likely to encounter:

CFP (Certified Financial Planner): The gold standard for holistic financial planning. It requires rigorous coursework, a comprehensive exam, and strict adherence to a fiduciary standard.

CPA (Certified Public Accountant): The gold standard for tax accounting. Keep in mind that while great for tax strategy, not all CPAs are trained in investment or retirement planning. Look for a CPA who is also a PFS (Personal Financial Specialist) if you want holistic advice.

CFA (Chartered Financial Analyst): The gold standard for investment analysis. This designation is focused on deep dive asset valuation rather than personal financial planning. It signals elite investment knowledge, but not necessarily expertise in estate planning or insurance.

ChFC (Chartered Financial Consultant): Very similar to the CFP curriculum but offered by a different organization. It's a respected designation, though it doesn't require the comprehensive board exam that the CFP does.

Brokerage-Based Planning Services

Major firms such as Fidelity, Schwab, and Vanguard offer access to planners through their advisory programs. These services are often well organized, cost-effective, and closely integrated with your accounts. For investors who want a second set of eyes without committing to a long-term relationship with a specific advisor, they can offer a convenient and relatively frictionless option.

That said, the tradeoff is often personalization. The advice may be more standardized than tailored, meaning you're placed into a model rather than given a fully customized plan. You also may not work with the same person each time, and the planner assigned to you may be responsible for a large number of clients, which can limit continuity and depth.

It's also important to understand your advisor's obligation to you. Some advisors operate under a hybrid model, acting as a fiduciary in certain contexts but under a lower standard in others. For that reason, it's worth asking directly whether the advisor is acting as a fiduciary across the entire relationship.

How to Manage Your Advisor Without Getting Sold

Once you've found a strong candidate, the next step is making sure you stay in control of the relationship. The goal is to ensure the advice you receive actually serves your interests. One of the first things to understand is whether your advisor is held to a fiduciary standard at all times.

In financial services, two standards commonly come into play. Under the fiduciary standard, an advisor is legally required to act in your best interest. If one investment option is better for you but pays the advisor less, a fiduciary is expected to recommend the better option. Under the suitability standard, a recommendation only needs to be suitable for you, not necessarily the best or lowest-cost option. That's one reason high-fee products can still end up in portfolios. For some investors that's a deliberate and informed choice, but for others it's a cost they never agreed to and may not even know they're paying. A simple question can clarify a great deal: "Are you a fiduciary 100% of the time?" If the answer is vague, qualified, or hesitant, that tells you something important.

It's also important to understand how the advisor is paid, because compensation shapes incentives, and incentives shape advice. With assets under management, or AUM, you pay a percentage of your portfolio each year, often around 1%, for ongoing management. That can make sense if your situation is complex or you want continuous support, but over time that fee can take a meaningful bite out of long-term wealth. With an hourly or flat-fee arrangement, you pay for time or advice much like you would with a CPA or attorney. For investors who want guidance without giving up control, this is often a cost-effective option. Project-based planning usually means paying a one-time fee for a financial plan that you then implement yourself. Before hiring someone, it helps to ask a few direct questions such as:

"How do you get paid?"

"Do you act as a fiduciary at all times?"

"What does our working relationship look like?"

"What is included in the fee, and what is not?"

"Do you have experience working with someone in my situation?"

If clear answers are hard to get, that's an answer in itself.

Annual Check-In

To ensure your plan keeps pace with your life, schedule a dedicated annual review with your planner to take stock of where you stand. The primary goal of the meeting is to get absolute clarity on your path, your costs, and your risk. You'll want to ask your planner whether you're still on track to retire by your preferred date, whether your fees have changed over the past 12 months, and whether your asset allocation needs to be adjusted. A good planner should be able to answer all three clearly and quickly.

Your circumstances today probably aren't what they'll be tomorrow. Careers shift, priorities evolve, and the retirement you're picturing now may look different down the road. Your annual meeting is your opportunity to catch small misalignments before they become costly ones, and to make sure every decision is still pointing toward the same retirement destination.

Now let's move into foundations of investing, arguably the most important part of building your retirement.

Power of Compounding

Compounding is the quiet engine that drives long-term wealth. It's the process of earning returns on prior returns, which creates exponential growth over time. For example, let's say you invest $7,000 each year into a Roth IRA and earn an average return of 10%. Over time, your returns begin generating their own returns, and the growth accelerates.

Year 10: Your contributions total $70,000, but the account has grown to about ~ $111,580.

Year 20: Your contributions reach $140,000, and the balance grows to about ~ $400,890.

Year 30: After three decades, your $210,000 of contributions grows to ~ $1,151,430.

The most remarkable part is that $210,000 came from contributions, while the remaining $941,000 came from investment growth. This is why the years you save in your 20s and 30s often matter more than the years you save in your 50s. Time is the multiplier. When you combine time with tax-advantaged accounts, the difference in outcomes between someone who consistently invests and someone who doesn't can become enormous.

Passive Vs. Active

It's important to understand the fee structure of your investments, because it determines how much of your wealth stays in your pocket and how much flows to the financial industry. One of the key decisions you'll make in that regard is whether to invest actively, passively, or some combination of both.

Passive Investing

Passive investing, the approach championed by Vanguard founder Jack Bogle, is a strategy that mirrors the market rather than trying to beat it. By using broad passive funds, investors automatically own thousands of companies, from household giants to small firms you've never heard of. This ensures they capture the growth of the entire economy without the risk of a single bad company derailing their portfolio.

Cost is one of the biggest advantages. According to Morningstar and ICI data, the asset-weighted average expense ratio on passive index funds was just 0.05% in 2024, and the best providers like Vanguard charge as little as 0.04%. Warren Buffett himself has long championed low-cost index funds, famously advising that most investors would be better served by a simple S&P 500 index fund than by paying for active management.

Active Investing

Active investing is a strategy where managers try to beat the market by analyzing balance sheets, forecasting economic conditions, and timing purchases and sales. The challenge is that it's difficult to sustain over the long term. Study after study shows that over a 15-year period, the vast majority of active mutual funds trail the simple passive index funds they're compared against. And since past performance doesn't predict future results, picking a winning active manager ahead of time is more guesswork than science.

Active funds also cost significantly more. According to Morningstar data, the average expense ratio for actively managed U.S. equity funds was approximately 0.65% in 2024, meaning an active fund could be charging you 13 times or more what a comparable passive fund would cost, for the opportunity to potentially outperform the market, even though the data suggests that's unlikely to be the case.

Fees

Over time, higher fees can be devastating. Imagine you retire with a portfolio of $500,000. It grows at 8% per year for 25 years. Here's how the math works out when you account for fees:

Passive Funds: In a low-cost index fund, you pay a fee of say 0.05%. You take the 8% market growth and subtract that tiny 0.05% fee to get a net growth rate of 7.95%. When you compound $500,000 at 7.95% for 25 years, the result is $3.38 million.

Active Funds: In a typical active fund, you may pay a fee of 0.65%. You take the same 8% market growth but subtract the 0.65% fee to get a net growth rate of only 7.35%. When you compound $500,000 at 7.35% for 25 years, the result is $2.94 million. The difference is over $440,000. That's nearly half a million dollars that went to the fund company instead of your future self.

Siren Song of Trends

At some point, you'll be tempted to chase what's hot. Your brother-in-law will brag about new crypto. Your coworker will send you a video about an artificial intelligence stock that's "going to the moon." Financial media will hype whatever has gone up recently. Always keep this in mind: *Excitement is the enemy of wealth.*

Many seasoned investors and financial advisors will tell you that investments that make headlines tend to reward those who already have money, not those trying to build it. For most investors, boring investments are what create wealth. If you must scratch the itch, some experts suggest creating a small play account. Take no more than 5% of your total invested money and use that for experiments, trading, and concentrated bets. Treat it like a trip to Las Vegas. When the money is gone, the trip is over. The other 95% belongs in your boring, diversified, low-cost portfolio that you hold through good times and bad.

Building Blocks

Understanding how your money is invested matters because it affects how your portfolio actually performs over time. The basic building blocks can be easier to sort through when they're grouped into buckets. In this chapter, we'll focus on three main buckets found in many portfolios: Stocks, Bonds, and Alternatives.

Before we look at those three buckets, it may help to understand how investments are packaged. That means taking a quick look at mutual funds, index funds, and exchange-traded funds.

Packaging

Up until the late 1970s, building a portfolio mostly meant picking individual stocks or relying on actively managed mutual funds. That began to change in 1976, when Jack Bogle launched the first retail index fund. The investment landscape shifted again in 1993 with the arrival of the first U.S. exchange-traded fund. Those changes gave everyday investors access to baskets of investments that hold hundreds or even thousands of assets. Let's break down how each one works.

Mutual Funds

These are the traditional vehicle for actively managed investing. The term "mutual" refers to the shared ownership structure, where thousands of investors pool their money together and everyone participates proportionally in the gains, losses, and costs of the fund. A professional manager selects and trades the investments on your behalf, and as discussed, that hands-on management comes at a cost. Many mutual funds also charge sales loads, which are one-time commissions paid either when you buy into the fund or when you sell out of it. These were the dominant investment vehicle for decades, and while they still have a place, those layered costs can, as we've seen, quietly erode your returns over time.

Index Funds

Like mutual funds, index funds are also pooled investments where thousands of investors share proportionally in the gains, losses, and costs. The key difference is how the money is managed. Rather than relying on a professional manager to select investments and attempt to beat the market, index funds simply track it by mirroring a broad market index like the S&P 500, which is a collection of 500 of the largest publicly traded companies in the U.S. and is widely considered the benchmark for the overall health of the American stock market. There's no manager making daily decisions, which is why the fees are a fraction of what mutual funds charge and there are no sales loads. These are the classic passive Bogle-style funds. You invest a dollar amount, and the trade is processed once a day after the market closes. These are a great option if you want to automate your investing and keep your costs low without the temptation of watching the market day to day.

Exchange Traded Funds (ETFs)

Like index funds, ETFs are pooled investments that track a broad market index, which means they carry the same low fees and no sales loads. The key difference from index funds is how and when they trade. Rather than being processed once a day after the market closes, ETFs trade on the stock exchange throughout the day just like a single company's stock. Because you can buy and sell them instantly during market hours, you have precise control over your entry and exit prices without paying a premium. These are my personal preference.

The Golden Rule of Costs

Regardless of which you choose, the expense ratio deserves close attention. As Jack Bogle spent decades arguing, in passive investing every dollar you don't pay in fees is a dollar that stays invested and compounds in your favor. Warren Buffett has echoed that sentiment, repeatedly emphasizing that costs are one of the few variables an investor can actually control. Research consistently shows that expense ratios are one of the strongest predictors of a fund's long-term performance, and the lower the cost, the better the outcome tends to be. For passive funds, most experts suggest targeting an expense ratio of 0.10% or less, though index funds from providers like Vanguard, Fidelity, and Schwab often come in well below that.

Bucket 1: Stocks (Growth Engine)

When you buy an individual stock, you own a small slice of a business. When you buy a stock fund, whether that's a mutual fund, index fund, or ETF, you own shares of a fund that in turn owns many businesses. Over time, companies can grow their earnings, increase the value investors place on those earnings, and in some cases pay dividends. That combination is why the U.S. stock market has historically returned about 10% per year before inflation, or roughly 6 to 7% after inflation, over long periods. In the short term, stocks can be highly volatile. Over the long term, they have been one of the most powerful tools for building wealth.

Stocks by Size

Not all stocks, and stock funds, behave the same way. They are often categorized by market capitalization, which is simply the total market value of a company's outstanding shares, commonly referred to as "market cap." Companies are generally grouped into three categories: large cap, mid cap, and small cap, each of which tends to behave differently in terms of growth potential, stability, and risk.

Large Cap: These are the giants, such as Microsoft or Coca-Cola. They are global, established, and often pay regular dividends. They tend to be more stable but grow more slowly.

Example Large Cap Fund: Vanguard S&P 500 ETF – VOO

Mid Cap: These companies are past the startup phase and still growing quickly. They strike a balance between stability and growth potential.

Example Mid Cap ETF: Vanguard Mid-Cap ETF - VO

Small Cap: These are younger, smaller companies. They tend to be volatile and can move up or down dramatically. Over very long periods, small caps have often outperformed large caps because investors demand a premium for taking more risk.

Example Small Cap ETF: Vanguard Small-Cap ETF - VB

You don't necessarily need to pick individual sizes when creating or updating your portfolio. A *total stock market* fund or ETF automatically holds large, mid, and small caps for you.

Example Total Market ETF: Vanguard Total Stock Market ETF (VTI) or VTSAX.

Stocks by Geography

You'll also want to consider where in the world your companies are based. Geography matters because different economies grow at different rates, respond differently to global events, and can help balance each other out within a portfolio.

Domestic Stocks: Companies based in the United States. The U.S. represents roughly 60% to 65% of the global stock market, making it the largest and most liquid market in the world.

International Developed Markets: Economies like the United Kingdom, Japan, Germany, and Australia. These markets are well established, relatively stable, and offer meaningful diversification beyond the U.S.

Emerging Markets: Developing economies such as India, Brazil, and parts of Asia and Latin America. They can grow faster than developed markets but come with significantly more volatility and risk.

Owning both domestic and international stocks gives you more diversification. When one region is struggling, another may be thriving. And a total international stock fund usually combines both developed and emerging markets.

Example ETF: Vanguard Total International Stock ETF (VXUS)

Bucket 2: Bonds (Stabilizer)

If stocks are the growth engine, bonds are the stabilizer. A bond is simply a loan. You lend money to a government or a company, and in return they pay you interest and repay your principal at the end of a set period. Bonds aren't bought to get rich. They're bought so you don't get poor. When stocks drop, bonds tend to hold their value or even rise, though correlations can shift in some market environments. The bond market is broad, and understanding the landscape will help you make informed choices when working with your planner. Here's a look at the key categories most relevant to retail investors:

Government Bonds (The Gold Standard of Safety)
Because they're backed by the taxing power of the federal government, these are widely viewed as some of the safest investments in the market.

Treasury Bills (T-bills)
These are short-term government securities that mature in a year or less. You buy them at a discount and get the full face value back at maturity. The interest is the gap between what you paid and what you receive.

Treasury Notes and Bonds
These are the longer-term cousins of T-bills. Treasury Notes mature in two to ten years, while Treasury Bonds can stretch all the way to thirty. Both pay interest every six months.

Treasury Inflation-Protected Securities (TIPS)
These are government bonds built to help defend against inflation. Their principal adjusts with changes in the Consumer Price Index, and the interest is paid on that updated amount.

Agency Bonds
These are issued by government agencies or government-sponsored entities such as Fannie Mae. They tend to offer a little more yield than Treasuries, partly because not all of them carry the same level of government backing.

Corporate Bonds (Lending to Big Business)
When you buy a corporate bond, you're lending money to a company in exchange for interest payments along the way and the return of your principal at the end.

Investment Grade Bonds
These are bonds issued by financially strong companies with higher credit ratings. They're generally considered the steadier, more dependable side of the corporate bond market.

High-Yield Bonds (Junk Bonds)
These come from companies with lower credit ratings, which means there's a higher chance of missed payments or default. Because the *risk is greater*, these bonds usually pay higher interest rates.

Convertible Bonds
These work like regular bonds, paying interest on a set schedule, but they also come with the option to convert them into company stock under certain conditions.

Municipal Bonds
These are issued by states, cities, counties, and other public entities. Their main draw is that the interest is often exempt from federal income tax.

General Obligation (GO) Bonds
These are backed by the general taxing power of the city or state that issues them, rather than by revenue from a single project.

Revenue Bonds
These are repaid with money generated by a specific project or service, such as a toll road, airport, or utility system.

Specialized Bond Structures
These have quirks that change how you get your money.

Bond Type	Key Feature	Why It Matters
Zero Coupon	No regular interest payments	You buy it at a steep discount and get one big balloon payment at the end.
Callable	Issuer can pay it off early	If interest rates drop, the borrower might call the bond back, forcing you to reinvest at a lower rate.
Asset-Backed (ABS/MBS)	Backed by a pool of loans	Your bond is actually a slice of thousands of mortgages or car loans.

International Bonds

These are issued by foreign governments or companies outside the U.S., and they can offer decent returns along with diversification you won't get from domestic bonds alone. Different economies and interest rate environments give you a way to spread things out.

The catch is that they come with real complications. Financial experts often warn that currency swings, political instability, and inconsistent regulations can chip away at international bond returns more than they typically affect domestic bonds. And if you're looking at funds labeled "global," don't assume they're purely international. Many include U.S. bonds too, so it's worth taking a closer look before you buy in.

Advisors aren't exactly united on this one. Suze Orman tends to keep things simple and stick with high-quality domestic options, while Jack Bogle was more open to limited international exposure for diversification purposes.

For most investors, international bonds usually aren't the centerpiece of a portfolio. The can play a supporting role, with major fund providers like Vanguard generally framing them as a modest share of the bond allocation, often around 20% to 30%, rather than the foundation of a bond strategy.

Example: Vanguard Total International Bond ETF (BNDX)

All-in-One Option (Simplest Path)

Aggregate bond funds are essentially all-in-one funds for bonds. They don't hold just one type of debt. Instead, they give you a broad basket that often includes roughly 60% to 70% government-related bonds, such as U.S. Treasuries and agency securities, with the remaining 30% to 40% in high-quality corporate bonds and other investment-grade debt. They're designed to track the overall investment-grade U.S. bond market.

In plain English, these funds are trying to give you a little bit of the major pieces of the high-quality U.S. bond market in one fund. That's why aggregate bond funds typically hold a similar mix of government bonds, mortgage-backed securities (bonds built from pools of home loans with payments flowing to investors), and high-quality corporate bonds.

Because these funds give investors broad bond exposure in one place, financial educators such as Christine Benz, Allan Roth, and Rick Ferri often point to total bond market or aggregate bond funds as simple ways to make bond investing easier. These funds can give you that exposure without forcing you to build the whole bond side of a portfolio piece by piece.

Personally, I think that kind of piecing together could become a bit overwhelming for some investors. It would for me, which is why I prefer bond funds over picking individual bonds. But that may not be the best approach for you. This is the kind of decision worth discussing with your financial planner, especially now that you may have a clearer sense of the different bond options you can incorporate into your retirement portfolio.

Example: Fidelity U.S. Bond Index (FXNAX)

Bucket 3: Alternatives (Diversifiers)

Alternatives are investments that don't fit neatly into the usual stock and bond buckets. They can include real estate, commodities, managed futures, private credit, private real estate, and cryptocurrency. The main idea is diversification. Some alternatives may move differently from stocks and bonds, which can help smooth out a portfolio in certain markets. But they can also be more complex, more expensive, harder to sell, or more volatile, so they're usually treated as smaller additions rather than the foundation of a retirement portfolio.

Real Estate Investment Trusts

Real Estate Investment Trusts own portfolios of income-producing properties such as apartment buildings, warehouses, data centers, hospitals, and shopping centers. When you buy a Real Estate Investment Trust fund, you're buying shares in many properties at once, and you may receive your share of the rental income through dividends. Real estate can also behave differently from regular stocks, which is why some advisors use it as a diversifier. A small allocation, such as 5% to 10% of a portfolio, is often discussed as a way to add variety without letting real estate take over the whole plate.

Example: Vanguard Real Estate Index Fund ETF (VNQ)

Gold and Commodities

Gold has been used for centuries as a store of value. Commodity funds may hold gold, other metals, oil, or agricultural products. These assets can sometimes perform well during periods of high inflation or economic stress, and they may rise when stocks fall, which can soften the impact of a rough market. The tradeoff is that long-term returns are usually lower than stocks, prices can be very volatile, and fees are often higher than simple stock and bond funds. For most investors, gold or broad commodity exposure, if used at all, is usually kept to a small slice, such as 5% of the portfolio.

Examples: SPDR Gold MiniShares Trust (GLDM) or Invesco Optimum Yield Diversified Commodity Strategy No K-1 ETF (PDBC).

Managed Futures

A Managed Futures fund uses rules-based strategies to "go long", which means betting prices will rise, or "short", which means betting prices will fall. They can invest across different asset classes, including stocks, bonds, commodities, and currencies. The goal isn't necessarily to beat the market in good times. It's often to help reduce damage during big market drawdowns. Some advisors like them because certain managed futures strategies have historically done well when stocks fell sharply, which can make them a true diversifier. The caution is that they're complex under the hood, fees are often higher, and there can be long stretches where they underperform a simple stock and bond mix. If used, they're usually a modest slice for more advanced investors who understand the tradeoffs.

Example: iMGP DBi Managed Futures Strategy ETF (DBMF).

Private Credit and Private Real Estate

In recent years, many advisors have begun using private funds that lend to businesses, known as private credit, or invest in real estate projects that don't trade every day on public markets. These investments can offer higher income and may not move in lockstep with stocks. The tradeoff is that they often come with higher fees, less liquidity, and less transparency. That means you may not be able to get your money out quickly, and the values can be more subjective.

Example (Public Proxy): True private funds don't have tickers. However, you can access similar private credit loans via public Business Development Companies, such as the VanEck BDC Income ETF (BIZD).

Cryptocurrency

Cryptocurrency has entered many client conversations and some advisor portfolios. A 2026 Bitwise and VettaFi survey found that 32% of advisors allocated to crypto in client accounts in 2025, up from 22% the year before. Still, crypto is usually treated as a speculative alternative rather than a core holding.

The landscape has also changed with the approval of spot Bitcoin exchange-traded funds and evolving regulatory frameworks, which make crypto easier to access through traditional brokerage accounts. That can reduce some operational risks, such as losing your crypto keys, but it doesn't remove the price volatility.

Certain crypto assets, such as Bitcoin, have delivered strong returns historically and have sometimes moved differently from stocks and bonds. At the same time, the risks are real, including extreme volatility, regulatory uncertainty, hacking, and the possibility that a specific coin could go to zero. For holders, we've experienced that volatility in 2026, with Bitcoin falling from a record high of more than $125,000 in 2025 to the mid-$60,000s in February 2026. Where it goes from there, no one knows. In my opinion, you really do have to have a strong stomach and nerves of steel to hold crypto.

If you choose to include crypto, many advisors suggest keeping it to a small slice, such as 1% to 5% of your total portfolio. Treat it as a venture-style position, not the foundation of your retirement plan.

Examples: iShares Bitcoin Trust (IBIT) or Fidelity Wise Origin Bitcoin Fund (FBTC). You can also buy crypto directly through an exchange like Coinbase and store it in your own soft or hard wallet. I prefer a hard wallet, but that's just me. I recommend you research how to store crypto *securely* before you buy.

Due Diligence

There are thousands of funds available, and the ones mentioned here may not be the best fit for your brokerage, tax situation, risk tolerance, or overall plan.

Before buying any fund, it's smart to take a look under the hood. Don't guess. At a minimum, use free, high-quality tools to compare your options. Morningstar.com is a strong resource for fund data and ratings. ETF.com is helpful for comparing expense ratios and holdings of specific exchange-traded funds. Your brokerage screener can also be useful, since Fidelity, Schwab, and Vanguard all have built-in tools that let you compare funds side by side.

When comparing two similar funds, such as two different S&P 500 exchange-traded funds, focus on the basics. Look at the expense ratio, because lower is usually better. Check assets under management, since larger funds are often more liquid and less likely to shut down. And review the holdings, so you can make sure the fund actually owns what you think it owns.

Before you make trades to create or update your portfolio, it's wise to review your plan with your planner or advisor. They can help spot tax consequences, wash-sale issues, which can happen when you sell an investment at a loss and buy a similar one too soon, allocation overlaps, which happen when different funds own many of the same investments, and other details that are easy to miss. Use this book to build your knowledge, but use your professional team to validate your selections.

Retirement Accounts

Before building or updating a portfolio, it helps to understand the accounts that hold your investments. These accounts are the containers. They determine how your money is taxed, how fast it grows, and how much of your wealth you ultimately keep. The investments inside these accounts may be identical, meaning you can buy the same funds or securities across multiple accounts, but the account structure can create a massive difference in your final outcome.

Once you understand these accounts, you'll know what each one does, how it's taxed, and why it supports your long-term plan. And when you reach the next section, the execution steps should be clear because you'll know exactly where each dollar should go and how to direct it with confidence.

401(k): Workplace Wealth Builder

A 401(k) is the most common employer sponsored retirement plan. Money goes in automatically from each paycheck, which removes the need for willpower and creates consistent momentum.

The strongest feature is the employer match. When your employer adds money based on your contribution, the match becomes an immediate 100% return on that portion. If you contribute $4,000 and your employer matches $4,000, you doubled your money before it ever reached the market.

Traditional 401(k)

You contribute pretax dollars, which lowers your taxable income today and can create meaningful savings while you're in your highest earning years. The money grows tax deferred, and you pay taxes when you withdraw in retirement. For many investors, especially those currently in higher tax brackets, this can be a powerful tool because it allows you to invest more upfront and control when the tax bill is paid. This option works well when you expect your tax rate to be lower later in life, or when immediate tax relief helps free up cash flow for saving and investing.

Roth 401(k)

You contribute after-tax dollars, which means no tax break today, but the payoff can be enormous. All qualified growth and withdrawals in retirement are tax-free, which gives you certainty in a future where tax rates are unknown. For many savers, especially earlier in their careers, a Roth 401(k) can become one of the most valuable accounts they ever own because every dollar of growth belongs entirely to them. This is why financial experts like Suze Orman give it a "hands down" endorsement, stating, "In my opinion, you should absolutely be putting every single cent into the Roth version of your retirement account. I think the Roth is the way to go, hands down." If your employer offers both versions, you can split your contributions between them.

Thrift Savings Plan (TSP)

If you work for the federal government or the military, your workplace plan is called a Thrift Savings Plan, or TSP. Functionally, it plays the same role as a 401(k). Contributions come from payroll, the government provides a match for most participants, and you can choose between Traditional and Roth contributions. The main difference is the investment menu, which is smaller and built around a handful of very low-cost index style funds. Think of a TSP as a streamlined, low-cost version of a 401(k).

Traditional IRA: Tax Deferred Option

A Traditional IRA is a retirement account you open on your own. In many cases, the money you contribute can be deducted from your taxable income for that year, which lowers the taxes you pay today. The investments then grow without being taxed each year. When you withdraw the money in retirement, the withdrawals are taxed as ordinary income. Required minimum distributions must begin at age 73, ensuring the government eventually collects taxes on the deferred money.

Roth IRA: Tax-Free Growth Engine

As mentioned, a Roth IRA is one of the most powerful accounts available. You contribute after-tax dollars and the money grows tax-free, and withdrawals in retirement are also tax-free. You're never forced to take required minimum distributions during your lifetime, which gives you greater control over your retirement income.

Health Savings Account (HSA): Triple Advantage

The Health Savings Account is the only account with three tax benefits: contributions are tax deductible, growth is tax-free, withdrawals for qualified medical expenses are tax-free

If you pay your medical bills out of pocket and let the HSA grow, it can double as a stealth retirement account. After age 65, you can withdraw money for any reason. Medical withdrawals remain tax-free, and non-medical withdrawals are taxed like a Traditional IRA.

This combination makes the HSA one of the most efficient long-term savings vehicles available.

SEP IRA: Solo Earners and Small Business Owners

A SEP IRA is designed for self-employed individuals or small business owners. It allows very high contribution limits relative to income. The business makes the contribution, and the money is tax deductible. Growth is tax deferred until withdrawal. This account is simple, flexible, and ideal for anyone who earns self-employment income and wants to shelter a larger portion of profit.

SIMPLE IRA: Lower Cost for Small Employers

A SIMPLE IRA is another plan used by small businesses. The rules are easier than a 401(k), but the contribution limits are lower. Employers must contribute either a match or a fixed percentage of each employee's income. Contributions grow tax deferred and are taxed at withdrawal. This account is a practical alternative for smaller teams that want a retirement plan without the administrative costs of a 401(k).

Solo 401(k): Powerhouse for the Self-Employed

A Solo 401(k) is one of the most flexible and powerful accounts for anyone who earns income without employees. You qualify as both the employee and the employer, which allows you to contribute at two levels: employee contributions and employer profit sharing contributions.

This structure creates the highest potential contribution of any retirement account available to individuals. Solo 401(k)s can also be Traditional or Roth, and many providers allow Roth contributions on the employee portion.

For self-employed earners, a Solo 401(k) often becomes the single most valuable tool for tax planning and fast wealth building.

Taxable Accounts

After you've taken advantage of your retirement accounts, the next place to invest is in taxable accounts. These are simply accounts that don't come with special tax breaks, so you pay taxes along the way on interest, dividends, and any realized gains. The most common example is an individual taxable brokerage account, but this category also includes joint accounts, trust accounts, and custodial accounts such as Uniform Transfers to Minors Act (UTMA) and Uniform Gifts to Minors Act (UGMA) accounts. Even everyday bank accounts like savings or money market accounts fall into this bucket since any interest earned is taxable.

The tradeoff is flexibility. Unlike retirement accounts, there aren't contribution limits, there aren't early withdrawal penalties, and you can access your money at any time. That makes taxable accounts ideal for goals outside of retirement or for building wealth once your tax advantaged space is full. While they're less efficient from a tax standpoint, they offer complete control over when and how you invest and withdraw your money.

Foundation Set

We've covered a lot of ground. Risk capacity and risk tolerance. Why volatility is the toll, not the trap. The quiet but relentless power of compounding, the real cost of fees, the value of a planner who can challenge your thinking, and what's actually inside the stock, bond, and alternative buckets. Plus, the accounts that hold them and how to evaluate a fund before clicking buy.

For some readers, much of this was a refresher. For others, it filled in gaps that have been there for years. Either way, the goal of this chapter wasn't to make you a portfolio manager. It was to make sure the foundation underneath your investment decisions is solid, whether you've been investing for decades or are just getting started. Knowing the parts is the easier half. Putting them together into a portfolio that fits your life is where the work shifts, and that's where we're headed next.

Chapter Nine Actions

Understand Your Risk (Complete this week)

[ ] **Assess Your Risk Capacity.** Based on your age, income stability, and years until retirement, write down whether your capacity for risk is high, medium, or low.

[ ] **Assess Your Risk Tolerance.** Be honest about how you handled the last market downturn you experienced. If you sold or panicked, your tolerance may be lower than you think.

Build Your Team (Complete this month)

[ ] **Find or Confirm a Planner.** If you don't have a Certified Financial Planner, use one of the directories in this chapter (cfp.net, napfa.org, garrettplanningnetwork.com, or xyplanningnetwork.com) to find one.

[ ] **Ask the Right Questions.** Before you commit, ask: "How do you get paid?" "Do you act as a fiduciary at all times?" "What's included in the fee, and what isn't?"

[ ] **Schedule an Annual Check-In.** Put a recurring date on your calendar to review your plan, fees, and asset allocation with your planner each year.

Audit What You Own (Complete this month)

[ ] **Identify Active vs. Passive.** For each fund you currently own, find out whether it's actively managed or a passive index fund.

[ ] **Look Up Expense Ratios.** Note the net expense ratio for each holding. Anything over 0.10% in a passive fund is worth a closer look.

10
Building Retirement Wealth

The last chapter gave you the foundation. This chapter is about putting that foundation to work. We'll look at how portfolios can be built at different levels of complexity, how open-market accounts differ from employer-sponsored plans, and how contributions, rebalancing, taxes, and written investment rules can shape your results over time. The goal is to give you enough clarity to understand what's happening in your portfolio and feel more confident in the conversations and decisions ahead. That way, when you sit down with your planner to talk through your plan and investment strategy, you can push back when something doesn't sound right and help ensure you're building a portfolio that reflects what you actually want.

We'll start with practical portfolio levels, from a hands-off robo-advisor to the kind of simple, Bogle-style three-fund portfolio introduced in the previous chapter, then move into more advanced strategies that may include alternatives, tax-smart placement, Roth conversions, charitable planning, values-based investing, and intentional tilts. From there, we'll cover where each additional dollar should go, how to keep contributions consistent, and how to keep a portfolio aligned with your plan through rebalancing, dividend reinvestment, and an investment policy statement.

You don't need to be a Wall Street pro to do this well. You need a clear system, steady discipline, and thoughtful guidance along the way. That's what we're building here.

Building Your Portfolio

A portfolio can be built in different ways depending on the account it sits in. This section uses a defined set of levels to explain common approaches to portfolio construction, including how much involvement each approach may require and how many moving parts it includes.

Before we get into those levels, it helps to divide accounts into two broad investing environments: open market accounts and employer-sponsored plans. Open market accounts usually give you broad investment freedom, while employer-sponsored plans usually limit you to a preselected menu of funds. Understanding that difference will make the levels easier to apply in real life.

Open Market (IRA, Roth IRA, Taxable Brokerage)

Open market accounts offer the most flexibility. You can select specific funds, adjust your allocation as needed, and apply the portfolio levels we'll review below with fewer limitations. Robo-advisors, alternative assets, and advanced tax strategies are all available here. Because the investment universe is so large, the examples in this chapter use specific funds to show how each level might look in practice.

The flexibility of these accounts also creates more responsibility. Because open market accounts give you access to a much wider investment universe than employer-sponsored plans, it's important to be intentional about costs, diversification, tax efficiency, and whether each holding serves a clear purpose. That freedom is valuable, but it can also make it easier to overcomplicate the portfolio.

Employer Walled Garden (401(k), 403(b), TSP)

Employer-sponsored plans come with a more defined investment menu. Your choices are usually limited to a preselected lineup, but that doesn't mean the portfolio levels won't work here. While some of the more advanced levels may require an open market account to fully implement, the same principles still apply within your employer plan using the options available to you.

Keep in mind that even with a limited menu, the quality of your decisions matters. You're choosing how much exposure you want to stocks versus bonds, domestic versus international markets, and high-cost versus low-cost options.

The menu options inside your plan likely won't match the exact funds mentioned in the examples below. So when selecting funds, instead of searching for a specific brand, such as Vanguard, Fidelity, or iShares, focus on the role the fund is meant to play. For example, when a level calls for broad U.S. stock exposure, review the fund options inside your employer plan's website or benefits portal for funds labeled "Equity Index," "Total Market," or "S&P 500." When a level calls for international exposure, look in that same fund menu for options labeled "International" or "Global."

A key consideration with these plans is that costs still matter, so it's important to check fees and expense ratios. To find them, log in to your plan's portal and look for the fund fact sheet or annual fee disclosure document. These documents should show the net expense ratio, which tells you how much the fund deducts each year to cover its operating costs. Since higher fees reduce returns over time, compare the available options and choose the lowest-cost fund that still fits the role you need it to play in your portfolio.

With that context in place, we can start looking at the levels that explain common portfolio approaches and the tradeoffs behind them.

Translating these ideas into actual investment decisions is something you should always do alongside a licensed professional.

Level 0: Robo-Advisor

If the idea of picking funds makes you want to throw this book across the room, there's an easier path. Robo-advisors, such as Betterment, Wealthfront, and many others, use software to build and manage a diversified portfolio for you. Robo-advisors are typically used with taxable brokerage accounts and some individual retirement accounts, but they are generally not offered inside employer-sponsored plans like 401(k)s.

My preference is a more hands-on approach using a simple ETF portfolio, mainly because it can offer lower costs and more flexibility than many robo-advisors. But for many investors, robo-advisors are a viable option because they remove much of the stress of decision-making.

To create an account, you start by answering a short questionnaire about your age, risk tolerance, financial goals, and other basic details. From there, the software automatically selects a tailored mix of stock and bond index funds for you. After the portfolio is built, the robo-advisor handles the ongoing maintenance. It can automatically rebalance your portfolio to keep it on track, and in taxable accounts, it may also harvest tax losses to potentially lower your tax bill.

For this service, robo-advisors typically charge around 0.25% per year. That's more expensive than pure do-it-yourself investing, but it's usually much cheaper than a traditional human advisor who may charge 1% or more of your assets per year.

A robo-advisor can also create some helpful distance between you and emotional decision-making. When the market drops, the system keeps following the plan, rebalancing when needed instead of reacting to panic. In that sense, the 0.25% fee buys more than portfolio management. It buys a layer of discipline, especially if you allow the system to operate without interference during periods of market stress.

One important limitation is that robo-advisors are built around average assumptions. They tend to work best when income, expenses, health, and timelines are relatively predictable. They can become less useful when life gets more complicated and judgment matters more than automation.

Level 0 may appeal to investors who want a sensible, automated investment strategy without touching the controls. Just be careful not to treat a robo-advisor as a substitute for workplace retirement accounts or other tax-advantaged accounts. If your employer offers a match, that match is part of your compensation. Skipping it could mean leaving free money on the table.

Level 1: Core Three-Fund Portfolio

For many DIY investors, Level 1 is all you'll ever need. It's often called the Boglehead approach after Jack Bogle. You own only three funds: a total U.S. stock market fund, a total international stock market fund, and a total bond market fund. Together, they give you a slice of nearly every major stock market in the world, along with broad exposure to the U.S. bond market. The appeal of this structure is its simplicity. Three broadly diversified funds form a complete portfolio without adding unnecessary complexity.

Let's take a look at commonly used frameworks for building this type of portfolio.

Stock and Bond Mix

A common rule of thumb is the 120 Rule. Take 120 minus your age. The result suggests the percentage held in stocks, with the rest in bonds. For example:

Age 30: 120 – 30 = 90. That suggests 90% stocks and 10% bonds.
Age 50: 120 – 50 = 70. That suggests 70% stocks and 30% bonds.
Age 60: 120 – 60 = 60. That suggests 60% stocks and 40% bonds.

Adjustments should reflect individual risk tolerance. Investors who are young, have stable income, and remain disciplined during market volatility may be comfortable holding a higher stock allocation for a period of time. Others, particularly those who are more anxious or have had difficult experiences in past market downturns, may prefer a higher bond allocation than the formula suggests. The right portfolio is one that can be maintained through severe market declines without abandoning the plan.

Age-based rules are best viewed as general guides rather than strict requirements. In practice, risk capacity is also shaped by cash-flow reliability, expense volatility, health, and the timing of withdrawals, not just age.

The 120 minus age rule can be useful during the accumulation years, when the primary goal is building wealth and there's time to recover from market declines. As retirement gets closer, though, the same approach may become too aggressive because withdrawals are about to begin.

A market decline right before or right after retirement can be especially damaging because the portfolio has less time to recover while also supporting withdrawals. This is part of the sequence of returns risk we'll cover more fully in Chapter 12. For that reason, financial professionals often recommend reviewing the stock and bond split around five years before retirement and considering whether a more conservative allocation is appropriate. At that stage, a simple age-based rule like 120 minus age may become less useful than a plan tailored to the investor's retirement date, spending needs, and risk capacity.

US and International Stock Split

Once you know your preferred stock percentage, the next step is deciding how much of that stock allocation belongs in U.S. stocks versus international stocks. A simple split is 70% U.S. stocks and 30% international stocks. For example, with a 70% stock allocation, that would mean 49% in a total U.S. stock fund, 21% in a total international stock fund, and 30% in bonds.

The example split isn't a rule of finance. It's simply a reasonable default for many investors. Other splits can also work well depending on your income, spending needs, and comfort with seeing your portfolio perform differently from the overall market. What matters most is choosing an allocation you can stick with over time.

Here's a sample reference list with common low-cost index funds from which you'd select only one fund from each category (one total U.S. stock fund, one international stock fund, and one total bond fund):

Total US Stocks

Vanguard Total Stock Market Index Fund
Ticker: VTSAX
Description: A mutual fund that tracks the performance of the entire U.S. stock market, including large-, mid-, and small-cap companies.

Vanguard Total Stock Market ETF
Ticker: VTI
Description: The exchange-traded fund version of Vanguard's total U.S. stock market strategy.

Fidelity ZERO Total Market Index Fund
Ticker: FZROX
Description: A zero-expense-ratio mutual fund that tracks the broad U.S. stock market.

Fidelity Total Market Index Fund
Ticker: FSKAX
Description: A low-cost mutual fund providing exposure to the full U.S. stock market.

Schwab Total Stock Market Index Fund
Ticker: SWTSX
Description: A mutual fund designed to track the performance of the broad U.S. stock market.

Schwab U.S. Broad Market ETF
Ticker: SCHB
Description: An exchange-traded fund that provides diversified exposure to the U.S. equity market.

iShares Core S&P Total U.S. Stock Market ETF
Ticker: ITOT
Description: An ETF that tracks the total U.S. stock market across large-, mid-, and small-cap stocks.

Total International Stocks

Vanguard Total International Stock Index Fund
Ticker: VTIAX
Description: A mutual fund that tracks the performance of international developed and emerging markets.

Vanguard Total International Stock ETF
Ticker: VXUS
Description: The exchange-traded fund version of Vanguard's total international stock strategy.

Fidelity ZERO International Index Fund
Ticker: FZILX
Description: A zero-expense-ratio mutual fund providing exposure to international stocks.

Fidelity Total International Index Fund
Ticker: FTIHX
Description: A low-cost mutual fund that tracks international developed and emerging markets.

Schwab International Index Fund
Ticker: SWISX
Description: A mutual fund focused primarily on developed international markets.

Schwab International Equity ETF
Ticker: SCHF
Description: An ETF that provides exposure to developed international markets outside the U.S.

Schwab Emerging Markets Equity ETF
Ticker: SCHE
Description: An ETF focused on emerging market stocks, often paired with SCHF for broader coverage.

iShares Core MSCI Total International Stock ETF
Ticker: IXUS
Description: An ETF that tracks international stocks across both developed and emerging markets.

Total Bonds

Vanguard Total Bond Market Index Fund
Ticker: VBTLX
Description: A broad U.S. bond index fund that tracks the investment-grade U.S. bond market.

Vanguard Total Bond Market ETF
Ticker: BND
Description: The exchange-traded fund version of Vanguard's total bond market strategy.

Fidelity U.S. Bond Index Fund
Ticker: FXNAX
Description: A low-cost index fund that tracks the broad investment-grade U.S. bond market.

Schwab U.S. Aggregate Bond Index Fund
Ticker: SWAGX
Description: A Schwab mutual fund designed to track the U.S. aggregate bond market.

Schwab U.S. Aggregate Bond ETF
Ticker: SCHZ
Description: Schwab's exchange-traded fund for broad exposure to the U.S. investment-grade bond market.

iShares Core U.S. Aggregate Bond ETF
Ticker: AGG
Description: A widely used exchange-traded fund that tracks the broad U.S. investment-grade bond market.

What Level 1 Illustrates

In this type of portfolio, the focus is usually on broad-market funds, low expense ratios, and reputable providers. Like any allocation-based strategy, it requires periodic rebalancing to keep the stock and bond mix from drifting too far from its target. This approach illustrates how a simple global portfolio can be built at a low cost, with a balance between growth and stability.

That core model can be expanded by adding alternatives, which is the focus of the next level. Before covering that, target-date funds deserve a brief mention because they offer another way to apply the same basic idea.

Target Date Funds

Target-date funds often use a similar underlying structure to Level 1, built from the same types of broad-market funds. But rather than choosing each fund individually, you select a single target-date fund, such as a 2050 or 2060 target-date fund, based on your expected retirement year, and the fund automatically adjusts its allocation over time.

Early on, the portfolio may hold a high stock allocation, often around 90%, then gradually shift toward bonds as the target retirement year approaches. By retirement, the fund may hold closer to a balanced mix of stocks and bonds, and it may continue becoming more conservative afterward. This automatic shift is known as the glide path, and it means the investor doesn't need to rebalance the fund manually.

Under the hood, these funds are still simple. For example, Vanguard target-date funds are generally built from a small set of broad Vanguard index funds, including Vanguard Total Stock Market Index Fund, Vanguard Total International Stock Index Fund, Vanguard Total Bond Market II Index Fund, and Vanguard Total International Bond Index Fund. The allocation follows a fixed structure, typically around 60% U.S. and 40% international for stocks, and about 70% U.S. and 30% international for bonds. There are no tactical shifts, no concentrated bets, and no active managers trying to outguess the market.

It's important to note that not everyone views target-date funds as the best fit for every investor. Some financial professionals prefer a more customized approach because target-date funds follow the preset glide path, which means the investor doesn't control the stock and bond split over time.

Suze Orman, for example, has often encouraged investors to stay more involved and tailor decisions to their personal circumstances rather than rely entirely on a one-size-fits-all fund.

Rick Rieder, a senior investment leader at BlackRock, has also argued that traditional glide paths can be too rigid, especially when interest rates and market conditions are changing.

The takeaway is that target-date funds can be useful, but they should still be understood before being used.

Level 2: Alternatives

For this level, the core portfolio is still usually built around broad stock and bond exposure. Alternatives, if used, are typically added as a smaller piece rather than becoming the center of the portfolio.

At a high level, alternatives are investments that may respond differently to inflation, interest rates, economic growth, or market stress than traditional stocks and bonds. They're not required for successful investing, and their benefits depend on how they fit with the rest of the portfolio.

Broad stock market funds may already include companies tied to alternative assets, such as real estate, commodities, or infrastructure. So when you add a dedicated alternative fund, you may not be adding something entirely new. You may simply be increasing your exposure to that area.

If alternatives are used, they're often funded by trimming the U.S. stock allocation by roughly 5% to 15%. That creates room for diversification without disrupting the core structure of the portfolio.

Let's look at a few common alternative categories, including some we've touched on earlier.

Real Estate Investment Trusts (REITs)

REITs own income-producing real estate such as apartments, office buildings, warehouses, data centers, healthcare facilities, and shopping centers. Instead of buying a rental property directly, investors can buy shares of a REIT or REIT fund and get exposure to a diversified pool of real estate assets.

REITs can provide income because they're generally required to distribute much of their taxable income to shareholders. They may also add diversification to your portfolio because real estate is influenced by factors such as rent growth, property values, occupancy rates, and financing costs, which don't always move in lockstep with the broader stock or bond markets.

Broad stock market funds already include some REIT exposure, so adding a dedicated REIT fund usually means increasing your real estate allocation rather than adding something completely new.

Gold and Precious Metals

Gold doesn't produce income or cash flow. Its role, when used, is typically defensive. Gold has sometimes held up better than stocks during rough markets or inflationary periods, mainly because investors may treat it as a store of value when they're nervous about the economy. But gold can also underperform for long stretches. For that reason, many financial professionals view gold as a diversifier rather than a primary growth asset.

Precious metals can also include silver, platinum, and palladium. These metals may still be used as stores of value, but they also have more industrial uses than gold. Silver is used in electronics and solar panels, while platinum and palladium are tied closely to areas like automotive production. That means their prices can be affected not only by investor demand, but also by manufacturing, technology, supply shortages, and broader economic activity. So while they sit in the same general category as gold, financial professionals generally treat them as specialized diversifiers rather than core portfolio holdings.

Managed Futures and Trend-Following Strategies

Managed futures strategies invest across many global markets using rules-based systems that respond to price movements. When the price of an asset has been rising for a sustained period, the underlying fund or manager may buy that asset with the expectation that the trend could continue. When the price has been falling for a sustained period, the fund or manager may do the opposite by betting against that asset, which means it can potentially profit if the price keeps falling.

The purpose of these strategies is not necessarily to outperform stocks over time, but to provide a different source of returns. In some market environments, especially during sharp stock market declines, they may hold positions that rise in value or lose less than stocks, which can help reduce overall portfolio losses. During calm markets or long, steady stock market advances, often called bull runs, they may trail traditional stock investments. These strategies are more complex and can be more expensive, so they're usually discussed as a smaller, diversifying part of a broader portfolio.

Cryptocurrency

Crypto is a highly speculative asset class with extreme volatility and uncertain long-term outcomes. It doesn't generate cash flow and is largely driven by adoption narratives and market sentiment. When included at all, it's typically limited to a very small allocation and treated as speculative rather than foundational.

Commodities (Broad Commodity Funds)

Commodities are basic raw materials such as energy products, metals, and agricultural goods that are widely used in the global economy and largely interchangeable regardless of producer. Some investors use diversified commodity funds for inflation sensitivity, typically through funds that track commodity futures rather than holding physical materials. These funds can be volatile, cyclical, and difficult to understand. They often behave very differently from stocks and bonds and may go through long periods of poor performance.

Cash and Cash-Like Reserves

In some portfolio designs, investors intentionally hold extra cash so they don't have to sell investments at a bad time. Cash can help cover withdrawals, emergencies, or short-term spending needs when the market is down. It can also make the portfolio feel less stressful because part of the money is sitting in something stable like a money market fund or short-term Treasury bill.

The tradeoff is that cash usually earns less than stocks and bonds over long periods, so holding too much can drag down returns. That's why cash is usually used deliberately, not casually.

Now that we've covered alternatives, let's look at a few sample models for illustration. Each one keeps stocks and bonds as the core, then adds one alternative sleeve to show how the portfolio structure changes.

70% Stocks, 20% Bonds, 10% REITs

This portfolio holds mostly stocks, keeps a smaller bond allocation, and adds a 10% real estate investment trust sleeve for dedicated real estate exposure.

Example: Fidelity Real Estate Investment Portfolio (FRESX)

80% Stocks, 15% Bonds, 5% Gold
This portfolio stays heavily tilted toward stocks, includes a modest bond allocation, and adds a small gold position as a defensive diversifier.

Example: SPDR Gold Shares ETF (GLD)

60% Stocks, 30% Bonds, 10% Managed Futures
This portfolio is more balanced between stocks and bonds, with a 10% managed futures sleeve added as a potential diversifier during certain market environments.

Example: iMGP DBi Managed Futures Strategy ETF (DBMF)

95% Core Three-Fund Portfolio, 5% Crypto Exposure
This portfolio keeps almost everything in the core three-fund structure, then adds a small crypto sleeve as a speculative alternative.

Example: iShares Bitcoin Trust (IBIT)

What Level 2 Illustrates

These sample models are not meant to be templates. They represent how alternatives can be added without replacing the core stock and bond structure. In each case, the alternative position stays relatively small, which is the main point. Level 2 adds a specific diversifier while keeping the core portfolio intact.

The tradeoff is that alternatives add more moving parts. They may help during certain market environments, but they can also bring higher fees, more complex tax reporting, wider performance swings, and long stretches of underperformance compared with popular benchmarks like the S&P 500. That can feel frustrating, even when the portfolio is working as designed. I've experienced that firsthand, and the lesson is that alternatives should be understood before they're added. Before buying, it's important to know what role the investment is supposed to play, how it may behave in different markets, and what conditions would make it difficult to keep owning. It's wise to write those details into your investment plan so you can refer back to them when markets are volatile and you're tempted to make an emotional decision.

Keep in mind that alternatives don't automatically reduce risk. Their usefulness depends on how they're sized, how they interact with the rest of your portfolio, and whether you can stay patient when they underperform. A small alternatives sleeve should make your portfolio stronger without making it harder to manage or stick with.

Level 3: Advanced Optimization

Level 3 presents an optional approach to optimizing a portfolio by going beyond basic asset allocation and exploring how portfolios can be deliberately engineered. Let's walk through some of the different ways you can do that.

Core Portfolio With Targeted Additions

One way a portfolio can be deliberately engineered is by keeping a broad core in place, then adding smaller targeted positions around it. A good example of this approach comes from a model Suze Orman discussed on her podcast, *Suze Orman's Women & Money*.

Rather than relying on a single all-in-one fund, Suze describes building around a broad market foundation and then layering in additional investments. Her starting point is a diversified core portfolio, similar in spirit to the three-fund approach. Around that core, she introduces additional building blocks, including sector-specific exchange-traded funds and individual stocks.

The following page provides an example that preserves the core structure while incorporating a more customized, hands-on approach.

PORTFOLIO EXAMPLE

Core Three-Fund Foundation + Targeted Enhancements

CORE THREE-FUND FOUNDATION (85%)

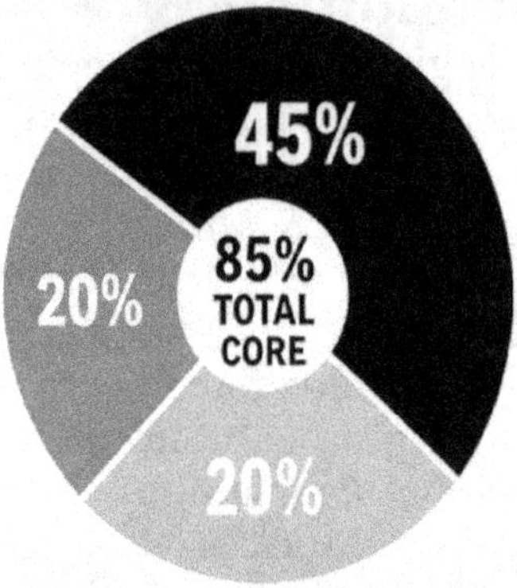

45% **Total U.S. Stock Market**
Vanguard Total Stock Market ETF (VTI)

20% **Total International Stock Market**
Vanguard Total International Stock ETF (VXUS)

20% **Total Bond Market**
Vanguard Total Bond Market ETF (BND)

ENHANCEMENTS (15%)

8%
Individual Stocks
(Selective Growth Exposure)

- Apple Inc. (AAPL)
- Microsoft Corporation (MSFT)
- NVIDIA Corporation (NVDA)

5%
Sector ETFs
(Targeted Exposure)

- VanEck Semiconductor ETF (SMH)
- Industrial Select Sector SPDR Fund (XLI)

2%
Alternatives
(Optional and Speculative)

- iShares Bitcoin Trust (IBIT)
- or SPDR Gold Shares (GLD)

This structure keeps most of the portfolio anchored in broad, diversified funds, while allowing a smaller portion to reflect more specific views, preferences, or opportunities.

With the targeted additions approach, the investor and advisor can work together to decide which targeted additions, if any, make sense. For individual stocks, that might mean looking at companies the investor already knows, uses, or follows, then reviewing things like earnings, financial strength, valuation, and long-term potential. For ETFs, it might mean identifying sectors, themes, or asset classes that complement the core portfolio without creating too much overlap.

The goal is to make sure any extra positions are intentional, appropriately sized, and aligned with the investor's risk tolerance, time horizon, and overall plan.

Tax-Smart Asset Location

Where you hold an investment can matter almost as much as what you own. This concept focuses on placing investments in the types of accounts where they may be most tax efficient, while keeping the overall portfolio aligned with the investor's goals.

Thoughtful asset location can help improve after-tax results by making better use of taxable and tax-advantaged accounts. It can also make a portfolio more efficient overall, especially when different investments generate income and gains that are taxed in different ways.

I've included the graphic below to show common examples of how certain investments are often prioritized across different account types. It doesn't mean these investments can only be held in the accounts shown. The best choice depends on your tax bracket and time horizon, as well as available account types and overall allocation. I strongly encourage you to discuss this with your financial advisor before deciding which types of funds to hold in which accounts.

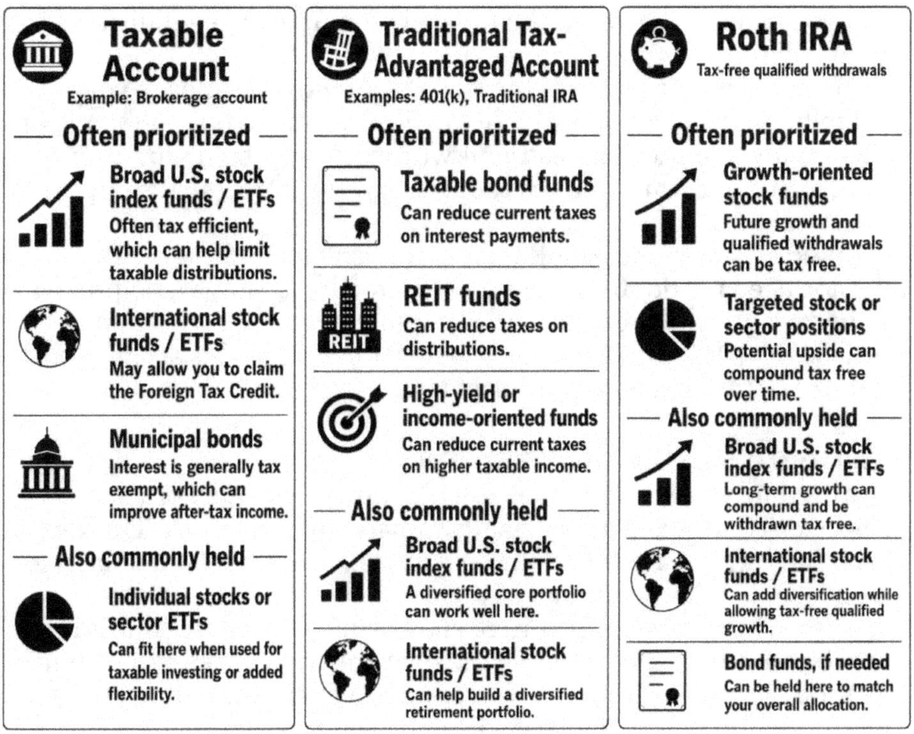

Tax-Loss Harvesting (For Taxable Accounts)

For investors interested in more advanced tax planning, tax-loss harvesting can be one way to reduce taxes without changing the long-term investment plan. The basic idea is that sometimes an investment you own temporarily goes down in value. If that investment is in a taxable brokerage account, you may be able to sell it and capture the loss for tax purposes. Then, you can buy a similar, but not substantially identical, investment so your money stays invested.

For example, suppose you bought a broad U.S. stock index fund in a taxable brokerage account for $10,000, and it later dropped to $8,500. If you sold it, you would have a $1,500 loss for tax purposes. You could then reinvest the $8,500 in a similar, but not substantially identical, fund so your money stays invested. That $1,500 loss could be useful if you also had a $1,500 gain from selling another investment that year. In that case, the loss could cancel out the gain for tax purposes, which may reduce or eliminate the capital gains tax you would have owed on that gain.

If you don't have gains to offset, the loss may be used to reduce up to $3,000 of ordinary income for the year. If the loss is larger than what you can use that year, the unused amount can generally be carried forward to future years.

The main rule to watch is the wash sale rule. This means you generally can't sell an investment at a loss and then buy the same, or a substantially identical, investment within 30 days before or after the sale. This rule can apply across accounts you control, so it's important to be careful.

Tax-loss harvesting is optional, and it isn't something every investor needs to do. But when used correctly, it can be a helpful way to improve after-tax results while keeping the portfolio invested. Because the rules can be tricky, it's smart to review this strategy with a financial or tax advisor before using it.

Strategic Roth Conversions

Advanced investors sometimes use a strategy called tax bracket arbitrage. This means intentionally moving money from a Traditional IRA or 401(k) to a Roth IRA and paying taxes now instead of later. The goal is to take advantage of years when income is relatively low, such as early retirement before Social Security or Required Minimum Distributions begin. In those years, investors may choose to "fill up" lower tax brackets with Roth conversions, which can reduce the amount that may be taxed at higher rates later in life.

Roth conversions can start at any age, as long as there's eligible retirement money to convert. There's no annual dollar limit like there is for Roth IRA contributions, but the converted amount is generally taxable in the year of the conversion. Roth conversions can be done from Traditional IRAs and, in many cases, from 401(k)s too. With a 401(k), the options depend on the employer's plan rules. Some plans allow money to be converted inside the plan to a Roth 401(k), while others may require the person to roll the money to a Roth IRA, often after leaving the employer.

A related strategy is a Roth conversion ladder. This means converting smaller portions of a Traditional IRA or 401(k) to a Roth IRA over time instead of converting one large amount all at once. Each conversion generally starts its own five-year clock. After that period, the converted principal may be withdrawn from the Roth IRA without additional tax or early withdrawal penalty, even before age 59½.

For example, suppose someone retires at age 55 and wants to use retirement savings before age 59½. They might convert $40,000 from a Traditional IRA to a Roth IRA each year. The $40,000 converted at age 55 could generally become available at age 60. The $40,000 converted at age 56 could become available at age 61, and so on. Over time, this creates a "ladder" of money that becomes available year by year. During that five-year period, the converted money can continue growing inside the Roth account, and qualified withdrawals should be tax-free because the taxes were already paid when the money was converted. The main catch is that the retiree needs another source of money to live on during the first five years while the ladder is being built.

The risk is converting too much. A large conversion can push you into a higher tax bracket unnecessarily, increase the taxability of Social Security benefits, or trigger higher Medicare premiums (known as IRMAA surcharges). It's important to do your homework before making any decisions. We'll come back to Roth conversions as they apply to specific retirement strategies in later chapters

Charitable Optimization (Donor Advised Funds)

If you give to charity, advanced portfolio design can integrate charitable giving with tax strategy.

Instead of giving cash, some investors donate highly appreciated stock or index funds directly to a charity or Donor Advised Fund, often called a DAF. This can help avoid the capital gains tax that would've been owed if the investment had been sold first, while still allowing the investor to potentially receive a charitable deduction for the fair market value of the donation.

A DAF can also make it easier to bunch donations. This means contributing several years' worth of charitable gifts in a single tax year to increase itemized deductions, then recommending grants to charities over time.

Tilts

Beyond basic asset allocation, some investors and advisors intentionally deviate from market weights. These deviations are commonly referred to as tilts. A tilt is an intentional overweight or underweight toward certain characteristics within an asset class, often implemented using diversified, rules-based funds rather than individual stock selection.

I personally like the idea of thoughtful tilts when they're used carefully and understood clearly. Tilts are not about predicting short-term performance. They're long-term structural decisions that can change how risk and return show up over time. Common equity tilts include:

Size (Small-Cap) Tilt: Overweights smaller companies relative to the overall market. Historically associated with higher expected returns, but also higher volatility and long periods of underperformance.

Value Tilt: Overweights stocks that trade at lower valuations. These companies are often priced conservatively and can provide better downside protection and higher long-term return potential when market leadership shifts, even though value strategies can lag growth-oriented markets for many years before reverting.

Quality or Profitability Tilt: Emphasizes companies with strong balance sheets, consistent earnings, and durable business models. These strategies often aim to reduce downside risk rather than maximize returns.

Momentum Tilt: Overweights stocks that have performed well recently (usually the last 6 to 12 months). The premise is that trends tend to persist for some time. This is a high-turnover strategy that can be tax-inefficient but historically powerful.

Low-Volatility Tilt: Focuses on stocks that have historically experienced smaller drawdowns. These strategies can help smooth portfolio returns and reduce the impact of market declines, even though they often give up some upside during strong bull markets.

Dividend Tilt: Overweights dividend-paying stocks. Often used for income stability or behavioral comfort, particularly near retirement, but less tax-efficient in taxable accounts.

Geographic Tilts: Intentionally overweight or underweight certain regions, often based on income sources, spending currency, or personal risk preferences.

Tilts are typically applied to a portion of the equity allocation rather than the entire portfolio. They require patience and discipline, as underperformance relative to broad market benchmarks can last for a decade or more. The greatest risk is abandoning a tilt during these periods.

Values-Based Investing (ESG)

Some investors want their portfolios to reflect their personal values. Environmental, Social, and Governance funds, often called ESG funds, attempt to emphasize companies with stronger scores in those areas while avoiding certain industries.

The main benefit is alignment. ESG funds can help investors feel that their money is invested in a way that better reflects their priorities. The tradeoffs are that these funds may have higher expense ratios, less diversification, and performance that can differ meaningfully from the broader market.

If values alignment is important, ESG versions of total market or international index funds can often be substituted into the core portfolio without changing its overall structure. Examples include Vanguard ESG U.S. Stock ETF or iShares ESG Aware MSCI USA ETF for U.S. exposure, and Vanguard ESG International Stock ETF or iShares ESG Aware MSCI EAFE ETF for international exposure.

What Level 3 Illustrates

Level 3 techniques are tools, not requirements. Just keep in mind that complexity acts as a multiplier. Used correctly, it can improve efficiency. Used incorrectly, it can increase costs and taxes. In many cases, a simple portfolio that's consistently maintained will outperform a more sophisticated strategy that's abandoned during periods of stress. No matter which level resonates with you, the strategy is only as good as your ability to stick with it.

Once you've settled on an overall approach, the next step is directing how new money flows into your portfolio. Whether you're building a new portfolio or refining an existing one, being intentional about where each dollar goes is critical. That's where the waterfall approach comes in.

Wealth Waterfall

The waterfall is a practical framework that helps you prioritize how your money flows into different accounts. Before applying it, keep in mind the cash strategies discussed in Chapter 8. You'll want to have a solid cash plan in place before you begin investing more aggressively. The following order is a general framework for deciding where each additional dollar of savings should go.

Company Match

First, contribute enough to your 401(k) or similar plan to get the full employer match. This is an immediate return on that portion of your contribution.

Toxic Debt

Next, pay off credit cards and other loans with high interest rates, which we covered in Chapter 7. The guaranteed return from paying off high-interest debt is hard to beat in the market.

Health Savings Account

As we covered in Chapter 9, the HSA offers a triple tax advantage and can also function as a retirement account for healthcare costs.

Roth IRA

Then, contribute up to the annual limit if you qualify. Your Roth IRA has tax-free growth and flexible withdrawal rules.

Back to 401(k) or Traditional IRA

If you still have savings capacity, increase your contributions to the maximum allowable amount. Check IRS.gov or your payroll portal for the current year's limit, since it's subject to annual adjustment and may be higher if you're over age 50.

Taxable Brokerage Account

Finally, any extra money can go here. To maintain your strategy, you can simply buy more of your core funds. Unlike retirement accounts, taxable brokerage accounts have no contribution limits and no age penalty for withdrawals, making them useful if you retire before age 59½.

The waterfall helps ensure your money is working as efficiently as possible.

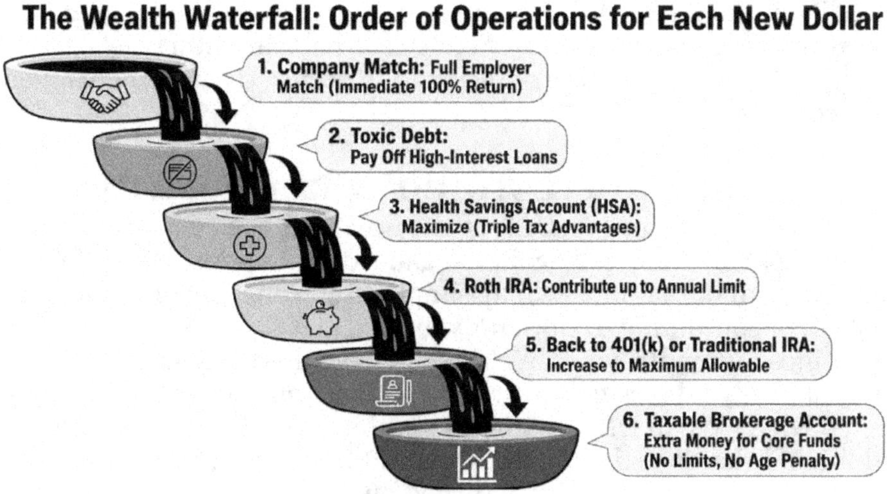

Dollar Cost Averaging

One of the biggest fears investors have is putting a large amount of money into the market right before prices drop. Dollar cost averaging is a way to reduce that pressure.

Instead of trying to pick the perfect day to invest, you invest a set dollar amount on a regular schedule. This is essentially what happens when you make monthly contributions to a retirement account, such as a 401(k) or IRA, and it can also be used in a taxable brokerage account. The same idea applies. You keep investing consistently, whether prices are up or down.

The key idea is that your purchase price averages out over time. When prices are high, your fixed dollar amount buys fewer shares. When prices are low, that same dollar amount buys more shares.

For example, suppose you have $6,000 to invest, and a fund is selling for $60 per share. If you invested the full $6,000 right away, you would buy 100 shares.

Now suppose you spread that same $6,000 over six months by investing $1,000 each month. In some months, the fund costs $60 per share. In other months, it drops to $50 or $40 per share. During the lower-price months, your $1,000 buys more shares.

By the end of the six months, you've still invested a total of $6,000. But because you bought more shares when the price was lower, you might own about 123 shares instead of 100 shares. If the fund later returns to $60 per share, those 123 shares would be worth about

$7,400. That's the benefit. The lower-price months helped you buy extra shares, and those extra shares helped when the price recovered. Dollar cost averaging doesn't always win, however. If prices rise steadily, investing the full amount right away may do better. But for many investors, dollar cost averaging can make investing feel less scary, reduces the pressure of picking the perfect day, and helps them stay consistent.

Dividend Reinvestment Plan (DRIP)

Many investments pay cash along the way. This can come from stock dividends, bond interest, or capital gains distributions. If you do nothing with it, that money may simply sit in your account as cash instead of continuing to work for you.

In most accounts, you can choose to have these payouts automatically reinvested by turning on dividend reinvestment, often called DRIP. When DRIP is turned on, the cash payout is used to buy additional shares of the same investment that paid it.

For example, without DRIP turned on, a $100 payout may sit in cash. With DRIP on, that $100 is automatically used to buy more shares of the investment. Now you own more shares, which can lead to larger future payouts, which can then buy even more shares over time.

Turning on DRIP means your portfolio keeps compounding quietly in the background. You don't need to remember to reinvest. You don't need to pay a trading fee. You just flip the switch once. Make this *mandatory*. You can't afford to have lazy cash sitting on the sidelines.

Log into your brokerage website and search for Dividends or Account Features. You'll see a list of your funds. Change the setting for each one from Deposit to Core or Cash to *Reinvest in Security*. Most platforms allow you to apply this to "All Current and Future Positions" with a single click. If you can't find it, type dividend reinvestment into the search bar or call customer support.

When you retire, you may want to flip the setting to Pay as Cash. Instead of buying more shares, the money will flow directly into your checking account and can be used for living expenses. This creates a natural paycheck from your portfolio so you aren't forced to sell shares during a market downturn just to pay bills. You live off the fruit (dividends) while leaving the tree (principal) alone.

Rebalancing

Markets move, and when they do, your portfolio mix can drift away from your original plan. For example, a 90/10 portfolio, meaning 90% stocks and 10% bonds, might become 85/15 after stocks fall, or 95/5 after stocks rise. Rebalancing is the process of nudging the portfolio back toward your target. A simple way to do this is to check your allocation once a year on a date you'll remember. That might be your birthday, the start of the year, or another easy calendar reminder. If your portfolio is off by more than 5 percentage points from your target, you can rebalance by trimming what has grown too large and adding to what has fallen behind.

For example, if your target is 90% stocks and 10% bonds, but stocks have grown to 95%, you may sell a small amount of stocks and move that money into bonds. If stocks have fallen and your portfolio is now 85% stocks, you may direct new contributions toward stocks or sell a small amount of bonds to buy more stocks.

Rebalancing can feel uncomfortable because it often asks you to do the opposite of what your emotions want. You may be selling part of what has recently done well or buying more of what has recently struggled. But that's the point. Rebalancing keeps your portfolio aligned with your plan and helps prevent market movements from quietly changing your risk level over time.

Investment Policy Statement

At this point, you've considered a lot of moving parts, such as asset allocation, account types, rebalancing, contributions, taxes, automation, and more. An investment policy statement brings those pieces together into one simple plan, and it's something your financial planner can help you create.

Think of it as a note you write to your future self. It reminds you why you're investing, what you're investing for, how much risk you're willing to take, and how you'll respond when the market is rising, falling, or making you and everyone around you nervous.

Your investment policy statement can include your goals, time horizon, target mix of stocks and bonds, contribution plan, rebalancing rules, and any investments you want to avoid. It's basically a way of saying, "Here's the plan I'm going to follow unless my life changes in a meaningful way."

I regularly reference my own investment policy statement before making any changes to my investments. It helps me slow down and make sure I'm making a logical decision, not an emotional one. Most importantly, it gives me a way to check that any change I'm considering still aligns with my long-term plan.

This document can be especially helpful when markets get noisy. When stocks are soaring, it can keep you from chasing whatever is popular. When markets are falling, it can remind you that downturns were already part of the plan.

Your investment policy statement isn't carved in stone. You can update it as your life changes, such as getting married, changing jobs, having children, approaching retirement, or shifting your financial goals. But it shouldn't change just because of a scary headline or a rough month in the market.

I've included an investment policy statement template in the appendix of this book. You can use it as a starting point if you don't already have one in place.

Transition to Ownership

Building a portfolio doesn't require perfect timing, insider knowledge, or complex strategies. It requires a clear framework, the right level of complexity for your life, the right accounts to support that structure, and the discipline to show up consistently over time. That's the work we've done in this chapter.

The framework we walked through is meant to educate and orient you, not replace personalized advice. Your circumstances are unique. Your income, timeline, tax situation, risk tolerance, and values all shape the decisions that make sense for you. Any meaningful changes you consider should be discussed with your Certified Financial Planner or another trusted advisor who knows your full picture.

Your goal is to become an informed participant in your own financial life. That's where confidence replaces guesswork and where investing stops feeling abstract and starts feeling intentional.

Once your investment strategy is defined and in motion, the next step is to see how well your overall retirement picture holds together. That means looking beyond the portfolio itself and asking whether your savings, income sources, spending needs, risks, taxes, healthcare costs, and timing all work as part of the same plan. The next chapter, Retirement Readiness, brings those pieces together so you can evaluate where you stand, what still needs attention, and how prepared you really are for the years ahead.

Chapter Ten Actions

Path 1. DIY Research Path

This path is best if you want to roll up your sleeves and understand the why behind every moving part before reviewing your findings with a professional.

Internal Audit (Complete this month)

[ ] **Fee Discovery.** Look up the net expense ratio for each holding. Note anything over 0.10% to review with your planner.

[ ] **Quality Review.** Use Morningstar, ETF.com, or another resource to verify the funds have sufficient assets (AUM) and that their underlying holdings match your expectations.

[ ] **Draft Your Allocation.** Based on the formula (120 - Age = Stock %), write down what your potential target mix would be.

[ ] **Identify the Misfits.** If you have an existing portfolio, list the legacy holdings that don't align with your new strategy or are too expensive.

Strategy Consultation (Complete this month)

[ ] **Engage Your Planner (or find one).** If you already have a planner, schedule a session specifically to review your research. If you don't, find a fee-only fiduciary using a database like NAPFA.

[ ] **Second Opinion.** Present your drafted allocation and fee audit. Ask: "I've designed this based on my research. What blind spots or tax landmines am I missing?"

[ ] **Finalize and Execute.** Based on the feedback from your consultation, decide on the final plan you'd like to implement and take the necessary steps to execute it.

Path 2. Educational Deep Dive

This path is your opportunity to bridge the gap between what you've learned in this book and your personal numbers as well as preferred timeline.

Complete this month

[ ] **Engage Your Planner (or find one).** If you already have a planner, schedule a session specifically to discuss your plan. If you don't, find a fee-only fiduciary using a database like NAPFA.

[ ] **Current State Meeting.** In your meetings, walk through your statements and your specific vision for the future. Your goal is to make sure your advisor understands that you aren't just chasing a return; you want a concrete plan that supports your preferred retirement timeline.

[ ] **Discovery Questions.** Beyond the planner-vetting questions from the previous chapter ("How do you get paid?", "Do you act as a fiduciary at all times?", etc.), use these prompts to help your advisor explain your current situation:

"What are my actual expenses?" Ask your advisor to help you calculate what it really costs to be you.

"What am I paying in total fees?" Ask for a single dollar amount or percentage that includes everything: their fee plus the internal costs of the funds you own.

"Does my current plan match my goal date?" Show them the timeline you've envisioned. Ask, "Is the plan we have today actually going to get me there, or do we need to adjust something?"

"Is there a simpler way to do this?" Now that you've learned about lower-cost options and straightforward allocations, ask whether your current strategy is the most efficient way to reach your goals.

"What happens if we change things?" If you decide to move to a new strategy, ask: "Will I owe the IRS money if we sell these old funds to buy new ones?"

Take a moment to listen to their logic. You're looking for a strategy that's sound and aligns with your preferred timeline. If their explanation feels too cryptic, ask them to break it down further until you feel confident in the plan.

[ ] **Finalize and Execute.** Review the findings from your meeting(s). Once you feel the plan matches your values and the timeline, work with your advisor to execute the necessary steps to get your portfolio in sync.

Maintenance Foundation — For Both Paths (Complete this week)

[ ] **DRIP Check.** Confirm your dividends are set to Reinvest (if accumulating) or Pay to Cash (if retired and it aligns with your strategy).

[ ] **Map the Waterfall.** Document your order of operations for future contributions (401(k) match, HSA, Roth, etc.) so the logic is clear and then setup the model.

[ ] **Retiree Bridge.** If you're nearing retirement, confirm you've set aside your 3 to 5 years of withdrawals in safe assets (Cash/Bonds) or have a plan to do so ASAP.

[ ] **Set a Strategy Day.** Pick a recurring date on your calendar to review this blueprint and ensure your financial status still matches your values and preferred retirement timeline.

Investment Policy Statement

[ ] **Write your Investment Policy Statement.** Document your goals, time horizon, target asset allocation, rebalancing rules, and decision-making guidelines so your investment plan is clear and repeatable. You can leverage Appendix A to help structure the document.

11
Retirement Readiness

Before I moved into corporate leadership, I spent years working as a Certified Project Management Professional. One project management concept I often had to consider was something called the triple constraint, sometimes known as the iron triangle. Every project, no matter how big or small, has three pieces that have to stay in balance: scope, time, and cost. Scope is what you're trying to accomplish. Time is your schedule. Cost is your budget. Quality lives in the middle of all three. Touch one, and the others feel it.

Retirement works the same way, just with different labels. I call it the retirement trifecta. Instead of scope, time, and cost, you're balancing **lifestyle, timeline, and resources.**

Your **lifestyle** is the retirement you actually want: where you live, how you spend your days, how much you travel, and what you want to do for the people you love. Your **timeline** is when you want to retire and how long that retirement needs to last. And your **resources** are everything available to support it, including savings, investments, income sources, benefits, home equity, and whatever else is in your hip pocket.

That's what we'll focus on next, determining whether those three pieces line up. It's something you'll want to revisit regularly as your life and the markets change because the last thing you want is to discover too late that you don't have what you need to retire on your terms. Doing this now, and keeping a close eye on it over time, can help you catch problems early enough to correct them.

You'll determine if you're right on track, close but not quite there, or staring down a shortfall that needs real attention. Then you'll decide how to manage it. Whatever you find, knowing where you stand is powerful because it keeps you in control.

Professional Guidance and Tools

So where do you actually start when it comes to assessing your retirement readiness? In my experience, there are two resources that make this process significantly easier and more reliable. The first is your Certified Financial Planner. They can help you stress test your plan, model different scenarios, compare retirement dates, and think through tradeoffs you might not have considered on your own. The second is planning tools, and this is something I personally lean on because the options available today are genuinely exceptional. These tools have become sophisticated enough to estimate future portfolio values, test different withdrawal rates, account for inflation, and run scenarios to show how your plan holds up under real-world conditions. Used together, your planner and the right tools can take you from a general sense of where you're headed to a much clearer picture of whether the plan actually works.

Some tools can also run what's called a Monte Carlo simulation. Think of this as a digital stress test. Instead of assuming one average return, the tool runs your plan through thousands of possible scenarios, including market declines, higher inflation, lower returns, and stronger growth periods. It then estimates how often your plan succeeds under those different conditions. That probability of success can help you see how likely your plan is to survive the unpredictability of the real world. I find this particularly useful because it looks at how the plan holds up when things don't go as expected, which is pretty much most of the time. There's no shortage of tools out there to leverage. Here are a few worth considering:

Boldin is one of the more comprehensive retirement planning tools available. It helps users build detailed retirement projections, including income, expenses, savings, investments, taxes, Social Security, Roth conversions, and withdrawal strategies. It also lets users set different spending amounts for different periods of retirement, which can be used to reflect the spending smile pattern we covered in Chapter 2.

Empower, formerly Personal Capital, connects to your actual accounts and gives you a real-time view of your net worth, savings, investments, spending, and asset allocation. Its retirement planner also uses Monte Carlo analysis to test how your plan might hold up under different market conditions, which can help you see whether your savings rate, retirement age, or spending assumptions need adjustment.

AARP Retirement Calculator is accessible and user-friendly, especially for getting a basic picture of retirement income, expenses, Social Security, and a potential income gap. It's a good starting point for those who want a simple estimate before moving into more detailed planning.

Major brokerages such as Fidelity, Vanguard, and Schwab also offer planning calculators that can help you run projections using your own numbers. These tools often work especially well if your accounts are already held there because they can incorporate your balances, savings rates, investment mix, and retirement assumptions more easily.

If you've got a planner, bring your numbers, your assumptions, and your questions to them. Let them help you compare scenarios, pressure-test your plan, and think through the tradeoffs before you make major decisions. A good planner can help you see what changes are realistic, what risks you may be overlooking, and which adjustments could have the biggest impact.

And if you haven't connected with a planner yet, this is a good point to revisit that idea. You don't have to figure out every variable on your own, especially when the decisions involve timing, taxes, income, investments, and lifestyle all at once.

Estimate Your Portfolio

In Chapter 1, you gathered the numbers that show where you stand today. You looked at your investable assets, retirement account balances, contribution amounts, employer match, debts, Social Security estimate, pensions, and other resources. In Chapter 3, you estimated your annual retirement spending and compared it with the guaranteed income you may receive. Those numbers gave you a snapshot. Now they serve a different purpose. They help you estimate what those resources could become and how much income they may be able to support.

This is the part I find most clarifying, because it's where the plan stops being abstract. You're not just tracking balances anymore. You're asking whether those balances can actually do the job.

Your estimate should include what you've already saved, what you're adding each year, any employer contributions you expect to receive, your timeline, your investment mix, and reasonable assumptions about returns, inflation, and taxes. It should also include other resources that may support the plan, such as cash reserves, rental income, business income, part-time work, REITs, or other income-producing investments.

The projection needs to answer two questions: What could your retirement assets become by the time you need them? And once retirement begins, how much income could those assets reasonably support? To answer the second question, use your preferred withdrawal strategy we'll cover in Chapter 12. That strategy helps turn a projected portfolio balance into a practical income estimate.

It's also important to separate total net worth from liquid net worth. You looked at this distinction earlier, but it matters even more here. Total net worth may include your home, vehicles, business interests, and other assets. Liquid net worth focuses on what can realistically fund retirement income, including cash, investment accounts, retirement accounts, and assets that can be accessed without major disruption.

Housing can play a major role too. A paid-off home may reduce your monthly expenses, while significant home equity may give you more flexibility later in retirement. Downsizing, relocating, or selling a higher-cost property can free up capital or reduce ongoing costs. But the opposite is also true. A large mortgage, rising insurance costs, property taxes, or expensive upkeep can put real pressure on the plan. For many, housing is one of the biggest variables in the entire retirement picture.

Projections must be honest in terms of reflecting what can actually be used. Someone can look wealthy on paper but still have a retirement income problem if most of their wealth is tied up in a home they don't plan to sell, a business they can't easily convert, or assets that are difficult to access. The point of estimating is to understand what your usable retirement resources may become and how much income they may be able to support.

Compare Projection To Target

Once you have a working estimate of what your retirement resources may become and how much income they may support, compare that projection to your freedom number from Chapter 3.

This is one of the most important checkpoints in the entire process, and honestly, it's the moment everything we've been building toward comes into focus. Your freedom number gives you the target. Your projected portfolio income, guaranteed income, and other expected resources show whether your current path appears strong enough to support it.

If the numbers suggest you're likely to have enough, that's encouraging. It means the plan is working. If, on the other hand, your numbers suggest you're close, that's useful information too. It may not be necessary to overhaul the plan, but you'll want to understand how narrow the margin is and which assumptions are doing the most work. If the numbers show a meaningful shortfall, that doesn't mean you've failed. There's a section ahead dedicated entirely to that situation.

This is where retirement readiness becomes really useful. It turns a vague concern into something you can actually evaluate. Instead of wondering whether you'll be okay, you can begin asking better questions. How large is the gap? How much time do I have? Which assumptions matter most? Which parts of the plan are helping, and which parts need more support? That's a whole lot better than flying blind.

When You're on Track

When the numbers show you're on track, that's a good sign. It means what you've been doing is working. But on track today doesn't mean on track forever.

Retirement readiness isn't something you check once and then forget about. Life changes. Markets change. Tax rules change. Inflation changes. Your goals may change too. Your income may rise or fall. Your expenses may shift. Healthcare needs will most likely change. Family responsibilities may change. So to stay on track, you have to keep paying attention. You'll want to continue saving and investing consistently, review your portfolio from time to time, rebalance when needed, update your assumptions as life evolves, and avoid emotional decisions because of short-term market noise.

A strong retirement plan doesn't need constant tinkering, but it does need regular attention. Think of it like a checkup. You're looking for signs that the plan still fits your life. Sometimes the right move will be to stay the course. Sometimes you'll need to save more. Sometimes you'll need to adjust your timeline. Sometimes you'll want to revisit investment risk, reduce expenses, or rethink certain goals. The value of retirement readiness is that it gives you a clearer way to make those decisions.

It's also important to be mindful of overconfidence. When markets are strong and account balances are rising, it's easy to assume the plan will keep improving on its own. That's when folks sometimes loosen discipline, increase spending, or take on new commitments without checking the long-term impact. It's an easy slip to make, but can be a difficult one to recover from.

Bottom line, being on track still requires consistent focus. Keeping the plan strong enough to handle changing markets, changing costs, and changing circumstances is what sustains it.

Close but Not Quite There

You may find you're close to being on track, but not quite where you want to be. That's a common place to land, and honestly, it's one of the more hopeful positions to be in. It means the foundation is there. It just needs a little more weight behind it.

The strategies we've covered so far, including contributions, expenses, timeline, investment consistency, and more, are the same tools that can close this kind of gap. Consider your trifecta and which of those tools has the most room to move in your situation. The difference at this stage is intentionality. Find it and focus there.

This is also a good time to revisit financial leakage. Leaks such as subscriptions, dining out, unused memberships, insurance overpayments, and lifestyle creep can quietly drain cash flow. And as we reviewed in Chapter 6, those dollars can be flipped into savings and investing, which is exactly where they need to be at this stage. Any reduction in monthly expenses is a bonus that may carry into retirement as well.

The earlier you work through this, and the more consistently you do it, the more time you'll have to make thoughtful changes before the gap becomes harder to close.

A Meaningful Shortfall

Finding a meaningful shortfall can be unsettling, but it's one of the most valuable things this process can reveal. If that's where you find yourself today, closing the gap may require more than a few small adjustments, but it's far better to know now than to find out later. When the gap is significant, the response usually needs to match. A hard look at your retirement trifecta is where to start.

On the resources side, it may mean revisiting your investment strategy to make sure your portfolio is working as hard as it reasonably can for your situation, or increasing income through a side gig, a career move, or additional skills development. It may also mean restructuring expenses more substantially, not just trimming at the edges but reconsidering fixed costs, housing, and longer-term spending goals.

On the timeline side, it may mean working longer to give your resources more time to grow, or phasing out of full-time work gradually rather than stopping all at once.

On the lifestyle side, it may mean adjusting the vision itself. Not abandoning it, but stress testing it. A more modest spending target in the early years or a different vision of what retirement looks like day to day can reduce pressure on your portfolio without giving up the life you're working toward. Closing a gap like this means the plan gets more focused, and in some cases, more creative. There's a compelling body of research on household financial resilience that points to the same lesson. Big gaps don't usually close with one dramatic move. They close through several deliberate choices made consistently over time. Taking it one piece at a time, rather than reaching for something drastic, is a good place to start.

Strategies to Bridge the Gap

When the projection shows a shortfall, several strategies can help close the gap. Again, some involve adjusting your timeline, others involve adjusting your resources, and a few involve rethinking lifestyle choices. The right combination depends on your situation, and a planner can help you weigh the tradeoffs. Here are some of the most common approaches worth considering:

The Power of One More Year

One of the strongest strategies, if it's an option, is staying in your current role a little longer. Even one additional year can improve the plan in several ways at once. New contributions keep coming in, existing investments continue to grow untouched, and there's one fewer year the portfolio needs to support. It may also allow you to delay Social Security, hold onto employer benefits a little longer, and cross into retirement with more confidence.

Part-Time Work

Part-time work in retirement can be a powerful strategy, and it's one that more folks are warming up to as the line between working and retiring becomes less rigid. Earning $20,000 per year for just five years is $100,000 you didn't have to pull from your portfolio during the years it needed time to grow. It can also help bridge the gap to Medicare eligibility if your goal is to retire before age 65.

Beyond the financial benefit, part-time work provides structure, purpose, and social interaction, all of which are often lost after leaving full-time employment.

This approach doesn't mean taking any ole' job just to bring in money. You may find something meaningful to do such as consulting, teaching, freelancing, seasonal work, or moving into a lower-stress role that gives you income without the demands of your former career. The point is that even modest income can reduce portfolio withdrawals and make the transition into retirement less abrupt.

Geo-Arbitrage

Geo-arbitrage is worth mentioning here because for some of us it can do more for a plan than years of budget cuts or working longer. The idea is simple. If you live in a high-cost area, relocating to a lower-cost one such as a different city, state, or even country can drastically reduce ongoing expenses while potentially freeing up capital. It's a strategy that deserves its own conversation, and we'll have that later in the book.

Home Equity

If you're a homeowner, home equity can play a meaningful role in retirement. The challenge is that it doesn't create income on its own. Unless you sell, borrow against it, rent part of the home, or use another strategy, that wealth stays locked inside your property.

If there's a meaningful shortfall and you're house-rich but cash-poor, the equity in your home may be part of the solution. But it needs to be handled thoughtfully. A home can be tied to family, identity, community, and daily comfort, so any decision around it carries more weight than a typical financial move.

Some folks consider borrowing against home equity, including a reverse mortgage. That can work in certain situations, but it's complex, expensive, and easy to misunderstand. We cover reverse mortgages more fully later in the book. For now, the key point is that home equity can be a meaningful part of the plan, but it should never be treated as a casual solution for lifestyle spending.

Late Starter

Starting later means the plan has to work even harder. But harder isn't the same as impossible.

If you're younger and have a shortfall, time can do a lot of the heavy lifting. Someone in their 20s, 30s, or even 40s may have decades for increased income, additional savings, and more time for compounding. But if you're in your 50s or early 60s, the window is narrower and what you do with it matters more. Small adjustments may not be enough on their own. You'll want to use your remaining working years to aggressively leverage the concepts we've discussed in this book as smartly and efficiently as possible.

It may also require adjustments to your trifecta and other strategies such as a smarter Social Security strategy, possible housing changes even if that's not currently part of the plan, and portfolio adjustments. Most professionals emphasize the importance of maintaining a growth-oriented portfolio at this stage and not being too conservative too soon. This is where your planner can make sure you've got the best investment plan in place.

Maximize Catch-Up Contributions

For late starters, catch-up contributions are worth understanding well. Certain retirement accounts allow those age 50 and older to contribute beyond the standard annual limit, including 401(k)s, 403(b)s, IRAs, and Roth IRAs.

At this stage, the goal may not be simply contributing enough to receive the employer match, though the match still matters and capturing the full amount is worth doing. The bigger opportunity may be pushing toward the maximum contribution limit if cash flow allows it. For a late starter facing a shortfall, every additional dollar saved in a tax-advantaged account carries more weight than it did earlier in their career.

If you're age 60 to 63, SECURE 2.0 created an additional catch-up opportunity for many workplace retirement plans beginning in 2025. During those years, the catch-up limit is higher than the standard age 50 catch-up amount. These are your sprint years. Always check the IRS site or your plan administrator to verify the current limits and whether your plan offers the higher catch-up amount.

If your employer plan allows after-tax contributions and either in-plan Roth conversions or in-service withdrawals, ask your benefits department or plan administrator about the mega backdoor Roth. This expert-level move may allow you to contribute beyond the regular employee deferral limit, up to the broader annual plan limit, and then move those after-tax dollars into a Roth account. Talk to your planner or tax professional before pursuing this one because the rules are plan-specific and the tax details matter.

A Sample Ten-Year Catch-Up Path

Here's a sample plan for those who have roughly ten years to catch up before retiring on their preferred timeline. It can be adjusted to move faster or slower depending on the situation. I've organized it in phases to show how focused action can be structured over time.

Phase 1: Foundation (Years 1 and 2) Your goal is to stop the leaks, organize data, and build a safety net.

Year 1: Radical Transparency and Stabilization

Calculate your liquid net worth separately from your total net worth. Cash and investments are what fund retirement, not the house (unless you use equity) or the car.

If you haven't already, set a preliminary freedom number based on the rule of 25, which is your annual estimated retirement expenses multiplied by 25, or use a planning tool to get a more precise estimate.

Track every dollar for 90 days using a budgeting tool or a simple spreadsheet. Your goal is to find the phantom expenses quietly draining cash flow without much to show for it.

Confirm you're contributing enough to your 401(k) to capture the full employer match. That's an immediate 100% return on your money and it's the first place to start.

List all debts by interest rate and attack anything above 6% aggressively. The avalanche method, highest interest rate first, is mathematically optimal. The snowball method, smallest balance first, can be psychologically powerful. Either works. Pick the one you'll stick with.

Build an initial emergency fund of three months of essential expenses in a high-yield savings account.

Confirm you have adequate insurance in place.

Define a plan to increase your income while still staying in your current job. Leverage the methods covered in the income chapter.

Review all investment expense ratios. For core index funds, aim to pay no more than 0.10% in fees. Remember, small differences in fees compound over time just like returns do.

Year 2: Acceleration
Push your savings rate toward 20% of gross income if cash flow allows it.

Aim to hit the IRS maximum contribution limits for your 401(k) and IRA.

Expand your cash reserves to a full six months of expenses. Consider options for creating side income. Can you consult, teach, or rent property for example? Any income earned here should bypass your checking account and go straight to investments.

Phase 2: Optimization (Years 3–6)

Your goal is to maximize efficiency and let compound interest do more of the work.

Years 3–4: Efficiency Audit
Push your savings rate toward 25% to 30% if your shortfall calls for it.

If housing costs exceed 30% of take-home pay, it's worth considering whether downsizing or relocating makes sense. In a catch-up scenario, a large expensive home can be an anchor on the plan.

Once 401(k) and IRA limits are being hit consistently, decide your next step for additional investing by referring back to the Wealth Waterfall we covered in Chapter 10.

Years 5–6: Debt Freedom and Expansion
At a minimum, eliminate all non-mortgage debt. No car payments. No credit card balances carrying interest.

If you're 60 or older, look into the SECURE 2.0 provisions that allow for higher catch-up contribution limits. Those extra years of elevated saving can make a real difference.

Phase 3: Transition (Years 7–10)

Your goal is to test the plan and prepare for the landing.

Years 7–8: Strategic Positioning
If you haven't already, determine whether your existing assets will grow enough on their own to support retirement at 65 without additional contributions. If they will, it may open the door to stepping back from a high-pressure role into something lower-stress without derailing the plan.

If relocating to a lower-cost area is part of the vision, use vacation time to actually spend time there. Visit during the off season, not just when everything looks its best. Retirement should work in real life, not just on paper.

If retiring before 65 is the goal, map out the healthcare bridge to Medicare now, not later. Whether that's an ACA marketplace plan, a spouse's coverage, or COBRA, healthcare costs can significantly affect the plan and deserve serious attention well before the transition.

Years 9–10: Dress Rehearsal and Prep
Live on the projected retirement budget for at least six months before pulling the trigger. If the budget holds up, that's a good sign. If it doesn't, better to find out now.

If you plan to move, set aside a specific cash reserve for one-time transition costs. Moving expenses, home purchase closing costs, home repairs, and other surprises have a way of showing up right when the plan is most sensitive to unexpected withdrawals.

Eyes Wide Open

Retirement readiness turns your freedom number from a target into a working plan. It helps you compare where you want to go with the resources you're building to get there. If the plan shows that you're on track, protecting that progress and keeping an eye on the assumptions is what sustains it. If the plan shows that you're close, the adjustments that can strengthen your position are often smaller than they seem. And if the plan shows a shortfall, that information is a signal, not a verdict.

That's the retirement trifecta doing its job. Your lifestyle, your timeline, and your resources working together, or telling you where they need to. The more clearly you understand where those three pieces stand today, the better prepared you'll be to build, protect, and use the money that can support the retirement you want.

Chapter Eleven Actions

Data

[ ] **Pull Together Your Numbers.** Gather your liquid net worth, retirement account balances, contribution amounts, Social Security estimate, pensions, and any other income sources. Make sure to separate total net worth from liquid net worth so you know what can actually fund retirement income versus what's tied up in property, vehicles, or other assets.

[ ] **Update Your Freedom Number.** If you haven't calculated it yet, use the rule of 25 as a starting point or use a planning tool to get a more precise estimate.

Run the Numbers

[ ] **Choose a Planning Tool.** Run a projection using your current numbers, savings rate, timeline, and investment mix. Boldin, Empower, or your brokerage's calculator are good starting points.

[ ] **Run a Monte Carlo Simulation.** If your tool supports it, stress test the plan across thousands of market scenarios to see how it holds up when things don't go as expected.

[ ] **Compare the Projection to Your Freedom Number.** Note whether you're on track, close, or facing a shortfall.

[ ] **Bring It to Your Planner.** Share your numbers, assumptions, and questions and ask them to stress test the plan and identify blind spots.

If You're on Track

[ ] **Schedule a Recurring Review.** Set a date on your calendar to revisit the plan regularly as life and markets change.

[ ] **Check for Overconfidence.** Confirm your savings rate, spending, and investment mix haven't drifted without a reason.

If You're Close

[ ] **Review Your Retirement Trifecta.** Identify which lever, contributions, expenses, or timeline, has the most room to move in your situation and focus there.

[ ] **Revisit Financial Leakage.** Track every dollar for 90 days if you haven't recently and flip any leaks into savings or investing.

If There's a Meaningful Shortfall

[ ] **Take a Hard Look at Your Trifecta.** Evaluate your lifestyle, timeline, and resources and identify where adjustments are most realistic.

[ ] **Consider Bridging Strategies.** Decide whether working longer, phasing into retirement, or pursuing part-time work makes sense for your situation to reduce pressure on your portfolio.

[ ] **Evaluate Home Equity.** If you're house rich but cash poor, discuss the options with your planner to understand whether equity could play a role in the plan.

[ ] **Explore Geo-Arbitrage.** If relocating to a lower-cost area is a possibility, begin researching cities, states, or countries that could reduce ongoing expenses.

If You're a Late Starter

[ ] **Maximize Catch-Up Contributions.** Confirm you're contributing beyond the standard limit if you're 50 or older.

[ ] **Check Your SECURE 2.0 Eligibility.** If you're age 60 to 63, verify whether your plan offers the enhanced catch-up limit and consider maxing it out if cash flow allows.

[ ] **Ask About the Mega Backdoor Roth.** If your employer plan allows after-tax contributions, ask your benefits department or plan administrator whether this strategy is available to you.

[ ] **Review Social Security Projections.** Log into SSA.gov and review your projected benefits at ages 62, 67, and 70. Discuss your claiming strategy with your planner.

[ ] **Audit Housing Costs.** If housing costs exceed 30% of take-home pay, evaluate whether downsizing or relocating makes sense.

[ ] **Reference the Wealth Waterfall.** Once 401(k) and IRA limits are being hit consistently, refer back to the wealth waterfall to determine your next step for additional investing.

[ ] **Work Through the Ten-Year Catch-Up Phases.** Use the phase framework in this chapter as a guide for focused action if you have roughly ten years before your preferred retirement date.

Prepare for the Transition

[ ] **Do a Budget Dress Rehearsal.** Live on your projected retirement budget for at least six months before retiring. If it doesn't hold up now, address it before the paycheck stops.

[ ] **Build a Transition Cash Reserve.** Set aside funds for one-time costs such as moving expenses, closing costs, and home repairs that often surface right at the point of transition.

[ ] **Map Your Healthcare Bridge.** If retiring before 65, evaluate ACA marketplace options, a spouse's coverage, or COBRA now, not later.

12
Your Retirement Paycheck

Many of us spend the better part of our careers focused on the accumulation side of retirement. Save consistently. Invest wisely. Stay disciplined through the good times and the bad. That part gets a lot of attention, and rightfully so.

But there's another side of the equation that often gets far less thought, and that's how those hard-earned savings actually turn into income once the paycheck stops. In my younger years, retirement was so far away that figuring out how to eventually draw income from my savings just wasn't on my radar. If that sounds familiar, you're in good company.

The data backs it up. In the 2024 Protected Retirement Income and Planning Study, fewer than one-third of respondents said they had a specific income plan in place for retirement. The same study found that 41% didn't know how to stage withdrawals from their accounts, and fewer than half knew how to handle required minimum distributions or minimize taxes.

Having a clear plan for turning your savings into income once your work paycheck stops is crucial. Without one, it's easy to make unforgiving mistakes. I've listened to enough financial professionals and podcast stories from retirees to know this is real. They withdrew too much too soon, created unnecessary tax bills, left too much sitting in cash, or didn't keep enough of the portfolio invested for future growth. These aren't small mistakes. They can be difficult to recover from.

I had a conversation not long ago that perfectly illustrates how easily this could happen. A repair technician working in my home struck up a conversation about 401(k)s and asked me a question I wasn't expecting. "I've never understood how people actually use the money. You put like $500,000 into a 401(k) for years and then what? On the day you retire, do you just sell everything and put the cash in your savings and checking accounts?"

I explained that depending on how much he had and what type of account it was in, cashing it all out at once could trigger a huge tax bill, bump him into a higher tax bracket, and stop his money from growing.

It's unlikely that cashing everything out was the right move for him, so I did what I've done throughout this book, something you've probably grown tired of hearing by now. I suggested he talk to a Certified Financial Planner to set up a proper plan. What he will need is a paycheck replacement plan. And that's the concept this chapter will cover.

The idea of the replacement plan is to turn assets into a stream of income that can hit your checking account each month, similar to the way your salary once did. But unlike a paycheck from work, a retirement paycheck has to be deliberately structured around taxes, inflation, market cycles, healthcare costs, and the need to keep part of the portfolio growing over time. Done well, this approach can help create more stability, reduce unnecessary tax surprises, and give your money a better chance of lasting throughout retirement.

Everything we've covered so far has been about building a portfolio large enough to support your retirement goals. Now the question shifts. How do you turn what you've built into income that actually works? Let's walk through the common strategies for modeling your guaranteed income alongside your savings to create a retirement paycheck.

Floor and Upside

With this approach, you divide your retirement paycheck plan into two pillars: floor and upside. Each pillar serves a different purpose, and each should be built intentionally.

Floor: Essential Lifestyle

These are your non-negotiable expenses, the core costs required to maintain your standard of living, including housing, utilities, food, insurance, taxes, healthcare, transportation, and other essential recurring bills. The goal is to cover these expenses with guaranteed lifetime income so that, no matter what the markets are doing, your basic needs are always covered, your lights stay on, and your fridge stays full.

In an ideal plan, guaranteed lifetime income covers the full floor. But that won't be true for everyone. If Social Security, pensions, and annuity income don't cover all of your essential expenses, then the remaining portion has to come from somewhere else, usually portfolio withdrawals, cash reserves, part-time income, or another reliable income source. That doesn't mean the plan is broken, but it does mean the uncovered part of your floor needs special attention. Money used to cover essential expenses should generally be invested and withdrawn more conservatively than money used for discretionary spending. When defining your floor, long-term care expenses should be considered because they're one of the biggest risks to any retirement plan. Medicare doesn't cover custodial care, such as nursing homes or assisted living, which can cost anywhere from $5,000 to more than $20,000 per month, and without a plan, these expenses can quickly deplete your portfolio.

To prepare, you can purchase traditional long-term care insurance, use a hybrid life insurance policy with a long-term care rider that locks in premiums, or self-insure by setting aside a dedicated portion of your portfolio, for example $300,000, that's not used for lifestyle spending and is reserved specifically for long-term care needs.

Floor Components

The strongest income sources are those designed to last for life because they help cover essential costs without depending on the stock market or ongoing portfolio withdrawals. For most retirees, the primary components are Social Security, defined benefit pensions, and income annuities. Let's take a look at each of them.

Social Security: Social Security is a key component of your floor. If you've worked for at least 10 years, or earned 40 credits, you're generally eligible for Social Security retirement benefits. Once that income begins, it can provide a guaranteed stream of income that may last for the rest of your life.

What makes Social Security especially valuable is that it's designed to rise with inflation. That feature is often overlooked. Nationwide Retirement Institute's 2025 Social Security Survey found that more than two-thirds of Americans didn't know Social Security is protected against inflation.

What does inflation protection mean? Well, each year, Social Security benefits typically increase through a cost-of-living adjustment, or COLA, which is designed to help benefits keep pace with rising prices. For example, if your monthly benefit is $2,000 and the COLA is 3%, your benefit would increase by about $60 per month, bringing your new monthly benefit to roughly $2,060. That annual increase helps Social Security remain a valuable part of the retirement paycheck as essential expenses rise over time.

Defined Benefit Pensions: A defined benefit pension is another powerful component of the floor because it can provide a predictable monthly paycheck for life. Unlike a 401(k) or IRA, where the responsibility for investing and withdrawals falls on you, a pension is designed to provide income on a regular schedule. That makes it especially valuable when you're trying to cover essential expenses. The pension payment is added on top of your Social Security benefit, increasing both the size of your floor and the retirement paycheck you're trying to build.

If you're fortunate enough to have a pension, you'll typically face a choice between taking a lump sum or receiving monthly payments. If your pension is intended to support your floor, the monthly payment option is often viewed as the better fit because it shifts both market risk and longevity risk to the company that sponsors the pension rather than leaving those risks on your shoulders.

A lump sum payment gives you more control over the money, but it also places the long-term responsibility for investing the funds and managing withdrawals squarely on you. For some retirees, that flexibility may be appealing. But when the goal is reliable income for essential expenses, financial and retirement professionals often view the monthly payment as the cleaner fit.

When you set up pension payments, it can be tempting to choose the higher life-only benefit. That option may be perfectly reasonable in some situations, but it comes with an important risk. If you're married and pass away first, that income may disappear immediately, leaving your spouse financially exposed. Unless your spouse has their own strong pension or you have sufficient life insurance in place to replace the income, the better choice is often the 100% joint and survivor option.

Income Annuities: These can function like a personal pension by turning a portion of your savings into a predictable paycheck. Annuities are a broad category, and they don't all serve the same purpose. Some are designed primarily to create guaranteed income, while others combine insurance features, investment options, fees, surrender rules, and other moving parts.

That distinction matters because annuities become more controversial when they move beyond simple guaranteed income. Other annuities may still be presented as income solutions, but the added features often come with added trade-offs, which is why some well-known voices in personal finance take a cautious view.

Dave Ramsey is one of the most aggressive critics. He's been especially critical of variable annuities, which he describes as mutual funds stuffed inside an annuity. His broader objection is that annuities are often complex, expensive, restrictive, and unnecessary for investors who can use lower-cost mutual funds instead. In Ramsey's view, most investors are better off avoiding annuities altogether and building wealth through growth stock mutual funds.

Suze Orman is more nuanced. She doesn't dislike all annuities, but she's selective. Suze strongly warns against variable and indexed annuities because of their high fees and restrictive surrender periods. Her concern is that these complex products often benefit the sales representative more than the investor. On the flip side, she supports Single Premium Immediate Annuities, or SPIAs, in certain situations. She's also generally more open to standard fixed deferred annuities, which can function somewhat like CDs issued by insurance companies. They offer a fixed interest rate for a set period of time and avoid direct stock market exposure, though they're backed by the insurance company rather than FDIC insurance and may include surrender charges.

Clark Howard, a longtime voice in consumer finance, advises avoiding the vast majority of annuities. He does make exceptions for SPIAs and Deferred Income Annuities, or DIAs, which he believes can serve a legitimate retirement income purpose by helping retirees avoid outliving their money.

For building a secure floor, we'll focus on SPIAs and DIAs because they're designed primarily to create guaranteed income. With a SPIA, you pay an insurance company a lump sum, for example $200,000, and in exchange, the company guarantees a monthly check for the rest of your life, or for a period you select. The payment is designed to include both a return of your original money and earnings built into the insurance company's payout calculation. For example, a $200,000 income annuity might ultimately pay out far more than $200,000 if the annuitant lives a long life. Schwab gives an example of a 65-year-old woman who could collect more than $417,000 by age 95 from a $200,000 annuity contract.

With a DIA, you also pay a lump sum now, but the income doesn't begin until a future date, such as age 75. Because payments are delayed, the insurance company can factor in both the waiting period and the shorter expected payout period, which can result in a higher monthly income than an immediate annuity would provide. This can act as longevity insurance, helping protect against the risk of running out of money later in retirement.

Used this way, an income annuity can earn its place in your floor by turning part of your savings into a predictable paycheck that keeps arriving month after month, helping cover essential expenses for as long as the contract guarantees payments.

Now that we've covered the key components of the floor, we can turn to the second pillar of the retirement paycheck: upside.

Upside: Discretionary Lifestyle

Upside is where retirement becomes more than simply covering essential expenses. It's the part of your plan that supports the flexible, enjoyable parts of life, the experiences, comforts, and opportunities that make retirement feel rewarding. These expenses matter, but they don't need to be funded with the same certainty as your floor. Your floor is designed to protect your essential lifestyle. Your upside is designed to provide flexibility, choice, and the opportunity to enjoy more when markets and circumstances allow.

Because discretionary spending can adjust, it can be funded from your investment portfolio, including accounts such as your 401(k), IRA, Roth IRA, brokerage account, and other investment assets. In stronger markets, your portfolio may support more upside spending. In weaker markets, you can scale back without threatening your basic standard of living.

That separation is powerful. Your essential needs are protected by guaranteed lifetime income, while your discretionary lifestyle has the flexibility to benefit from market growth. You don't have to choose between safety and opportunity. You can build a plan that gives each dollar a job.

Because upside spending is flexible, portfolio withdrawals should be reviewed regularly and adjusted when needed based on portfolio performance, market conditions, and your discretionary spending priorities. With that flexibility in mind, let's look at several common strategies that can help turn your investments into cash flow for the discretionary side of retirement.

Systematic Withdrawals: This is the most common approach, allowing you to maintain full control of your money while selling shares to pay yourself. In practice, you can set this up directly through your brokerage firm, such as Fidelity, Vanguard, or Schwab, by establishing automatic withdrawals. For example, you might instruct the account to send you $2,000 on the first of each month, with the platform automatically selling the necessary shares and transferring the cash.

Systematic withdrawals can be taken from taxable accounts, Roth accounts, or traditional pre-tax retirement accounts such as 401(k)s and IRAs, but each carries different tax implications, so it's important to structure them thoughtfully while working with your advisor.

Growth Mutual Funds with Systematic Withdrawals: This approach builds on systematic withdrawals but takes a different view of how a portfolio can generate income. Rather than relying on income-producing assets such as dividends, bonds, or real estate, this philosophy relies primarily on long-term growth and uses withdrawals as the source of cash flow. In other words, systematic withdrawals aren't just a tool in this framework. They're the income strategy.

The portfolio is intentionally constructed using broadly diversified, growth-oriented stock funds, and income is generated by selling shares as needed. Cash flow comes from converting portfolio growth into spendable income, rather than from built-in distributions.

Portfolios following this approach are typically diversified across several growth categories, which may include large-company growth, growth and value blends, aggressive or small-company growth, and international growth funds.

Proponents favor this approach for its simplicity, liquidity, and focus on long-term growth. It avoids income-targeted strategies and instead treats the portfolio as a total return engine. The trade-off is that it requires discipline, especially during market downturns, since income depends entirely on selling shares.

Dividend and Income Strategies: Instead of selling shares, you can invest in assets that generate cash flow through distributions. This typically includes dividend-paying stocks, income-focused ETFs, and Real Estate Investment Trusts, or REITs.

A common strategy is to focus on dividend aristocrats, which are companies like Procter & Gamble or Johnson & Johnson that have increased their dividends for at least 25 consecutive years. While some investors build portfolios of individual companies, many choose to implement this strategy through diversified funds, such as the Vanguard Dividend Appreciation ETF or income-focused ETFs like the Schwab U.S. Dividend Equity ETF, to reduce company-specific risk. The goal is to create a stream of cash flow through regular distributions without having to sell the underlying investments.

It's important to remember that dividend and REIT payouts aren't guaranteed and can be reduced or eliminated, especially during economic downturns. For that reason, these strategies belong in the upside pillar and shouldn't be relied upon to fund essential expenses.

Real Estate Income: REITs: As we covered in Chapter 9, REITs own income producing properties and are generally required to distribute most of their taxable income to shareholders. These payments are typically made as regular cash dividends, which can be directed into a cash or money market account to help fund living expenses. Because of this structure, REITs often provide higher income than standard stocks, although that income isn't guaranteed.

Bond Ladders: This is the same laddering principle we covered with CDs in Chapter 8, applied to bonds. A bond ladder can be used to create a more predictable stream of cash flow by staggering bond maturities over time. This approach is often built with professional support to help manage credit quality, interest rate risk, and reinvestment decisions. This involves purchasing individual bonds, such as Treasuries or high-quality corporate bonds, that mature in different years, for example $30,000 in 2026, $30,000 in 2027, and so on.

As each bond matures, it returns principal and interest directly into your account, creating a scheduled source of cash flow that can be used to support discretionary spending. In effect, you're structuring a portion of your investment portfolio to provide more predictable income while maintaining control over the underlying assets.

Now that you have insight into these common strategies, it's helpful to understand how they may work together. In practice, retirees often use a combination of approaches rather than relying on a single method. Systematic withdrawals may provide flexibility, bond ladders or short-term fixed income may provide more predictable cash flow, and dividend or real estate income may provide additional upside income. The appropriate mix depends on market conditions, tax planning, risk tolerance, and how much discretionary spending can be adjusted from year to year. Investors often work with a financial advisor, and in some cases a tax professional, to coordinate these strategies within their broader retirement income plan.

Portfolio Spending Methods

With cash flow strategies in mind, the next question is how much spending the portfolio can reasonably support each year. In an ideal structure, the floor covers essential expenses and the upside covers discretionary lifestyle spending. In reality, some retirees may need portfolio withdrawals to support the floor, either fully or partially, as well as the upside.

The methods that follow can apply in either situation. They're designed to help determine how much can be withdrawn from the portfolio each year, whether those withdrawals are used to support the floor, the upside, or both.

Common Man's Rule (Guardrails): Best for those who want a practical rule of thumb without overcomplicating things. Retirement spending isn't linear, so this approach balances simplicity with flexibility. You begin with a withdrawal rate of about 3.5% to 4%, then adjust each year based on market performance and your needs. If markets are strong and your portfolio has grown, you can give yourself a modest raise. If markets are weak and your balance declines, you temporarily reduce spending, for example by 10%. The strength of this approach is adaptability. Even small adjustments, such as delaying a major expense during a downturn, can significantly improve the likelihood that your portfolio lasts 30 years or more.

RMD Method (Autopilot): Best for those who prefer a simple, structured approach and want to reduce the risk of running out of money. This method uses the IRS Uniform Lifetime Table. Each year, you divide your portfolio balance by your life expectancy factor, which determines your withdrawal amount. The percentage naturally increases as you age, which can align with rising healthcare costs later in life. Because the formula adjusts continuously, the portfolio is designed to last indefinitely.

For example, a retiree with $1,000,000 at age 73 would divide by a factor of 26.5, resulting in a withdrawal of about $37,736, or roughly 3.8%. By age 83, if the portfolio has grown to $1.2 million and the factor declines to 17.7, the withdrawal increases to about $67,797, or roughly 5.6%. The process requires no guesswork and automatically adjusts over time.

Income-Only Method (Preservationist): This approach is typically used by retirees who have substantial assets and want to preserve principal for future needs, heirs, charitable giving, or other long-term goals. Instead of selling investments to create cash flow, spending is generally limited to the income the portfolio produces, such as dividends, interest, and other distributions.

The benefit is that the underlying portfolio is largely preserved because principal isn't intentionally sold to fund spending. The trade-off is that income can vary from year to year, and the portfolio must be large enough to generate meaningful cash flow without relying on asset sales. For that reason, this method may provide stability for the portfolio itself, but less consistency for annual spending.

4% Rule: Best for those who want a steady and predictable paycheck. You withdraw 4% of your portfolio in the first year of retirement, then increase that dollar amount each year with inflation, regardless of market performance. This creates consistency, but it's rigid and can be vulnerable to poor market returns early in retirement.

While widely used, the 4% rule isn't universally accepted. Research from Morningstar suggests that a lower starting withdrawal rate, currently estimated at around 3.9%, may provide a higher probability of success in today's market environment. At the same time, William Bengen, who originally developed the rule, published updated research in 2025 raising his safe withdrawal rate to 4.7%, which he calls "Universal Safemax." His updated analysis incorporates broader asset class diversification and a more thorough historical review. The right choice ultimately depends on individual circumstances, flexibility, and risk tolerance.

Advisor-Managed Paycheck Method: This approach is typically used by retirees who prefer to delegate the ongoing spending decision to a financial advisor. Instead of personally deciding how much to withdraw each month or when to adjust spending, the advisor helps establish a monthly paycheck from the portfolio and reviews it over time based on the retiree's broader plan.

The benefit is that it can add discipline, structure, and accountability. It may also help reduce emotional decisions during periods of market volatility, since spending adjustments are made through a planning process rather than in reaction to short-term market movements.

The trade-off is that it may limit flexibility and can add cost, since this approach is typically part of an ongoing advisory relationship. If spending needs change, the retiree may need to discuss the adjustment with the advisor before increasing withdrawals. For some retirees, that structure is helpful. For others, it may feel restrictive.

Sequence of Returns Risk

As we touched on in Chapter 8, it's important to understand that retirement income depends on more than how much your portfolio earns over time. Once you begin taking money out, it matters whether the good market years or bad market years happen first. This is called sequence of returns risk, and I believe it's one of the most important concepts to understand before retiring.

A downturn early in retirement can do more damage than a similar downturn later, after the portfolio has had more time to grow. That timing can determine whether your portfolio stays on track or comes under pressure early in retirement.

Imagine two retirees who both start with $1 million, withdraw $40,000 per year, and average 8% returns over 30 years. Retiree A experiences a strong bull market in the first five years, allowing the portfolio to grow while withdrawals are being taken. Retiree B, however, retires into a market downturn and sees the portfolio drop 20% in the first year while still taking the same $40,000 withdrawal.

Even with the same average return over time, Retiree B faces a much greater risk of running out of money. Losses early in retirement are especially damaging because withdrawals may force investments to be sold at lower values, leaving fewer assets available to recover when markets rebound.

This is why your retirement paycheck can't be based only on a withdrawal percentage. The percentage matters, but so does the process behind it. A strong income plan considers how withdrawals may change during difficult markets, which accounts should be tapped first, how taxes may affect the order of withdrawals, and which parts of the portfolio should remain invested for future growth.

Your goal should be to build enough flexibility into your retirement paycheck so a bad market early in retirement doesn't automatically force the worst possible decision, which is selling long-term investments when they're temporarily down.

Sequence of returns risk doesn't mean portfolio withdrawals are unsafe. It means they need to be managed carefully, especially in the early years of retirement.

If your portfolio is supporting only the upside, you may have more flexibility to reduce or delay discretionary spending during a downturn. If your portfolio is also supporting part of the floor, the withdrawal strategy becomes even more important because some of those withdrawals may be tied to essential expenses.

This is where the spending method, investment mix, tax plan, and cash reserves need to work together. The spending method helps determine how much can be withdrawn. The investment mix helps determine where those withdrawals may come from. The tax plan helps decide which accounts to use and when. Cash reserves, discussed earlier, can provide a buffer during difficult markets.

When you know which income sources cover the floor, which assets support the upside, and how withdrawals may adjust when conditions change, the retirement paycheck becomes easier to monitor and refine over time.

Real-World Example: Sarah, Age 55, Teacher

Sarah's a 55-year-old public school teacher who plans to retire at 65. She earns $70,000 and has saved $350,000 between her 403(b) and Roth IRA. She expects a modest teacher pension. For planning purposes, we'll estimate her combined pension and Social Security income at about $40,000 per year.

Her expected retirement spending is $70,000 in today's dollars. That means her portfolio may need to provide about $30,000 per year. In her case, the pension and Social Security create a meaningful floor, while portfolio withdrawals help support the remaining lifestyle spending.

Ten years before retirement, Sarah begins checking whether her projected income plan is realistic. She reviews expected expenses, estimates future guaranteed income, and calculates how much her portfolio may need to provide each year. Instead of making major changes all at once, she increases her savings rate and becomes more intentional about how future contributions are invested.

Seven years before retirement, her portfolio has grown to about $420,000. She keeps most of her long-term money invested for growth, but she also begins paying closer attention to the portion of the portfolio that may eventually support early retirement withdrawals. Her pension helps reduce pressure on the portfolio because a meaningful portion of her essential expenses is already covered by guaranteed income.

Two years before retirement, her portfolio has grown to about $525,000. Sarah begins finalizing her retirement paycheck plan. She works through how much will come from her pension and Social Security, how much may need to come from portfolio withdrawals, which accounts may be tapped first, and how her cash reserves can support the plan during difficult markets.

By the time Sarah retires, she has a coordinated income plan. Her guaranteed income supports the floor, her portfolio helps support the remaining spending need, and her withdrawal strategy gives her flexibility if market conditions change.

Real-World Example: James and Maria, Ages 60 and 58
James and Maria are behind on retirement savings. They have $175,000 saved across a 401(k) and IRA. They plan to retire at 70 so they can receive a larger Social Security benefit. Their combined Social Security at age 70 is estimated at about $48,000 per year.

Their expected retirement spending is $75,000 in today's dollars, which means their portfolio may need to provide about $27,000 per year. Unlike Sarah, their guaranteed income may not fully cover the lifestyle they want. That means their portfolio may need to help support both the floor and the upside.

Ten years before retirement, James and Maria start testing the numbers. They review expected expenses, projected Social Security income, taxes, healthcare costs, and the amount their portfolio may need to provide each year. The estimate shows that the numbers are tight, but it also gives them time to respond.

They increase their savings rate, avoid taking on new debt, and begin reducing fixed expenses so their future retirement paycheck will be easier to support. They also decide that delaying Social Security is an important part of their plan because it strengthens their floor without requiring additional savings.

Seven years before retirement, their savings have grown to about $240,000. They're still behind, but their position is improving. They continue saving, keep part of the portfolio invested for growth, and become more intentional about building conservative assets that may help support early retirement withdrawals. They also continue strengthening their cash reserves so unexpected expenses don't derail the plan before retirement begins.

Four years before retirement, inflation increases their projected spending need. Rather than starting over, they adjust. They revisit their retirement date, spending assumptions, savings rate, and Social Security timing. Delaying Social Security still makes sense because it reduces the amount their portfolio will need to provide later.

Two years before retirement, their portfolio has grown to about $350,000. They realize their retirement paycheck will require flexibility. Instead of relying on a fixed withdrawal amount no matter what happens, they plan to use a more flexible spending method. They also decide to work part-time during their first three years of retirement, earning about $20,000 per year. That income reduces the strain on their portfolio during the early years, when sequence of returns risk can be most damaging.

At age 70, they claim Social Security at the larger benefit amount. Their floor is stronger, their portfolio withdrawal need is smaller, and their plan becomes more workable. Their retirement paycheck relies on delayed claiming, higher savings, lower fixed expenses, part-time income, and a flexible withdrawal strategy.

James and Maria's example is important because not every retiree enters retirement with a fully funded plan. When the numbers are tight, the goal is to create more room for the plan to work. As you know, that may mean spending less, working longer, delaying Social Security, earning part-time income, adjusting withdrawals, or combining several of those strategies.

Ultimate Goal

We've spent this chapter walking through how to create a retirement paycheck, but the mechanics are only part of the transition. As we explored in Chapter 4, one of the hardest adjustments is the shift in mindset. After decades of saving, investing, and watching balances grow, it can feel unsettling to start drawing from the very accounts you worked so hard to build.

Before retirement, success is usually measured by how much the numbers in your accounts grow. Once retirement begins, success has to be measured differently. It should be measured by how well those numbers support the life you want to live.

That shift can be difficult. You may feel a twinge of guilt the first time you sell shares to pay for a trip, help family, or enjoy something meaningful. You may worry that you're depleting your safety net. But it's important to remember that money is a tool, not a high score.

A retirement paycheck helps turn years of saving into confidence. When you know where your next check is coming from, which expenses it's meant to cover, and how the plan can adjust over time, retirement can start to feel less like watching a scoreboard and more like living the life you worked so hard to build.

Chapter Twelve Actions

Build Your Floor

[ ] **Confirm Your Essential Expenses.** Pull up the essential expenses you've already calculated and confirm they still reflect your expected retirement costs. Update anything that has changed.

[ ] **Map Your Guaranteed Income.** Add up your expected Social Security, pension, and any annuity income. This is what covers your floor.

[ ] **Run the Gap Test.** Compare your guaranteed income to your essential expenses. If there's a gap, identify what will fill it, whether that's portfolio withdrawals, part-time income, or an income annuity.

[ ] **Optimize Your Social Security Timing.** If you haven't already, decide on your claiming age. Delaying to 70, if possible, maximizes the guaranteed, inflation-adjusted income that strengthens your floor.

[ ] **Address Long-Term Care.** Decide how you'll handle potential long-term care costs. Options include a traditional policy, a hybrid life insurance policy with a long-term care rider, or a dedicated self-insurance fund set aside specifically for this purpose.

[ ] **Protect Your Spouse.** If activating a pension, confirm whether the joint and survivor option makes sense for your situation to avoid leaving a spouse financially exposed.

Build Your Upside

[ ] **Choose a Spending Method.** Select the approach that fits your situation, whether that's the guardrails method, the RMD method, the income-only method, or the 4% rule. Write it down and review with your planner.

[ ] **Select Your Cash Flow Strategy.** Decide how the upside will be funded, whether through systematic withdrawals, dividend and income strategies, a bond ladder, real estate income, or a combination of approaches.

[ ] **Plan for Sequence of Returns Risk.** Consider how the plan will hold up if markets decline early in retirement. Identify which accounts will be tapped first and how discretionary spending might adjust during a downturn.

Get the Logistics Right

[ ] **Set Up Systematic Withdrawals.** When ready, coordinate with your brokerage to establish automatic withdrawals from the appropriate accounts in the right order, typically taxable accounts first, if that's part of your strategy.

[ ] **Review RMD Requirements.** If you're 73 or older, confirm your required minimum distributions are set up correctly to avoid penalties.

[ ] **Run a Tax Check.** Ask your planner or CPA whether low-income years create a Roth conversion opportunity and whether planned withdrawals could trigger higher Medicare premiums through IRMAA.

[ ] **Consider Qualified Charitable Distributions.** If you're 70½ or older and support charitable causes, explore using QCDs to satisfy charitable giving while reducing taxable income.

[ ] **Review Early Withdrawal Rules.** If retiring between 55 and 59½, check whether the Rule of 55 applies before rolling a 401(k) into an IRA. The Rule of 55 may allow penalty-free withdrawals from a 401(k) if you leave your job in or after the year you turn 55, but that option is generally lost once the money is rolled into an IRA.

[ ] **Maximize HSA Spending in Retirement.** Once you turn 65, consider using HSA funds tax-free for qualified medical expenses including Medicare premiums, long-term care premiums, dental, and vision.

[ ] **Practice the Retirement Paycheck.** Live on your projected retirement budget for at least six months before retiring to confirm the plan works before the paycheck stops.

13
Alternate Paths

Up until now, we've primarily focused on the standard path to retirement. You earn a salary, you save a percentage of it, you invest it in the market, and you let compound interest do the heavy lifting. That strategy works. It's the foundation of almost every financial success story. But it has one major challenge. It takes time.

If you follow the standard script, the math often dictates a timeline of 20, 30, or even 40 years. For some, that's simply too long. For example, maybe you've defined a preferred timeline that's more aggressive and the standard path isn't getting you there fast enough. In that case, you need a shortcut.

What follows is a different kind of conversation. These are the creative, nontraditional strategies that go beyond saving and investing, things like navigating the tax code to access your money early, redefining your cost of living through geo-arbitrage, or rethinking your healthcare strategy entirely. Some of these may surprise you. Others may not be right for your situation at all. But understanding what's possible is the first step toward deciding what's worth pursuing.

FIRE Movement: A New Way to Think

The concept of retiring early has been revolutionized by the FIRE movement, which stands for **F**inancial **I**ndependence, **R**etire **E**arly. While traditional retirement planning focuses on age, FIRE focuses on math.

The foundation of the FIRE movement is the Rule of 25, which we covered in Chapter 3. This rule states you're financially independent when you've saved 25 times your estimated annual expenses in retirement. The distinction is that we use estimated expenses in retirement because your consumption needs might be structurally lower than they are today, due to eliminating major debts like a mortgage, stopping savings contributions, and removing work-related costs like commuting. Most of us focus on saving more. The FIRE movement proves that spending less is actually the more powerful variable.

Savings Rate Accelerator

To calculate the FIRE timeline, you must establish a conservative rate of return. For example, using a 5% real rate of return, which is the expected return after accounting for inflation, ensures the model has a large margin of error.

The most powerful data point is the direct link between your savings rate and your working years. This simple math allows you to test your preferred timeline against reality. Take a look.

Illustrative Timeline Example

Assumes 5% Real Return and a 4% Annual Withdrawal Rule

SAVINGS RATE	WORKING YEARS REQUIRED
10% (Standard Advice)	~51 years
30% (Aggressive Saver)	~28 years
50% (FIRE Path)	~17 years
70% (Extreme Path)	~9 years

Illustrative example only. Results depend on income, expenses, investment returns, and withdrawal assumptions.

Timeline Test

This table connects your goal to a required savings rate. Let's say you're 45 years old and want to retire by 55, a 10-year timeline. The math shows that to hit that goal, you'd need a savings rate approaching 70%. If you're currently only saving 15%, the math proves you won't hit your target without a massive lifestyle change. The path to your preferred timeline is clear. You must aggressively move your savings rate up. Here's an example:

The Tale of Two Spenders

Two couples earn $100,000 a year. The first is Bob and John. The second is Ted and Alice. Bob and John spend $80,000 a year. To retire, they need $2 million, which is $80,000 multiplied by 25. At a 20% savings rate, saving $20,000 per year, they'll need to work for roughly 37 years.

Ted and Alice optimize their lifestyle and spend $40,000 a year. To retire, they need $1 million, which is $40,000 multiplied by 25. At a

60% savings rate, saving $60,000 per year, they'll need to work for roughly 12.5 years.

The result is that Ted and Alice might retire 25 years sooner because they reach their finish line much faster.

It's worth noting that the standard Rule of 25 calculation assumes your portfolio must carry the entire load. It intentionally ignores Social Security. This is largely because early retirees face a long gap between their last paycheck and their first government check. By excluding those future benefits from the math, the formula ensures they are financially self-sufficient from day one. In this model, Social Security is treated as a safety buffer for later in life, not a requirement for survival.

Choosing Your Flavor of Freedom

The FIRE movement is a spectrum. To use this approach, decide which version fits your vision and your tolerance for delayed gratification.

Lean FIRE (Minimalist Path) achieves freedom with a modest annual spending level of $30,000 to $40,000. This is the fastest path but offers the smallest margin for error. It requires embracing a perpetually frugal lifestyle.

Fat FIRE (Abundance Path) is the opposite of Lean FIRE. This is for high earners who want to retire early but with a large annual spending level of $100,000 or more for travel and luxury. It requires a significantly larger portfolio and a longer accumulation phase but provides maximum safety and comfort.

Barista FIRE (Hybrid Path) achieves a portfolio size large enough to cover the floor during the years before Social Security begins. You then quit your high-stress career and work a low-stress, part-time job that covers discretionary spending, and crucially, health insurance premiums. This removes corporate pressure while ensuring continuous cash flow and solving the healthcare gap.

Coast FIRE (Front-Loaded Path) is ideal for those who want to be finished saving decades ahead of schedule. You save aggressively early in your career until your portfolio reaches a coast number, which is the exact amount that, if left untouched, will automatically grow to your full retirement target by age 65. From that point, you only need to earn enough to cover current living expenses, giving you immediate freedom to pursue lower-stress or passion-driven work.

FIRE Perspectives

Two well-known voices offer perspectives worth considering before committing to the FIRE approach.

Ramit Sethi, author of I Will Teach You to Be Rich, offers a powerful warning about FIRE psychology. He argues that those who pursue extreme frugality for decades often struggle to spend money even after they've hit their goal. They may reach financial independence, but as we explored in Chapter 4, a scarcity mindset can still make it hard to spend from the wealth they worked so hard to build. With that in mind, don't just plan your savings. Plan your spending too, or you won't enjoy the freedom you earned.

Suze Orman takes a harder stance. During an appearance on the Afford Anything podcast, she famously declared her strong opposition to the movement and labeled early retirement the biggest mistake you'll ever make. Her critique is rooted in the math of catastrophe. She warns that retiring early on a tight budget leaves you exposed to things markets can't fix, like massive inflation, a decade-long market downturn, or a major health crisis. To Suze, true independence isn't just having enough to live. It's having enough to survive when life goes wrong.

Exit Before 59½

The IRS generally requires you to wait until age 59½ before withdrawing from tax-advantaged retirement accounts like 401(k)s and IRAs without penalty. Withdraw before then and you'll typically owe a 10% early withdrawal penalty on top of any income taxes due. But that rule has exceptions, and for early retirees, those exceptions matter. There are several strategies financial professionals recommend for accessing retirement funds before 59½ without triggering penalties. Here are a few to know:

Roth Conversion Ladder is the planner's choice for those retiring in their 30s or 40s. You can always withdraw your original Roth IRA contributions tax-free and penalty-free. However, early retirees often need access to more than just their contributions before age 59½. The strategy is to convert pre-tax account money to a Roth, pay taxes on the conversion today, and then wait five years. After five years, that converted amount is treated like principal and can be withdrawn penalty-free. By converting a chunk every year, five years later the first chunk becomes available, creating a rolling stream of accessible cash.

Rule 72(t) is the break-glass option for early retirees who need access to pre-tax retirement accounts before age 59½ and don't have a Roth conversion ladder or enough taxable-account savings. The IRS allows substantially equal periodic payments from an IRA at any age penalty-free. The catch is that it's rigid. Once started, the exact same payments must continue for five years or until age 59½, whichever is longer. If payments are stopped or modified, all penalties are owed retroactively.

Rule of 55 is the cleanest option for people who leave work in or after the year they turn 55. If you separate from service at 55 or later, you may be able to withdraw money from that employer's 401(k) or 403(b) without the 10% early withdrawal penalty. You'll still owe ordinary income tax on pre-tax withdrawals, but the penalty may be avoided. The key limitation is that this rule applies to the workplace plan tied to the job you just left, not to IRAs. Rolling the account into an IRA too soon can eliminate this option.

Company Stock Loophole (NUA) is a special-case strategy for those who hold highly appreciated employer stock inside a 401(k). Instead of rolling those shares into an IRA, they may be able to transfer the company stock in-kind to a taxable brokerage account. They pay ordinary income tax on the stock's original cost basis, while the built-in growth, called net unrealized appreciation, may later be taxed at long-term capital gains rates when the shares are sold. According to tax professionals, such an approach can result in significant tax savings, but it's not a general early-access tool like a Roth ladder, Rule 72(t), or the Rule of 55. If it sounds like something worth exploring, a conversation with your tax advisor is a good place to start.

Healthcare Hacks

Healthcare costs and availability tend to be the biggest reality check when thinking about early retirement. Medicare doesn't begin until 65, and without an employer plan, coverage can be expensive and complicated to navigate. If you retire early, you'll need a bridge to get you there, and the good news is that there're more options than you may realize. Here are three to be aware of:

Silver Loading and Cost-Sharing Reductions give early retirees one of the most powerful healthcare options available. The Affordable Care Act offers subsidies based on income, and early retirees have extraordinary control over their taxable income because they can choose where their money comes from. By withdrawing from Roth accounts or using cash savings, income stays low and subsidies stay high. If you keep your taxable income between 100% and 150% of the

Federal Poverty Level, which is roughly $15,000 to $22,000 for a single person as of 2025, you may qualify for Cost-Sharing Reductions. These reductions are only available on Silver plans, and when they kick in, they can dramatically lower deductibles and out-of-pocket costs, making a Silver plan far more valuable than its sticker price suggests.

Health Sharing Ministries are nonprofit organizations where members pool money together to cover each other's medical bills. Because they aren't regulated insurance, monthly costs tend to be lower than traditional coverage. But that tradeoff comes with real limitations. Pre-existing conditions and routine care are often excluded, and if a claim is denied, you have far fewer legal protections than you would with a traditional insurance plan. They work best for healthy individuals who want lower monthly costs and are comfortable with the added risk.

Direct Primary Care pairs a monthly subscription to a primary care physician with either a high-deductible plan or a health sharing arrangement. You pay a flat monthly fee in exchange for unlimited visits, direct access to your doctor, and reduced costs on many services. It works best as a complement to one of the other coverage strategies rather than a standalone solution.

Geo-Arbitrage: Adventure as a Strategy

In the context of early retirement, geo-arbitrage is about thriving. It's the act of earning money in a strong currency like the U.S. dollar and spending it in a weaker currency or lower-cost economy.

Domestic Geo-Arbitrage (State-Line Strategy)

You don't have to leave the country to find freedom. Moving from a high-tax and high-cost city to a lower-cost area can perform financial miracles. For example, selling a Manhattan property in the range of $1.2 million and relocating to Atlanta, where the median home price is roughly $440,000, could allow a retiree to purchase a home for cash and still add approximately $760,000 to the investment portfolio before transaction costs. The same principle applies to someone selling in San Francisco, where the median home price is currently around $1.69 million, and relocating to Knoxville, Tennessee, where the median is roughly $307,000, potentially adding over $1.3 million to the portfolio before transaction costs.

Done thoughtfully, moves like these can reduce monthly expenses, increase portfolio flexibility, and create a larger margin of safety without requiring a move overseas.

The tax impact can be just as meaningful. California's top marginal state income tax rate is 13.3%, while Tennessee has no broad-based state income tax. The actual tax savings for any individual retiree will depend on income level, income sources, and deductions, but the difference can be substantial. For someone earning $120,000 per year in retirement income, the effective California state tax bill could easily run $7,000 to $8,000 or more annually. In a state with no broad-based income tax, that money stays in the portfolio. States with no broad-based personal income tax include Alaska, Florida, Nevada, New Hampshire, South Dakota, Tennessee, Texas, Washington, and Wyoming as of this writing. Note that Washington does impose a capital gains tax on certain higher-income earners, so it's worth verifying your specific situation before making a move.

That said, financial advantages are only part of the picture. Access to quality healthcare, climate preferences, and proximity to family can carry equal or greater weight in the final decision.

International Geo-Arbitrage (Global Citizen)

Many retirees move abroad to make their money stretch, and it's more common than most people realize. As of 2024, approximately 1.26 million Americans of retirement age were living abroad, with over 760,000 of them receiving Social Security payments overseas. Research consistently points to rising housing and healthcare costs as primary drivers of the trend.

A U.S. retired couple living on roughly $5,500 per month from Social Security and retirement-account income may feel squeezed by American housing and healthcare costs, yet that same income can support a comfortable lifestyle in many countries, as the data ahead suggests.

Before packing your bags though, there's plenty to research. A few items I've looked into are currency fluctuations, which can affect purchasing power in ways that are hard to predict, U.S. tax obligations, which don't go away just because you've moved abroad, and healthcare quality and availability, which can vary significantly by country and region. The distance from family and friends should be considered before committing.

Some of the best, common sense advice I've read is to spend meaningful time in a location before committing, ideally during the less glamorous season, not just when everything looks perfect.

With those considerations in mind, here's a look at how the cost of living compares across some of the more popular destinations. The numbers may surprise you.

Average Monthly Cost of Living for Retired Couples

Estimated 2026 monthly budget for a couple, including housing, utilities, food, transportation, and routine healthcare

RANK (MOST AFFORDABLE)	COUNTRY	TYPICAL MONTHLY COST (FOR A COUPLE)	MONTHLY BUDGET (USD)	BUDGET NOTE
1	Portugal	$1,500–$2,000	$1,750	Comfortable in smaller cities; private healthcare included
2	Thailand	$1,750–$2,500	$2,125	Comfortable expat lifestyle with private care
3	Mexico	$2,000–$2,800	$2,400	Typical in popular retirement areas; healthcare included
4	Spain	$2,100–$2,800	$2,450	Affordable Western Europe option; outside biggest cities
5	Costa Rica	$2,300–$3,000	$2,650	Comfortable in many expat hubs; healthcare included
6	USA	~$5,100+	$5,100	Average retired household spending; includes healthcare

COST SCALE (APPROXIMATE MONTHLY COST IN USD): $0 · $1,000 · $2,000 · $3,000 · $4,000 · $5,000 · $6,000

Figures are approximate 2026 monthly budgets for a retired couple and include housing plus healthcare. Actual costs vary by city, housing choice, and lifestyle.

Source basis: *U.S. retiree spending averages and 2026 retirement cost-of-living guides for Portugal, Spain, Costa Rica, Mexico, and Thailand.*

Visa Guide (as of 2026)

You can't just move abroad. You need permission. The options below represent some of the more popular retirement visas available at the time of writing, each requiring proof of income rather than employment. Visa requirements, income thresholds, and program availability change frequently, so it would be wise to verify current requirements with the appropriate embassy or a qualified immigration attorney before making any decisions.

Panama (Pensionado) is widely considered the gold standard. It requires approximately $1,000 per month in lifetime income and grants permanent residency along with significant discounts on utilities, healthcare, transportation, and entertainment.

Costa Rica (Pensionado) is a classic favorite requiring proof of approximately $1,000 per month in lifetime pension income. It offers a path to permanent residency after three years.

Spain (Non-Lucrative Visa) is the gateway to Europe, requiring roughly $2,400 per month in passive income, including Social Security, or equivalent savings. Local employment isn't permitted, but it grants access to the European lifestyle.

Portugal (D7) is the European favorite, requiring proof of passive income of approximately $900 per month per person. It offers a path to EU citizenship after five years.

Malaysia (MM2H Silver) is a premium Asian option requiring a bank deposit of approximately $150,000 USD. It grants a five-year renewable visa with tax-free remittance of foreign income.

Thailand (LTR Wealthy Pensioner) is the luxury option, requiring $80,000 per year in income or $40,000 per year in income combined with a $250,000 investment. It comes with a ten-year visa and premium government services.

Unique Lifestyle Hacks

The Golden Girls Strategy (Senior Co-Living) is all about preservation. Two or three single retirees pool their resources to share a high quality home. Instead of paying $2,500 per month for a one bedroom apartment, three people might each pay $1,500 per month to share a $4,500 home with far more space and amenities such as a pool. The result is lower individual cost and a built in social environment.

Housesitting Hack (Rent-Free Living) eliminates housing costs entirely for those willing to watch pets and care for a home while traveling. Platforms like TrustedHousesitters charge an annual fee of around $180. In exchange, you stay in someone's home, often a high end property, for free while handling simple responsibilities like walking a dog or watering plants. Some full time nomads use this strategy to live in cities like London, Sydney, or New York with zero nightly housing cost.

House Hacking doesn't require being a traditional landlord to benefit from real estate. By purchasing a duplex or a home with an accessory dwelling unit, you live in one portion of the property and rent out the other. The rental income can cover part or even all of the mortgage, significantly reducing living expenses and in some cases eliminating them entirely.

University-Based Retirement (UBRC) attracts some retirees to communities built around major universities. More than 100 schools, including Duke, Stanford, and Arizona State, offer these setups. Residents can audit classes, attend events, and often access university affiliated healthcare facilities. It creates a lifestyle that blends intellectual engagement, community, and convenience.

Micro Retirement

Micro retirement is the practice of taking planned breaks from work before traditional retirement age. Instead of saving all retirement time for later in life, you'd intentionally step away from employment for several months or longer, then return to work afterward. It's typically handled as a structured pause built into the larger financial plan.

The biggest benefit is time. A micro retirement can provide rest, reduce burnout, create more space for family, and offer a preview of what retirement may actually feel like. With this approach, you'd get a clearer sense of your real spending habits, how comfortable you are living without a paycheck, and whether your retirement assumptions are realistic.

The financial side must be planned carefully. The money used for a micro retirement should be separate from an emergency fund and shouldn't weaken long-term retirement savings. You'd also need to factor in lost income, missed employer retirement contributions, slower investment growth, taxes, and ongoing expenses during the break.

Health insurance is one of the most important issues. If coverage is tied to employment, leaving work may require COBRA, a marketplace plan, a spouse's plan, or private insurance. These costs can be significant, especially for a family, so coverage should be priced and confirmed before stepping away.

There are also career risks. Some employers may allow a sabbatical, but others may not hold a position open. A gap in employment can affect future job searches, so it helps to maintain professional contacts, keep licenses or certifications current, and have a clear plan for returning to work.

Micro retirement can offer rest and perspective while you're still healthy enough to enjoy it, but it works best when the freedom it creates doesn't come at the expense of your long-term security.

Reimagining the Road Ahead

There's no single path to retirement. Whether it means embracing geo-arbitrage to change where you live, using NUA strategies to manage taxes more efficiently, or restructuring housing costs through approaches like house hacking, alternative paths can change your timeline in meaningful ways. One of the keys to retiring sooner, if that's your goal, is flexibility. The path to financial independence is rarely linear, and plans often evolve as life does.

The ideas in this chapter are meant to expand your sense of what's possible. By understanding and selectively using these approaches, you may gain more control over when and how you step away from full-time work, even if you once assumed you'd need to work longer. If any of these paths resonate, take the time to understand how they work and whether they improve your situation. When something aligns with your goals and circumstances, it's worth exploring. Life is short, and financial freedom is ultimately about creating more choice in how you spend your time.

Chapter Thirteen Actions

FIRE Planning

[ ] **Calculate Your Lean Number.** If early retirement is something you're exploring, start by figuring out the bare minimum you could live on. Multiply that by 25. That's your Lean FIRE number and a useful starting point for understanding how far you are from financial independence.

[ ] **Check Your Coast Status.** If you're wondering whether you could stop contributing and let your existing savings grow to your retirement target on their own, search for a Coast FIRE Calculator online. You may discover you're closer than you think.

[ ] **Choose Your Flavor of Freedom.** If you plan to pursue a FIRE strategy, decide which version best aligns with your goals and lifestyle, whether Lean FIRE, Fat FIRE, Barista FIRE, or Coast FIRE. Write it down and think about how it connects to your broader retirement vision and timeline.

[ ] **Set Your Target Savings Rate.** Once you've chosen your FIRE flavor and have a target timeline in mind, calculate the savings rate you'd need to get there. Compare it to your current rate and identify your first realistic adjustment step.

Accessing Money Early

[ ] **Rule of 55 Check.** If you're planning to retire between ages 55 and 59½ and still have money in a current employer's 401(k), call your plan provider and ask whether partial withdrawals are allowed under the Rule of 55 if you separate from service. Some plans force a lump sum, which can undermine the strategy, so confirm it before making any moves.

[ ] **Determine Your Early-Access Strategy.** If you plan to retire before 59½ and will need to draw from pre-tax retirement accounts, decide whether a Roth conversion ladder or Rule 72(t) makes more sense for your situation. If either approach applies, it would be wise to work with your financial planner to design and implement a plan that fits your timeline and tax situation.

[ ] **Check for NUA.** If you have highly appreciated company stock inside your 401(k), don't roll it over until you've spoken with your CPA

or financial planner about whether NUA treatment could result in significant tax savings.

[ ] **Income Bridge Check.** If you're retiring before 59½ or before Medicare kicks in at 65, map out how you'll cover living expenses during that gap. Consider how taxable accounts, Roth funds, and early access strategies can work together to keep income flowing without triggering unnecessary taxes or penalties.

Healthcare

[ ] **Silver Audit.** If you're planning to retire before 65 and will need to find your own coverage before Medicare begins, go to Healthcare.gov and look at the Silver Plans in your area. If you have control over your taxable income in retirement, which many early retirees do, check how low the deductibles drop with cost-sharing reductions. The savings can be significant.

[ ] **Explore Health Shares.** If you're in good health and looking for a lower cost alternative to traditional insurance, get a quote from a health sharing ministry like Zion Health or Sedera and compare it to what traditional coverage would cost. Keep in mind that these aren't insurance and come with limitations, so understand what's covered and what isn't before deciding.

Geo-Arbitrage and Location

[ ] **Cost of Living Research.** If you're considering a move to a lower-cost area, use a tool like Numbeo or Expatistan to compare your current monthly cost of living to your target location. Look beyond housing to include food, transportation, healthcare, and utilities to get a complete picture before drawing any conclusions.

[ ] **Zillow Search.** If a lower-cost city or region has been on your radar, spend some time looking at home prices and comparing them to your current home equity. If the numbers look compelling, consider booking a trip to experience the location in real life, not just on paper.

[ ] **Visa Reality Check.** If retiring abroad is something you're seriously considering, look up the basic visa or residency requirements for your top country choice and confirm whether your income or savings would qualify. Requirements change, so verify with the

appropriate embassy or an immigration attorney before making any decisions.

[ ] **Pick a Location.** Once you've done the research, make a preliminary decision about where you plan to live in retirement, whether that's your current home, a new home, a new state, or another country. Estimate the major expenses associated with that choice, including housing and healthcare. This doesn't have to be final and can be refined over time.

Lifestyle Hacks

[ ] **Golden Girls Reality Check.** If you're single or know others in a similar situation who are facing high housing costs in retirement, explore whether co-living with one or two others could meaningfully reduce monthly expenses. Run the numbers on what shared housing might look like in your target location to see if it changes the math.

[ ] **Housesitting Test Drive.** If the idea of traveling in retirement while eliminating housing costs sounds appealing, visit TrustedHousesitters and browse available sits in locations you're curious about. Consider signing up for a trial sit before retirement to see if the lifestyle is a realistic fit before committing to it full time.

[ ] **House Hacking Analysis.** If you own or are considering purchasing a home, research whether a duplex or a property with an accessory dwelling unit makes sense in your target area. Estimate what rental income could realistically cover and how it would affect your overall retirement math.

[ ] **UBRC Exploration.** If intellectual engagement, lifelong learning, and a built-in community sound like an appealing way to spend retirement, research which universities near your preferred retirement location offer university-based retirement communities and what they include in terms of access and amenities.

Update Your Plan

[ ] **Update Your Vision and Timeline.** Once you've worked through the sections above and made decisions about FIRE strategy, location, healthcare, and lifestyle, go back to your retirement vision and timeline and update them to reflect what you've learned. The goal is to make sure your plan is still pointing in the direction you actually want to go.

14
The Personal Equation

I've found that a lot of financial advice is written for a specific avatar. It's written for a married couple, both working W-2 corporate jobs, who stay married for 40 years and retire at 65. If that's you, the standard playbook works perfectly. But the reality of modern life is far more complex. You might be single, self-employed, divorced later in life, or managing a chronic illness. You might be part of a nontraditional family structure or navigating the financial headwinds of systemic inequality. If you don't fit the standard mold, following the common advice can actually work against you, leaving gaps in your legal protection and blind spots in your savings strategy.

This chapter covers specific considerations for unique life paths. It's not meant to be read cover to cover. Feel free to focus on the sections that apply to your situation, and skip the ones that don't.

Women and Investing

Women face a specific set of financial headwinds that, based on research, appear to require a more aggressive savings strategy than what's typically recommended. The core challenge isn't simply a longer retirement, since everyone should plan to age 95 or 100, but the need to fund that same long period with, in some cases, significantly less capital. Researchers and financial professionals often refer to this as the longevity tax, and it appears to be driven by three compounding factors.

The first is an income gap. Recent data shows a 32.6% gap in retirement income between men and women, largely driven by what's often called the motherhood penalty, time out of the workforce for caregiving. The second is a longevity gap. Women live, on average, roughly five years longer than men. While everyone should plan for the longest possible life, this means some women are more likely to spend their final, higher-cost years without a spouse or partner. The third is cash drag. Financial platform Ellevest has reported that women tend to keep more of their wealth in cash than men, a form of risk awareness that their analysis suggests costs the average woman roughly $100 a day in lost market returns over a lifetime.

Based on my research, aiming to save 12 to 15% of income rather than the standard 10% can create an important buffer against the wage gap. For women who are widowed, understanding Social

Security survivor benefit rules matters enormously. A survivor benefit can be claimed as early as age 60, while delaying your own retirement benefit until as late as age 70 allows it to continue growing. Later, the larger of the two can be used, which is especially important since the surviving spouse often relies on that income for many years. And because some women may outlive their spouses, a robust long-term care plan is worth prioritizing early rather than treating it as an afterthought.

BIPOC Investors

Research and data widely point to the fact that Black, Indigenous, and People of Color households often face distinct structural barriers that can make building wealth and preparing for retirement more difficult. Lower access to employer-sponsored retirement plans is one piece of it. In many cases, there's also a cultural expectation to provide financial support to extended family members, which can quietly limit both the ability to save and the consistency of long-term planning.

The data reflects real disparity. The median white family holds roughly $285,000 in wealth compared to about $44,900 for the median Black family. About 62% of white workers have access to employer-sponsored retirement plans compared to roughly 54% of Black and Asian workers. A higher likelihood of working in lower-wage or part-time roles at smaller firms that don't offer benefits plays a role, as does the lingering effect of historical labor market inequities.

A few things come up consistently for those navigating these headwinds. If an employer doesn't offer a 401(k), opening a Roth IRA and a Traditional IRA right away creates a personal retirement foundation without waiting for the system to catch up. For those whose cultural norms include financially supporting parents or siblings, building a specific budget line item for family support and holding that boundary when the money runs out is one of the most protective moves available. And where it aligns with the broader financial plan, homeownership comes up again and again as one of the most meaningful ways to build intergenerational wealth, locking in housing costs and creating something that can be passed down.

LGBTQ+ and Non-Traditional Families

While legal protections have evolved significantly over the years, the data points to the fact that LGBTQ+ families still face unique financial challenges rooted in long-standing disparities in wealth accumulation and social structures. Three compounding factors tend to show up consistently in the data. The first is a savings gap. Studies indicate that 51% of LGBTQ+ adults have less than $5,000 in savings, largely due to higher debt loads and wage discrimination, which makes building an initial financial foundation more difficult. The second is a care gap. LGBTQ+ seniors are reportedly twice as likely to be single and four times less likely to have children than their peers, which means reliance on chosen family for care, a structure that carries no legal standing and creates a real need for self-funded long-term care planning. The third is an income gap. Research shows LGBTQ+ workers tend to have lower median retirement account values than non-LGBTQ+ workers, often due to decades of discrimination that limited access to employer-sponsored plans.

From conversations with my personal legal team and attorneys who specialize in this area, a few things stand out as particularly important. Having the three core legal documents in place, a will, a power of attorney, and a medical directive, is essential. Without them, a biological relative could legally take control of medical decisions and lock a partner out of the hospital room entirely. For unmarried couples who own a home together, a cohabitation agreement that details who owns what equity is worth the investment of an attorney's time. And because chosen family carries no legal standing in a care setting, self-funding long-term care through either a dedicated cash account or an insurance policy tends to be one of the most important financial moves available to LGBTQ+ individuals who may not have adult children to rely on later in life.

Single Parent

Single parents carry the financial weight of a dual-income household on one pair of shoulders, and the margin for error is slim. Raising a child to age 18 costs roughly $300,000 according to widely cited estimates. Doing that on a single income requires a level of financial discipline that most standard advice doesn't fully account for, and it deserves a more specific conversation.

Life insurance tends to be at the top of every list when it comes to single parent financial planning, and for good reason. As the sole financial provider, a term life insurance policy worth ten to twelve times annual income is widely cited as the minimum needed to protect children if something happens. Disability insurance is equally important and often overlooked. If illness or injury makes it impossible to work, own occupation disability insurance can replace the paycheck that keeps everything running.

One of the harder conversations in this situation involves college funding. The temptation to put a child's college savings first is completely understandable. But the guidance that comes up most consistently is worth paying attention to. A child can borrow for college. A parent can't borrow for retirement. Putting the IRA first isn't selfish. It's the financially responsible move for both generations.

The Sandwich Generation

As we looked at earlier, being sandwiched between caring for aging parents and raising your own children is one of the most financially demanding positions a person can be in. You're supporting two generations at once, often serving as both the emotional anchor and the financial backup. The data points to the fact that nearly half of those in this position report significant financial strain, which can delay savings and stretch everyday budgets thin. The trend is also growing, with about one in three adults now claiming a parent as a dependent due to limited savings.

A few things come up consistently when looking at what's commonly recommended for those navigating this situation. If you're providing regular care for a parent, formalizing that arrangement through a Personal Care Agreement can be worth exploring. This is a legal document that allows a parent to pay a family caregiver from their own assets, and when drafted correctly, it can also help the parent spend down assets in a way that may support Medicaid eligibility later. An estate planning attorney can help determine whether this makes sense for the specific situation.

On the tax side, if you're paying more than 50% of a parent's support costs, claiming them as a dependent may unlock the Credit for Other Dependents and potential medical expense deductions. A tax professional can help clarify whether this applies.

There's only so much one income can carry across three generations. Perhaps the hardest part of navigating this situation is knowing where to draw the line. Children may need to consider community college. Parents may need to sell a home to fund their care. These are difficult conversations, but protecting your own financial footing isn't a selfish act. It's what makes it possible to keep showing up for everyone else.

Solo Ager

More than 22 million Americans over age 50 live alone, and that number keeps growing. Solo agers, those who are single, divorced, or widowed without children or without close connections to them, face a version of later life that the standard financial plan doesn't fully address. Without a built-in support system, critical moments become more uncertain. Who steps in to make medical decisions if you can't? Who notices early signs of cognitive decline? Who helps navigate a health crisis or a major life decision? Aging without a close support network goes beyond living alone. It means facing some of the most important decisions of your life without someone naturally there to help.

What comes up consistently in this area is the importance of putting formal support structures in place before they're needed. Rather than relying on a casual friend for legal and medical decisions, hiring a Professional Fiduciary or an Aging Life Care Professional (sometimes still called a Geriatric Care Manager), licensed professionals who can serve as a power of attorney and health proxy, should be looked into. An estate planning attorney or local aging services agency can help with referrals.

On the housing side, Continuing Care Retirement Communities, or CCRCs, are frequently mentioned as worth considering for solo agers. These communities offer independent living, assisted living, and nursing care all on one campus, with the ability to pre-pay for future care. For someone aging without a built-in support network, that kind of continuity can provide real peace of mind.

Small Business Owner

Many business owners report that the business itself is where they expect most of their retirement wealth to come from. But a business is an illiquid asset. You can't buy groceries with inventory, and you can't fund retirement with a valuation that exists only on paper.

A key distinction that comes up early in this kind of planning is the difference between succession and exit. Passing the business to family members is a completely different process, legally and financially, than selling it to an outside buyer. The earlier that decision gets made, the more options tend to be available.

Valuation is another area that business owners frequently report being surprised by. What an owner believes the business is worth and what the market will actually pay are often two different numbers. Getting a professional valuation five or more years before retirement gives enough runway to fill the gap if the number comes back lower than expected.

The third piece worth understanding is diversification. Putting all profits back into the business concentrates risk in one place. If the industry hits a rough patch, a business owner whose entire net worth is tied up in that company has no cushion. Pulling cash out regularly and investing it elsewhere builds a parallel financial foundation that doesn't rise and fall with the fate of one business.

Gray Divorce

Gray divorce has become a widely discussed topic in personal finance articles and the media, and the data behind it is striking. In 1990, only

8.7% of people divorcing in the United States were age 50 or older. By 2019, that share had risen to roughly 36%, and more recent research suggests that nearly 40% of divorcing individuals are now in this age group. Researchers point to several contributing factors, including longer life expectancy, changing expectations for marriage, greater financial independence, and more optimism about finding fulfillment in the years ahead. Whatever the reason, the financial consequences of divorcing later in life deserve serious attention.

According to research in this area, wealth typically drops by around 50% following a gray divorce, while the cost of maintaining two separate households rises. Studies suggest the standard of living drops by roughly 45% for women and 21% for men in the aftermath.

A few things come up consistently when looking at what's commonly recommended for those navigating this transition. The first is making sure a Qualified Domestic Relations Order, or QDRO, is part of the divorce settlement. This legal document allows a 401(k) or pension to be split between spouses without triggering taxes or penalties, and without it, that division can get complicated and costly. An attorney who specializes in divorce at this stage of life can help ensure it's handled correctly.

Social Security is also a factor here. If the marriage lasted ten years or more, it may be possible to claim spousal Social Security benefits based on an ex-spouse's record, even after divorce, as long as the claimant hasn't remarried. In some cases, that benefit may be higher than the one earned independently, which makes it important to review before making any claiming decisions.

On the practical side, the financial reset that comes with gray divorce often requires a hard look at housing and spending. Two people who built a life together on combined income now have to maintain separate lives on individual income. Downsizing sooner rather than later is a move that comes up frequently in this conversation, not as a defeat but as a way to protect liquidity and create breathing room while rebuilding.

Public Servants

Teachers, firefighters, police officers, and other public servants have historically faced a significant financial penalty through two provisions called the Windfall Elimination Provision, or WEP, and the Government Pension Offset, or GPO. Both reduced Social Security benefits for those who also received a government pension, creating a situation where decades of public service came with an unexpected retirement income hit.

That changed with the passage of the Social Security Fairness Act. As of 2026, the WEP and GPO penalties have been repealed, which means public servants can now collect their full pension and their full Social Security entitlement without one reducing the other. For those already retired, the SSA has been automatically adjusting benefits and issuing retroactive payments back to January 2024, with most adjustments completed in 2025. If you're affected and haven't seen the change reflected, verify your mailing address and direct deposit information in your mySocial Security account, and contact the SSA only if your benefit hasn't been recalculated.

One other area for public servants to pay attention to, particularly teachers, is the 403(b) plan. Many educators are enrolled in 403(b) plans through their districts, and some of those plans have historically been loaded with high-fee annuity products that quietly erode returns over time. Checking the expense ratios on any investments inside a 403(b) is a worthwhile exercise. If fees are above 1%, it may be worth asking the district whether lower-cost options through providers like Fidelity or Vanguard are available.

Late-Career Immigrant

Immigrants who arrive in the United States later in life often face a retirement planning challenge that the standard advice doesn't fully address. Building toward Social Security benefits requires at least 40 work credits, which typically translates to roughly ten years of covered employment. For someone who arrived in their 40s or 50s, that timeline is compressed in ways that may require a more deliberate approach.

One thing that comes up in research on this topic is the existence of totalization agreements between the United States and a number of other countries. These agreements allow work credits earned in both countries to be combined when determining eligibility for Social Security benefits. For those who worked in their home country before immigrating, look into whether a totalization agreement exists and what it might mean for benefit eligibility.

On the savings side, the compressed timeline is something that wealth managers and retirement specialists who work with this population frequently flag. Someone who arrives at 45 has roughly 20 years to build what most people spend 40 years accumulating. Maxing out a 401(k) and IRA every year during that window is widely cited as one of the most important moves available.

For those who plan to retire outside the United States, cross-border tax planning is an area that comes up consistently in this conversation. The United States taxes citizens and permanent residents on worldwide income regardless of where they live, which creates a layer of complexity that most tax professionals suggest working through with a cross-border specialist.

Early-Life Disability

For individuals born with disabilities or who become disabled early in life, the financial challenge is rooted in a fundamental mismatch with a system built around steady work, rising income, and delayed need for care. The data points to the fact that people with lifelong disabilities often face lower earnings and higher unemployment rates, even when fully capable of working, due to gaps in accommodation and persistent employer bias. At the same time, programs like SSI and Medicaid enforce strict asset limits, which makes building any meaningful financial cushion genuinely difficult. Many individuals also live long lives with ongoing care needs, which increases costs without a corresponding increase in earning power.

A few things come up consistently when looking at what's commonly recommended for those navigating this situation. ABLE accounts, which stand for Achieving a Better Life Experience, are one of the most important tools available. These accounts allow individuals with qualifying disabilities to save and invest without triggering the asset limits that would otherwise affect benefit eligibility.

Maintaining higher cash reserves than traditional advice recommends is another consideration that comes up frequently, given the unpredictability of care disruptions and benefit delays. Financial planning in this context also tends to require ongoing attention to benefits navigation, including recertifications and appeals, in ways that standard planning doesn't account for. Estate planning with family members or trustees should be a priority to avoid accidental benefit disqualification down the road.

Chronic Illness

Chronic illness creates a different kind of financial constraint than most standard advice accounts for. Income may still be possible, but it often isn't reliable. Health costs can rise and fall unexpectedly, energy comes in limited supply, and the ability to work can change without warning. Traditional financial planning assumes consistency, but the data points to the fact that chronic illness demands flexibility, backup plans, and quicker access to cash.

This unpredictability tends to show up in several interconnected ways. Income often becomes unstable, with reduced hours, job changes, or periods out of the workforce, which limits long-term growth and access to employer benefits. Even with insurance, ongoing medical expenses can quietly drain savings and push people toward high-interest debt. Career gaps can also reduce opportunities for advancement, weaken benefits eligibility, and shrink retirement contributions over time, creating a compounding disadvantage that builds year after year.

From what comes up consistently in research and among those who work in this area, a few adjustments tend to make a meaningful difference. Favoring work arrangements that allow remote options, contract pacing, or benefits portability over maximum salary is something that comes up frequently as a way to protect both income and health over the long term. Keeping a larger emergency fund than standard advice recommends helps absorb flare-ups without derailing longer-term plans.

On the account side, Roth accounts are frequently highlighted for their flexibility in this situation. Contributions can be withdrawn at any time tax and penalty free, and in certain circumstances, including disability or high medical expenses, earnings may also be accessible without penalty. Building a mix of account types that can be drawn from when income changes is a strategy that tends to come up consistently for those managing chronic illness. And short and long-term disability insurance are widely viewed as core protections rather than optional add-ons when health is uncertain.

Sudden Disability

A cancer diagnosis, serious accident, or acute illness can rewrite a financial life overnight. The real risk, according to those who study and work in this area, isn't just the lost income. It's the tendency to assume things will return to normal, which can delay the adjustments needed to protect long-term financial stability. The impact tends to hit from multiple directions at once. Income can drop sharply or disappear for extended periods during treatment and recovery. At the same time, expenses often surge, from medical bills and insurance gaps to travel and recovery costs, draining savings quickly.

A few steps tend to matter most in the aftermath of a sudden disability. Reassessing income, expenses, and savings as early as possible and making appropriate adjustments is widely cited as the most important first move, even when the situation feels temporary. A thorough review of employer benefits, disability coverage, Social Security eligibility, and healthcare options should be handled sooner rather than later, since many of these have time-sensitive enrollment or filing windows that can be missed during a health crisis.

Career redesign is another area that comes up frequently, and it's often one of the harder conversations. Returning to the same role at the same capacity may not be realistic, and planners who work in this space often suggest that accepting a lower-stress or lower-intensity role sooner rather than later can actually extend working years and protect long-term health. And planning for partial recovery rather than best-case recovery is an approach that tends to produce more financially resilient outcomes, even if a full recovery eventually happens.

Securing Your Custom Path

If your path deviates from convention, whether you're navigating the complexities of a gray divorce, the headwinds of a wealth gap, or the demands of the sandwich generation, the financial vulnerabilities are unique and may require equally unique adjustments.

The strategies in earlier chapters form the foundation. What this chapter adds are the adjustments that help that foundation fit your actual life. From understanding Social Security survivor rules to putting the right legal documents in place for a chosen family, these aren't replacements for the core work. They're the layer that makes the core work for you specifically.

Whatever your situation, the goal is the same. A financial plan that accounts for the life you're actually living, not the one the standard playbook assumes you have.

Chapter Fourteen Actions

Custom Audit

[ ] **Women.** Run a longevity stress test. Does your money last to age 95 to 100 without a spouse or partner? If not, consider increasing your savings rate to 12 to 15% and review your Social Security survivor benefit strategy if widowed.

[ ] **BIPOC.** If you don't have access to a workplace retirement plan, set up an automatic monthly transfer to a Roth IRA. Review the IRS annual contribution limits each year as they may change.

[ ] **LGBTQ+.** Review your beneficiary designations and confirm your partner is named specifically. Make sure the three core legal documents are in place, a will, a power of attorney, and a health directive. If you own a home with an unmarried partner, look into a cohabitation agreement.

[ ] **Single Parents.** Verify you have term life insurance equal to at least ten times your income. If you haven't already, look into own occupation disability insurance to protect your paycheck if you can't work.

[ ] **Sandwich Generation.** Have the money conversation with your parents. Do they have a long-term care plan? If not, explore options together. Look into whether a Personal Care Agreement makes sense if you're providing regular care, and check whether you qualify to claim a parent as a dependent on your taxes.

[ ] **Solo Agers.** Interview a Professional Fiduciary or Geriatric Care Manager to serve as a future power of attorney and health proxy. Look into Continuing Care Retirement Communities if you don't have a built-in support network.

[ ] **Public Servants.** Log into SSA.gov to see your updated benefit estimate following the repeal of the WEP and GPO provisions. If you're already retired and haven't seen your benefit adjusted, verify your contact information with SSA and reach out only if the recalculation hasn't happened automatically. Check the expense ratios in your 403(b) and ask your district about lower-cost options if fees exceed 1%.

[ ] **Business Owners.** Schedule a professional business valuation at least five years before your target retirement date. Decide whether your exit plan is succession or sale and make sure the legal structure reflects that decision. Review how much of your net worth is tied up in the business and consider pulling cash out regularly to invest elsewhere.

[ ] **Gray Divorce.** Confirm that a Qualified Domestic Relations Order, or QDRO, is part of your divorce settlement to split retirement accounts without triggering taxes or penalties. Check your Social Security statement to see whether an ex-spouse benefit applies if you were married ten years or more. Review housing costs and consider whether downsizing makes sense to protect liquidity.

[ ] **Late-Career Immigrant.** Check whether your home country has a totalization agreement with the United States that could allow you to combine work credits for Social Security eligibility. Max out your 401(k) and IRA every year without exception given the compressed timeline. If you plan to retire outside the United States, consult a cross-border tax specialist.

[ ] **Disability From Birth or Early Life.** Open and fund an ABLE account and confirm contributions won't jeopardize SSI or Medicaid eligibility. Review any family gifts or inheritances with an attorney to ensure they flow through a special needs trust if needed. Maintain a minimum six-month cash reserve to cover benefit delays or care disruptions.

[ ] **Chronic Illness.** Build a larger emergency fund to cover income interruptions and higher medical expenses. Review disability insurance, employer leave, and health coverage annually and address any gaps. Prioritize Roth retirement contributions for flexible, tax-free access if your work capacity changes.

[ ] **Sudden Disability.** Within 90 days of a diagnosis or significant health event, review employer benefits, disability coverage, and Social Security eligibility. Rebuild your financial plan based on reduced income and ongoing medical costs. Create a flexible return to work plan that protects long-term capacity over short-term income.

15
Avoiding Retirement Traps and Financial Landmines

Up to this point, we've been in building mode. Defining the retirement you want, understanding the tradeoffs, and figuring out which financial pieces need to be in place to support your vision. With that foundation set, you can focus on accumulating the resources to make it possible. But the work doesn't end there. Building wealth is only part of the job. Protecting it matters just as much, yet it's a part of retirement planning that too many of us overlook.

As your wealth grows, so does the need to protect it. And the greatest threats are not always things like dramatic market crashes. More often, they arrive quietly. A relative with a can't-miss opportunity. A medical expense that shows up without warning. A tax bill no one told you was coming. A contractor, an advisor, or a stranger online who says exactly the right thing at exactly the right time. Any one of them can undo years of careful planning.

Think of everything up to this point as your offense. This chapter is your defense. Not because you should expect the worst, but because a strong retirement plan has to account for what can go wrong. And the folks who come out ahead are usually the ones who saw the risks coming before they arrived.

The Traps

The 12 traps that follow can quietly undo years of careful planning. Some show up disguised as good advice. Others come from people you trust. A few hide inside the tax code, the market, or your own decisions. Unfortunately, some retirees don't recognize them until they've already paid the price. With that in mind, walk through each carefully, and use this chapter as a reference whenever something feels off.

Trap 1: The Family Bank

One of the most common reasons retirements fail isn't market performance. It's the inability to set boundaries with adult children. Wealth researchers call this Economic Outpatient Care, subsidizing an adult child's lifestyle to the detriment of their independence and your retirement. Recent studies show that roughly 50% of parents provide regular financial assistance to adult children and spend an average of $1,400 or more per month.

For some, giving an adult child $1,400 a month doesn't feel like a fortune, but it's financially violent to a portfolio. That $16,800 a year would require an additional $420,000 saved to sustain under the 4% rule. Financial expert Suze Orman is famous for her tough love stance on this. Her mantra is "Put your own oxygen mask on first."

If you must help, make it a one-time gift like a wedding contribution or a single student loan payment rather than an ongoing subsidy like a cell phone bill or rent. Instead of cash, contribute to a 529 plan for a grandchild. It's tax-advantaged, locks the money for education, and ensures it won't be wasted on lifestyle creep.

A defensive move is to avoid saying yes immediately when a child asks for a loan or help with a bill. Instead, say, "I need to check my retirement projections first." Then wait 24 hours, because the urgency often fades.

Offer non-financial help first, such as advice, babysitting, or networking. If you give cash, write a letter or card stating it's a one-time gift so expectations are clear.

Trap 2: Fraud Epidemic

Retirees lose over $3 billion annually to financial scams. Retirees are a target specifically because scammers know they likely have access to a lifetime of savings. They use psychology, technology, and sometimes brute-force performance to bypass your skepticism.

Imposter Scam

Scammers call pretending to be a grandchild or child in trouble. They often know your name and your child's name from social media. In the modern era, they may use AI voice cloning to sound exactly like your loved one.

This threat isn't theoretical. It happened to my senior parents. A scammer called them pretending to be me and knew my first name. To disguise his voice, the imposter slurred his speech, sounding drunk and terrified. He claimed to be in jail after hitting a pregnant woman with his car and begged them to send bail money immediately. The scenario was designed to bypass logic and trigger pure panic.

Instead of reacting by sending money, my parents questioned the caller. "Which jail are you in?" "Where did the accident happen?" The scammer was vague, which was the giveaway. My parents immediately sent me a text and were relieved to learn that I was safe in a business meeting, impressively sober. At that point, they realized it was a scam and hung up.

The takeaway is that scammers will use family names and act out horrific scenarios to make us panic. Verify everything before acting.

A defensive move is to hang up immediately and not speak. Then call your grandchild or child on the number saved in your phone. If they don't answer, call their spouse, partner, or a close friend. Verify their location and the validity of the issue before doing anything.

Pig Butchering Scam

This is a long con. You get a wrong number text from a polite stranger who strikes up a friendship. They're kind, patient, and successful. But remember the old saying about putting lipstick on a pig? It's still a pig. The politeness is just the lipstick disguising the intent to slaughter your bank account.

Eventually, they mention they're making huge returns on a specific crypto app. They walk you through investing a small amount and let you withdraw the profit to build trust, which fattens the pig, then convince you to wire your life savings right before the slaughter.

A defensive move is to never take investment advice from someone you've never met in person and never send money. Perform a reverse image search of their profile photo, because you may find it belongs to a model or influencer. Then block the number.

Tech Support Scam

A terrifying popup appears on your computer claiming, "VIRUS DETECTED. Call Microsoft Support Immediately." You call and a fake agent asks for remote access to fix it. Once inside, they drain your bank accounts while you watch.

A defensive move is to avoid clicking any link or calling the number on the screen. Disconnect your computer from the internet and close your web browser completely. If the popup won't close, restart your computer. The popup is usually just a browser tab designed to look scary, and restarting kills it.

If needed, contact a trusted tech source directly. Use official websites or saved contacts, never the popup. If you gave access or entered any information, secure your accounts immediately. Change passwords and contact your bank.

Medicare Scam

A caller claims to be from Medicare and states you're eligible for a refund or a new card. They ask for your Social Security number. They aren't trying to help you. They want your Social Security number to commit medical identity theft.

A defensive move is to terminate the call immediately. Medicare, the IRS, and Social Security won't call you out of the blue demanding information or money.

If you're concerned, call Medicare directly using the official number on their website or on the back of your card. Never use the number the caller gives you. Never give your Social Security number or Medicare number to anyone who calls you.

Romance Scam

You meet someone on a dating site. They seem perfect, attentive, loving, and successful. But there's always a reason they can't meet in person. They work on an oil rig or are deployed military. After months of love bombing, a crisis hits, and they ask for a wire transfer.

A defensive move is to demand a video call. If a dating prospect refuses to meet in person or do a live, spontaneous video call within a few weeks, block them immediately. Scammers refuse because they don't look like their stolen profile pictures.

Perform a reverse image search of their profile photo, because you may find it belongs to a model or influencer. If anyone you've met online requests money, a wire transfer, or a gift card for any reason, including an emergency, it's a scam. Block them and walk away.

Trap 3: Costly Emotional Errors

The stock market will crash. A 10% to 20% drop happens every few years. The danger isn't the crash. It's your reaction to it.

Consider Mark, an investor who had $500,000 in his 401(k). When the pandemic hit, the S&P 500 dropped 34%. Terrified, Mark sold his stocks on March 20. He felt smart for three days. But on March 24, the market began a violent recovery. By August, it hit new all-time highs. Mark was still sitting in cash. By selling, he locked in a $170,000 loss and missed the recovery. He didn't just lose money. He lost years of freedom.

A defensive move is to do nothing for 24 hours. Never trade on emotion. Open the Investment Policy Statement your retirement or financial planner provided, or the one you developed, and refresh yourself on the plan. Then contact your planner. They can talk you off the ledge.

Trap 4: Bad Advice

As we've covered, not all financial advisors are created equal. Taking advice from the wrong person can cost you thousands in hidden fees.

High Expense Ratio Trap
Many "advisors" who are actually sales representatives will put you into active mutual funds that carry high expense ratios of 1% or more. If the market returns 8% and your fund charges 1.5%, you lose nearly 19% of your growth to fees. Over decades, that compounding drag can reduce your ending wealth by hundreds of thousands of dollars.

Annuity Trap
Avoid equity indexed annuities with long surrender periods. These are insurance products tied loosely to the stock market, with limited upside and restricted access to your money. An agent might lock your money up for 10 or 15 years with a massive penalty, called a surrender charge, if you try to leave.

Trap 5: Social Security Landmines

There are two landmines that can catch sophisticated retirees off guard.

Earnings Test Trap
If you claim Social Security early and continue to work, benefits may be temporarily withheld. In 2026, Social Security withholds $1 for every $2 you earn above $24,480. Any withheld benefits are later credited back after full retirement age.

Widow's Trap
Many couples assume it makes sense for the higher earner to claim Social Security early to bring in more money now. The problem appears later. When one spouse dies, one Social Security check disappears entirely. The surviving spouse doesn't keep both checks. They keep only the larger one. If the higher earner claimed early, that larger check is permanently smaller. Waiting until age 70 increases the benefit the surviving spouse will depend on for the rest of their life.

Trap 6: Inflation Creep

Inflation is one of the quietest threats in retirement because it doesn't feel like a crisis at first. Nothing breaks overnight. No account statement suddenly flashes red. Instead, the same groceries, insurance premiums, utility bills, home repairs, property taxes, and healthcare costs simply become more expensive year after year.

That slow pressure can be dangerous. A retirement paycheck that feels comfortable at age 65 may feel stretched by age 75 and inadequate by age 85 if income doesn't keep pace. This is especially important for retirees whose floor isn't fully inflation protected. Social Security includes cost-of-living adjustments, but many pensions, annuity payments, and portfolio withdrawal plans may not automatically rise enough to match real-world expenses.

The biggest mistake is assuming today's spending number is permanent. It isn't. Retirement can last 20, 30, or even 40 years, and inflation has decades to work against you. Even modest inflation can quietly double the cost of living over a long retirement. That means a plan that looks safe on day one may become fragile later if it doesn't include a way to keep income growing.

The defensive move is to build inflation into your retirement projections instead of treating today's expenses as fixed forever. Identify which income sources have inflation protection and which ones don't. Keep part of the portfolio positioned for long-term growth so the plan has a better chance of keeping up with rising costs. Then review spending annually and adjust before inflation pressure becomes a crisis.

Trap 7: Tax Traps

Earlier chapters covered the mechanics of withdrawing money in retirement, including the different account types, the order in which they're typically tapped, Roth conversions, and required minimum distributions. This section is about what goes wrong when those decisions aren't coordinated.

Retirement income doesn't behave like a paycheck. A withdrawal that looks small in isolation can ripple through the rest of the plan, spike Medicare premiums, push more of your Social Security into taxable territory, or knock you off the ACA subsidy cliff. None of these traps announce themselves. They just show up on a tax return months later.

Social Security Taxation Surprises

Many retirees are surprised to learn that Social Security can become taxable. The amount taxed depends on a formula that includes other income, such as withdrawals from traditional IRAs and 401(k)s.

As pre-tax withdrawals increase, more of a Social Security benefit may become taxable. This can create a multiplier effect. A withdrawal from a traditional IRA may not only add taxable income by itself, but it may also cause more Social Security income to be taxed. That means the effective tax rate on a withdrawal can be higher than expected. That's why these decisions can't be made in isolation.

ACA Healthcare Cliff

If someone retires before age 65, health insurance can become one of the biggest planning challenges. Before Medicare begins, many early retirees rely on Affordable Care Act (ACA) coverage, where premiums and subsidies are tied to modified adjusted gross income, or MAGI.

For ACA subsidy purposes, MAGI can include income that doesn't feel obvious from a spending perspective, including traditional IRA and 401(k) withdrawals, tax-exempt interest such as municipal bond interest, and the non-taxable portion of Social Security benefits. That means a withdrawal that looks manageable from an investment perspective can still affect healthcare subsidy eligibility. If MAGI rises too much, subsidies may fall and premiums can increase sharply. In 2026, the ACA subsidy cliff has returned for people above 400% of the federal poverty level, so crossing the threshold by even one dollar can eliminate premium tax credit eligibility.

A withdrawal that seems modest on its own can therefore create a costly healthcare surprise. This is why retirees who use ACA coverage before Medicare should coordinate withdrawals, Roth conversions, capital gains, and other taxable income with their healthcare subsidy thresholds before making year-end decisions.

Medicare Premium Surprises

Medicare premiums are income-tested. Higher income in retirement can increase monthly Medicare costs through surcharges known as IRMAA, or **I**ncome-**R**elated **M**onthly **A**djustment **A**mount.

This can surprise retirees who make otherwise smart planning moves, such as large Roth conversions, big capital gains, or unusually high withdrawals in a single year. The problem is that Medicare surcharges are based on prior tax returns, so a high-income year can increase future premiums.

This doesn't mean Roth conversions or larger withdrawals are always bad. It means they need to be coordinated. Tax planning in retirement should consider not only income tax brackets, but also Medicare premium thresholds. Keeping income more evenly distributed over time can sometimes help reduce both tax and healthcare cost surprises.

RMD Mistakes

Once required minimum distributions begin, the IRS requires annual withdrawals from tax-deferred retirement accounts whether the money is needed for spending or not. The trap is that RMDs can increase taxable income at exactly the wrong time, pushing retirees into higher tax brackets, triggering more Social Security taxation, and raising Medicare premiums.

Missing an RMD can also create penalties, so systems matter. Many custodians allow automated RMD calculations and distributions. Consolidating old accounts may also make RMD tracking easier.

For retirees who give to charity, a Qualified Charitable Distribution, or QCD, can be useful. A QCD allows money to be sent directly from an IRA to a qualified charity, which can satisfy an RMD while keeping the distribution out of taxable income.

Rollover Mistakes That Lock You Out

Earlier chapters covered the Rule of 55 and Roth conversion ladders as ways to access retirement money before 59½. Both share the same trap: one wrong rollover can permanently lock you out of a strategy you spent years planning for. Roll a 401(k) into an IRA too soon and the Rule of 55 benefit may be gone. Run a Roth conversion ladder without modeling the impact on ACA subsidies and Medicare premiums and the tax surprise can wipe out the benefit it was meant to deliver.

The defensive move is the same for both. Don't rush the rollover. Don't execute either strategy without modeling the tax impact across multiple years with a planner or tax professional.

Trap 8: Home Equity and Relocation Landmines

Housing can be one of the most powerful retirement levers, but it can also be one of the easiest to miscalculate.

Reverse Mortgage Cautions

A reverse mortgage can turn home equity into cash flow, but it's a high-consequence tool and should be approached carefully.

For homeowners age 62 and older, a Home Equity Conversion Mortgage, or HECM, may allow access to home equity without selling the home or making monthly mortgage payments. Funds may be available as a lump sum, monthly payment, or line of credit. The loan is typically repaid when the homeowner dies, sells the home, or no longer lives there as a primary residence.

A reverse mortgage doesn't transfer ownership. The homeowner remains on title, but the lender places a lien on the property.

The risks are significant. Fees can be high. Interest accrues over time, which can reduce home equity and affect what's left to heirs. The homeowner must continue paying property taxes, insurance, maintenance, and any HOA fees. Failure to meet those obligations can lead to foreclosure. For that reason, a reverse mortgage shouldn't be viewed as a lifestyle upgrade tool. It's usually better understood as a last-resort or backup strategy, especially for retirees who need to remain in the home and have few other options.

Housing and Geo-Arbitrage Decisions

Geo-arbitrage was covered as a strategy in Chapter 13. Here, it's worth flagging as a trap. The math needs to be honest. Selling a home can involve real estate commissions, closing costs, moving costs, repairs, new furnishings, taxes, and emotional tradeoffs. A lower-cost area may also come with different healthcare access, climate risks, travel costs, or distance from family.

The trap is making the decision based only on the difference in home prices or state income taxes. Before selling or relocating, calculate the net proceeds, ongoing cost savings, tax implications, healthcare access, and lifestyle impact. The goal is to improve your retirement plan, not just move somewhere cheaper.

Trap 9: Forced Exit

We often assume we'll work until 65 or 70 on our own terms. The data says otherwise. A recent report found that nearly 60% of retirees left the workforce sooner than they planned due to health issues, layoffs, or caring for a spouse.

I've seen this happen throughout my career. Layoffs are a regular occurrence, and they seem to target the older workforce more often than not. Once you reach a certain age and pay level, there's an unspoken understanding that you have a target on your back. The defense is to lean hard into experience, knowledge, and the value you bring that newer hires can't easily replicate. That helps, but it doesn't make anyone immune. Being prepared for an earlier-than-planned exit is just smart, not pessimistic. And keep in mind, a forced exit doesn't necessarily mean you're out of the workforce. For many, it turns out to be a blessing in disguise, the push that opens the door to a meaningful pivot.

If this happens to you, avoid signing the severance package immediately. You legally have time to review it and may be able to negotiate, so contact an employment attorney right away. Stop all discretionary spending and switch to a wartime budget. Leverage your cash reserves as needed. Don't roll over your 401(k) yet. If you're age 55 or older, check the Rule of 55 to see if you can access those funds penalty-free, if needed. Contact your planner to discuss options.

Trap 10: The Catch-Up Investment Trap

Late starters often face a difficult emotional choice. They know they need growth, but they also know they have less time to recover from mistakes. That pressure can lead to two opposite traps.

The first is speculation. A late starter may take oversized risks in individual stocks, crypto, options, or other high-volatility investments in hopes of catching up quickly. That isn't a plan. It's gambling with a shorter recovery window.

The second is excessive safety. A late starter may become so afraid of loss that they move too much money into cash or low-return investments. That may feel safe, but it can make it harder for the portfolio to keep up with inflation or support a retirement that could last 30 years or more.

The balance is disciplined growth. Late starters may still need meaningful exposure to broad, diversified equities, but the focus should be on a thoughtful allocation, not home-run bets. The goal is to give the portfolio a chance to grow without taking risks that could permanently damage the plan.

A defensive move is to avoid trying to fix a shortfall with speculation. A home-run investment can just as easily become a permanent setback. Don't confuse safety with progress, because too much cash or too much conservatism can create inflation risk and longevity risk.

Review your allocation with your planner and focus on disciplined growth, diversification, and a realistic retirement timeline.

Trap 11: Boredom Tax

You're not just retiring *from* something. You're retiring *to* something. One of the most expensive traps in retirement is boredom, especially when there's no clear vision for what comes next. Retirees without purpose often fill the void with spending. When there's no plan for your time, it's easy for shopping, upgrades, and impulse purchases to become a substitute for meaning.

A defensive move is to implement the 72-hour rule. Put it in the cart and walk away for three days. Then ask, "Am I buying this because I need it, or because I'm bored?"

Rent it first, if that's an option. Before buying an RV, rent one for a week or two. If you hate driving it, you just saved $100,000 or more.

Trap 12: Flying Blind

Professionals don't guess. They follow a written set of rules, and so should you. That's what an Investment Policy Statement is for. Your IPS is your rulebook. It defines how you invest, how you respond to market swings, and what you will not do no matter how bad things look.

Most retirees don't have one. And when the market gets stressful, that's when it shows. Without a plan to follow, it's easy to react to headlines instead of sticking to a strategy. As we covered in Chapter 10, the IPS is your defense against that kind of thinking.

If you don't have one, get it done. If you have one, be sure to actually use it. It should explicitly prohibit panic selling and spell out what to do instead. Before any buy or sell decision, check it first. And if you feel the urge to deviate, pause. Seriously consider calling your planner before you make a move.

Different Planning Philosophies

Not all retirement philosophies agree with the tools and strategies presented in this chapter. Some approaches intentionally take a narrower view of retirement planning, prioritizing simplicity, personal discipline, and long-term growth over engineered income solutions or optimization techniques. We've already touched on a few of these perspectives, but it's helpful to group them together and address them directly. Understanding these objections is important because many of us encounter them elsewhere and may already hold strong views. A few of the most common perspectives are outlined below.

Rejection of Dividend-Focused Income Strategies

Some philosophies are skeptical of using dividends as a primary source of retirement income. In a dividend-focused approach, the portfolio is built around assets that generate regular cash payouts, such as dividend-paying stocks or REITs, with the goal of living off those distributions.

By contrast, these approaches follow a total return philosophy. The portfolio is designed for long-term growth, and income is created by selling shares as needed. Dividends and price appreciation are treated as interchangeable sources of return. From this perspective, dividends are considered incidental rather than reliable, since they can be reduced or eliminated, and building a portfolio around them may distort asset allocation decisions.

Avoidance of Bonds and Bond Ladders

Some philosophies deliberately avoid bonds, bond funds, and bond ladders, even in retirement. The concern is that bonds may limit long-term growth, expose retirees to inflation risk, and create a false sense of safety. Rather than using bonds for stability or income, these approaches accept greater volatility in exchange for higher expected returns over time.

Strong Resistance to Reverse Mortgages

Some financial voices take a hard line against using home equity as a source of retirement income, period. The objection isn't just about cost or complexity, which were covered earlier in the reverse mortgage trap. It's a deeper philosophical concern that the home should function primarily as a stability asset, not a financial one. Borrowing against it, in this view, treats shelter and security as something to be optimized rather than protected.

Consumer advocates often echo this concern. Clark Howard has described reverse mortgages as a last resort, generally appropriate only when there are no better options for remaining in the home. Jane Bryant Quinn, longtime personal finance columnist and author of *How to Make Your Money Last*, has warned that reverse mortgages can be hazardous when used too early and are often better considered as a backup source of liquidity rather than a primary way to fund lifestyle spending.

The underlying belief is that home equity should be treated as protection of last resort. Once it's accessed, it's gone, and the flexibility it represents disappears with it. From this perspective, the better path is to design a retirement plan that doesn't depend on tapping the home in the first place.

Discomfort with RMD Based Strategies

Some approaches avoid using IRS life expectancy tables or Required Minimum Distribution formulas as a guide for spending. These methods are seen as overly technical and disconnected from real-world needs. Critics prefer simpler frameworks, such as fixed withdrawals or flexible spending tied to portfolio performance.

Avoidance of Proactive Tax Strategies

While tax efficiency is recognized as important, some philosophies reject strategies such as Roth conversion timing, tax bracket management, or income smoothing across years. The concern is that these approaches add complexity, require ongoing monitoring, and increase the risk of execution errors. Simpler methods are preferred, even if they result in higher taxes over time.

Preference for Growth and Systematic Withdrawals

Instead of relying on income-producing assets, these approaches favor broadly diversified, growth-oriented portfolios combined with systematic withdrawals. Income is generated by selling shares as needed, rather than from dividends, bond maturities, or contractual payouts. The emphasis is on liquidity, transparency, and simplicity.

Emphasis on Behavior Over Optimization

Underlying all of these objections is the belief that retirement failures are more often behavioral than mathematical. Panic selling, rigid plans, overconfidence, and emotional reactions to market declines are seen as the primary risks. From this perspective, the goal of a retirement plan is not to optimize every variable, but to reduce the likelihood of poor decisions during periods of stress.

Securing Your Defenses

Building wealth is an act of optimism, but keeping it requires a healthy dose of paranoia. Protecting money demands a fundamental shift in mindset that many intelligent folks fail to make. For decades you played offense. You took risks, invested for growth, increased your income, and focused on expanding opportunity. If you made a mistake, time and another paycheck could repair the damage. But that playbook doesn't work when you retire. Retirement changes the rules.

Once retired, the margin for error narrows and the consequences of complacency rise. There's no guaranteed second stretch of peak earning years to rebuild from a major loss. You're no longer simply accumulating assets. You're stewarding a finite pool of capital that must sustain your lifestyle, your independence, and possibly your spouse for decades. That responsibility calls for discipline and vigilance. Playing defense doesn't mean living in fear. It means understanding where the real threats exist and addressing them before they cause harm. Excessive fees can quietly drain compounding. Poor tax decisions can trigger unnecessary erosion. Ill-timed withdrawals can lock in market losses. Fraud, cognitive decline, and misplaced trust can open the door to irreversible damage. None of these risks announce themselves loudly, yet each has the power to undermine a lifetime of work.

You have to think differently once retired. You're the Chief Executive Officer who sets direction and defines the mission. You determine what matters most and what risks are acceptable. You're also the Chief Financial Officer who allocates money wisely, oversees diversification, manages income streams, and approaches taxes with intention. And you're the Chief Security Officer who protects what you've built by installing safeguards against unnecessary risk, excessive costs, poor advice, and emotional decision-making. You can delegate tasks to professionals, but you can't delegate ultimate responsibility.

Guarding your wealth means building a system resilient enough to withstand volatility, uncertainty, and time. Wealth that took decades to build can be compromised in just a few careless years. Guard it deliberately. Avoid the traps. Defuse the landmines. Preserve the freedom you worked a lifetime to create.

Chapter Fifteen Actions

Fortifying Your Future

Family Audit (Complete this today)

[ ] **The Help Review:** List every dollar you currently give to family (children, siblings, etc.) and sum the annual total. Ask yourself whether this jeopardizes your retirement security.

[ ] **One-Time Rule:** If you're helping family financially with some form of ongoing payment, convert to a one-time gift, if anything. Write a short letter/card stating it's a one-time gift, not a loan and not a pattern.

[ ] **Non-Financial First:** Commit to offering advice, networking, or practical help before cash the next time you're asked for financial assistance from family.

Fraud Shield (Complete this week)

[ ] **Family Password:** Create a secret verbal password with family to verify real emergencies. If a family member contacts you for help, request the password if you're in doubt.

[ ] **Contact Tree:** Write down exactly who you'll call to verify any emergency involving family.

[ ] **Tech Safety:** Install or update antivirus software and enable automatic updates on all your devices. Make this a top priority.

[ ] **Credit Freeze:** Consider placing a security freeze or fraud alert with the major credit bureaus if you're at higher risk for identity theft.

Social Security Review (Complete this month)

[ ] **Earnings Test Awareness:** If you claimed early and still work, calculate whether the earnings test applies to you.

[ ] **Widow's Strategy Check:** If married, model what happens if the higher earner dies first.

Forced Exit Plan (Set up now, use later)

[ ] **Emergency Budget:** Identify what you'd cut immediately if income stopped.

[ ] **Rule of 55 Review:** Check whether your current 401(k) would be accessible penalty-free if needed.

[ ] **Planner Meeting Trigger:** Define what would prompt an immediate call to your planner, e.g., layoff.

Advisor and IPS Check (Confirm this year)

[ ] **Fee Audit:** List your investment funds and look up expense ratios. Flag anything over 0.10% to review with your planner.

[ ] **Advisor Alignment:** Confirm your advisor is a fiduciary and how they're paid (ideally fee-only, not commissions on products).

[ ] **IPS in Place:** Confirm you have a written Investment Policy Statement (IPS) that defines your target allocation, rebalancing rules, and when changes are allowed.

Anti-Boredom Plan (Complete this month)

[ ] **Purpose List:** Write three activities you'll pursue in retirement that aren't spending-based and add them to your retirement vision.

16

Estate Planning

"The only thing you take with you when you're gone is what you leave behind." - John Allston

Over decades, we build wealth while managing the familiar risks of investing and retirement planning. Estate planning addresses a different kind of risk, the possibility that what we've worked to build might not stay protected or end up where we intended. That's where a solid estate plan comes in, creating the legal framework to safeguard our assets and ensure they transfer according to our wishes.

Many of us think estate planning is only for the wealthy. In reality, it becomes relevant the moment we have something or someone worth protecting. Beyond just tax strategies, estate planning gives us control over three critical questions. Who will handle my affairs if I can't? Who will make important decisions on my behalf? And what happens to everything I own?

I'll admit, estate planning wasn't on my radar when I was younger. Like most in their twenties and thirties, I focused entirely on investing and saving for retirement. It's easy to feel invincible at that age, and I was no exception. Planning for death or incapacity feels abstract and far away. For me, getting married and facing unexpected health challenges changed everything. Suddenly, I realized estate planning had less to do with age or wealth and everything to do with protecting those I cared about most.

Without proper planning, state law steps in to make decisions you'd probably want to make yourself. The court might choose who manages your money, who gets your property, and even who makes personal medical decisions for you. The results rarely match what you would have chosen.

The statistics on this are pretty sobering. A 2024 Caring.com survey found that only 32% of Americans have a will. Even among those 55 and older, who you'd think would have this handled, nearly half still don't have basic estate documents. When planning gets put off indefinitely, family members are left to pick up the pieces during an already difficult time.

There's another critical aspect that doesn't get enough attention, and that's planning for incapacity. As we live longer, the chances of spending time unable to manage our own affairs increase significantly. The right planning ensures your bills get paid, your investments stay on track, and your medical preferences are respected, all without forcing your family through lengthy court proceedings.

At its heart, estate planning is really an act of love. It's one of the most concrete ways to take care of those who matter to you, even when you can't be there to do it yourself. And the foundation of any good estate plan starts with getting the right documents in place.

Foundation Documents

Everyone, regardless of net worth, requires a foundational legal triad. These documents act as your voice when you can't speak. Think of them as the essentials to keep in a Red Folder, which is a physical binder or secure digital folder where documents are stored and available to your trusted person. Let's look at what those documents are.

Last Will and Testament

The will is the cornerstone of traditional estate planning. At its most basic, it's a legal document that provides instructions to a probate court about how assets should be distributed after death. It names an executor, the person responsible for paying debts and distributing assets, and perhaps most importantly for parents, it's where guardians for minor children are appointed.

A common misconception is that having a will automatically keeps you out of court. It doesn't. In most cases, a will must be submitted to probate court to be validated and to authorize the transfer of assets that don't pass by beneficiary designation or trust. Probate is a public process, which means the contents of the will and the details of the estate become part of the public record.

The cost of probate should be understood before assuming a will alone is sufficient. Attorney fees, court expenses, and executor compensation can add up to several thousand dollars, depending on the size and complexity of the estate. In states like California and Florida, fee structures based on the gross value of the estate can push costs significantly higher into six figures. Formal probate commonly lasts anywhere from six months to two years, and during that time assets are generally frozen, which can create real hardship for surviving family members who depend on them. Even so, a will is still a foundational document and an essential starting point for anyone who hasn't yet put an estate plan in place.

Not all assets have to go through probate, and understanding which ones don't can make a meaningful difference in how smoothly things transfer. Retirement accounts, life insurance policies, and many financial accounts pass directly to named beneficiaries without court involvement. Joint ownership with survivorship rights can allow property to transfer automatically at death. Some states allow transfer on death deeds for real estate. And a properly funded revocable living trust can allow assets to pass privately without the court process entirely. With the right planning, many families can significantly reduce or even avoid most probate costs and delays.

Something I came across while researching this topic and through conversations with estate attorneys was just how exposed probate makes things. Once a will is submitted, anyone can look up who you owed, what you owned, and who received what. For families who value privacy, that's a meaningful reason to explore strategies that keep assets out of probate altogether. The broader estate plan should also include documents that appoint someone to manage finances and make medical decisions if you become unable to do so yourself. That way, your family can act without being forced into court proceedings at an already difficult time.

Durable Power of Attorney (Financial)

While a will handles death, a durable power of attorney handles life. This document designates someone, often called an agent or attorney-in-fact, to manage your financial affairs if you're unable to do so yourself. It's one of the most important documents in any estate plan and one of the most commonly overlooked.

There are two versions that are important to understand. A durable power of attorney is effective immediately and remains in effect if you become incapacitated. This is generally the preferred choice for spouses and trusted partners because it allows for seamless management without interruption. A springing power of attorney, by contrast, only becomes effective after a physician, or in some cases two physicians, declare you incompetent. While that might sound like a safer option, it can create serious delays during a medical crisis while family members scramble to get doctors to sign legal affidavits at an already chaotic time.

Without this document in place, even a long marriage offers less protection than most assume. Even if you've been married for 40 years, your spouse generally can't access an account solely in your name, such as an IRA or a specific checking account, without a power of attorney. Without it, your spouse may have to go to court to obtain conservatorship or guardianship, which can become an expensive and very public proceeding at exactly the moment when your family has enough to deal with.

Advance Healthcare Directive

An advance healthcare directive is often a combination of two distinct legal concepts that work together to protect your medical wishes if you're unable to speak for yourself.

The first is a living will. This is a written statement detailing your preferences regarding end-of-life care. It answers some of the hardest questions a family can face. Do you want a feeding tube? Do you want to be intubated? Do you want CPR in circumstances where recovery is unlikely? Having these answers documented in advance relieves your family of an enormous burden. Rather than guessing what you would have wanted, or disagreeing with each other at the worst possible moment, they can simply follow the instructions you've already provided.

The second is a healthcare proxy, sometimes called a medical power of attorney. This designates a specific person to make medical decisions that fall outside the scope of what the living will covers. Together, these two documents give your chosen person both a clear set of instructions and the authority to act when decisions need to be made quickly.

One piece that often gets overlooked is the HIPAA release. The Health Insurance Portability and Accountability Act was designed to protect patient privacy, but in an emergency it can become an unintended barrier. Without a signed HIPAA authorization, doctors are legally barred from discussing your condition with anyone, including your spouse and your children. Adding this document to your estate plan is a small step that can prevent a significant problem.

Beneficiary Designations

My estate attorney talked me through beneficiary designations years ago, and it was eye opening. I had always assumed the will trumped everything. It doesn't. Many of the largest assets we own, including 401(k)s, IRAs, life insurance policies, and annuities, don't pass through a will or trust. They pass through beneficiary designation forms held by the account custodian, such as Vanguard or Fidelity.

Because I'm a nerd, I read the majority opinion of *Kennedy v. Plan Administrator for DuPont Savings and Investment Plan* on Justia. The court ruled unanimously that a plan administrator must pay benefits to whoever is named on the beneficiary designation form on file, regardless of what a divorce decree or a will might say. That means a carefully drafted estate plan can be completely undermined by a single outdated form. For example, it's possible to draft a perfectly worded will leaving everything to a current spouse, and still have a 401(k) from twenty years ago pay out to an ex-spouse simply because the beneficiary form was never updated. Therefore, keeping designations current should be a high priority. You'll also want to understand exactly what you're choosing when you fill them out. One area that often causes confusion is how children are named, both on beneficiary designation forms and in a will.

When naming children as beneficiaries, there's often a choice between two options that sound similar but work very differently. Per capita, which means by the head, splits the money equally among surviving beneficiaries. If you leave money to three children and one dies before you, the remaining two split everything and the deceased child's family receives nothing. Per stirpes, which means by the roots, works differently. If a child predeceases you, that child's share passes down to their children. For many families that's the intended outcome, but per stirpes is rarely the default on beneficiary forms, so it has to be selected intentionally.

Inherited retirement accounts come with their own set of rules that can catch heirs off guard. For most non-spouse beneficiaries, inherited IRAs generally must be emptied within ten years under current law, and without a step-up in basis, heirs may owe taxes on the full amount of growth that occurred during the original owner's lifetime. Coordinating beneficiary designations on retirement accounts with the broader estate plan, and revisiting them after any major life change, is one of the most important steps in the entire process.

Planning for Digital Assets

In today's world, a significant portion of wealth is stored digitally. That can include cryptocurrency, brokerage accounts, retirement accounts, domain names, and revenue generating digital assets. For example, unlike previous generations who held physical stock certificates, that's now rare. For those who own stocks through index funds or other investments, that information lives digitally inside a brokerage account, such as one held at Fidelity or Vanguard. That applies to almost everything we own today, existing across platforms, apps, and devices that only we know how to access.

With that information spread across so many places, creating a secure inventory of digital assets and adding it to the Red Folder is critical. That inventory should include PINs for phones and laptops, financial account information including banks, brokerages, crypto wallets, social media, email accounts, and any subscription services that may carry value or recurring charges, along with instructions for accessing all of them.

Using a password manager, such as 1Password, Bitwarden, or LastPass, has become less of a convenience and more of a necessity.

Most of these tools offer an emergency kit or recovery document that can be printed and stored in a safe alongside other estate planning materials. Many major platforms also offer built-in legacy features that allow you to designate someone to access your account if it becomes inactive. These small steps can save your family an enormous amount of frustration at an already difficult time.

The legal side of digital assets is something most estate plans don't fully address, and that gap can cause real problems. Most states have laws governing who can access your digital life after you're gone, but without explicitly granting your executor or trustee access to digital assets in your legal documents, major technology and financial platforms may refuse to share information based on federal privacy laws. This is one of those areas where having the right language in your estate documents can make a significant difference.

DIY vs. the Professional

Online legal services have made it easier than ever to put together basic estate documents without hiring an attorney. For some situations, that may be perfectly adequate. According to estate planning attorneys and legal resources, if you're single, have no children, rent your home, and have relatively modest assets, a state approved form or a reputable online template may cover the basics.

For most situations though, going the DIY route can be a risky move. From what I've learned through my own estate planning process and conversations with my attorney, there are a few situations where working with a specialized estate planning attorney really matters.

Owning real estate is one of them, especially if it's in more than one state. That alone can trigger two separate probate processes, which is exactly the kind of headache a good plan is designed to avoid. Blended families are another one. Second marriages with children from prior relationships are apparently one of the most common sources of estate disputes, and a generic online template isn't going to sort that out.

When a beneficiary has special needs, careful planning becomes especially important. Leaving an inheritance directly to a child with a disability could jeopardize eligibility for government benefits such as SSI or Medicaid. To avoid that, you may need to have a special needs trust created so the inheritance can provide support without disrupting the benefits they rely on.

And if the estate might be large enough to trigger estate taxes, that's another area where professional guidance pays off. The federal exemption is $15 million per person in 2026 under the One Big Beautiful Bill Act, indexed for inflation going forward. State thresholds are often much lower though, which means more estates get caught than most people expect.

Finding the Right Attorney

When looking for an estate planning attorney, one credential to consider is the ACTEC designation, which stands for the American College of Trust and Estate Counsel. It's a sign of specialization in this area. One key question to ask any attorney you're considering is whether they help with funding the trust, meaning whether they help retitle assets into the trust after it's created. If the answer is no, you may want to look elsewhere. A trust that isn't properly funded doesn't work, and that's a detail too important to leave unfinished.

Asking how the attorney handles ongoing updates is an important part of the conversation. Life changes, and an estate plan that made sense five years ago may need adjustments today. An attorney who builds a relationship with you over time is more valuable than one who treats it as a one-time transaction. Getting referrals from your financial planner or CPA is a good starting point since they tend to work alongside estate attorneys regularly. They can point you toward a trusted professional you can build a relationship with.

One thing to be aware of is responsiveness. In the past I had an attorney who simply wasn't, and I wasn't okay with it. I secured a different attorney after that experience because responsiveness matters. If you request changes and it takes weeks to get a reply, updated documents, or a signing appointment, that's a signal you should pay attention to. A good estate attorney should be accessible and responsive, because requests for changes often arise from circumstances that require prompt attention.

Making Your Plan Work

Many estate plans fall short for a simple reason. They're created once and then ignored. Caring.com found that almost one in four people with an estate plan haven't touched their documents since creating them. Be sure to review your documents every 3 to 5 years, and sooner after a major change in your family, finances, wishes, or state of residence.

Communication is another weak spot. A Cambridge Trust report found that 52% of children don't know where their parents store their estate planning documents, and nearly half of named executors weren't aware they had been chosen. That's not a documentation problem. That's a conversation problem. Make sure your children know where the documents are stored and that your executor understands the responsibility you've asked them to take on.

The practical takeaway is straightforward. A plan only works if it's current, coordinated, and accessible. That means reviewing it after major life events, keeping your Red Folder updated, and making sure at least one trusted person knows where to find everything and how to step in if needed. Your goal is to have a system that actually functions when your family needs it most.

Speaking from experience after facing my own health scares, having the documents in place and knowing the beneficiaries are current brings a kind of peace of mind that's hard to put a price on. A relatively small amount of effort now can prevent years of stress for the people you care about most. Take the time to put the pieces in place, keep them updated, and make sure the plan can actually be carried out when it matters.

Chapter Sixteen Actions

Audit (Complete this week)

[ ] **Document Inventory.** Locate your existing will and trust documents. If they're older than five years or were created in a different state, it may be time to review and update them with an estate planning attorney.

[ ] **Beneficiary Sweep.** Log in to your 401(k), IRA, and life insurance accounts and verify that your primary and contingent beneficiaries are current. If the account offers per stirpes or per capita options, make sure your selection reflects your wishes.

[ ] **POA Check.** Confirm you have a financial power of attorney in place and note whether it's durable or springing.

[ ] **Healthcare Documents Check.** Confirm you have an advance healthcare directive, a healthcare proxy, and a signed HIPAA release. If any of these are missing, add them to the execution list below.

Execution (Complete this month)

[ ] **Select Your Agents.** Have conversations with and get permission from the people you want to serve as executor, trustee, and health proxy. Make sure they understand what the role involves and are willing to take it on.

[ ] **Agent Details.** Record full contact information and alternates for your executor, trustee, agent, and health proxy and add those to your Red Folder.

[ ] **Hire Counsel.** Schedule a consultation with an estate planning attorney. Look for the ACTEC designation as a sign of specialization in this area, and ask whether they help with the funding of the trust after documents are created.

[ ] **Special Situations.** If you have a disabled beneficiary, business interests, or property in more than one state, schedule specialty consultations with the appropriate advisors, such as a special needs attorney, a business succession advisor, or multi-state counsel.

Organization (Complete this month)

[ ] **Fund the Trust.** If you created a trust, retitle bank and investment accounts and record deeds for real estate. Your attorney may handle this, but verify it's been completed. A trust that isn't funded doesn't work.

[ ] **Funding Verification.** Create a short checklist of accounts retitled and deeds recorded. Date and initial each item when completed.

[ ] **Beneficiary Coordination.** Review retirement account distribution rules including the inherited IRA ten-year rule and spouse options, along with RMD and tax implications, before finalizing beneficiary designations. Confirm per stirpes or per capita designations reflect your intentions.

[ ] **Update Insurance.** If you retitled real estate into a trust, contact your homeowner's insurance agent to confirm whether the policy needs the trust named as an insured party.

[ ] **Digital Legacy.** Set up legacy contact features on major platforms and verify account recovery options. Store the password manager emergency kit or recovery file in your red folder.

[ ] **Safe Storage.** Decide where original documents will be kept, whether at your attorney's office or in a bolted fireproof safe at home, and note who has access.

[ ] **Confirm Documents.** Ensure all documents including the will, trust, directives, powers of attorney, and HIPAA release are complete, signed, and properly stored.

[ ] **Notification.** Tell at least one trusted person where the red folder is, who the named agents are, and how to access the documents if needed.

Ongoing Maintenance

[ ] **Regular Review.** Schedule estate plan reviews every three to five years and after any major life event including marriage, divorce, birth, death, significant asset changes, or a move to a different state.

[ ] **Update Beneficiaries.** Recheck beneficiary forms after any major life change and confirm per stirpes or per capita designations still reflect your intentions.

[ ] **Trust Funding Audit.** Do an annual check to make sure any new accounts or property acquired since the trust was created are properly titled to the trust.

When Additional Help Is Needed

[ ] **Special Needs Planning.** If you have a disabled beneficiary, a special needs trust may be necessary to protect their government benefits. An attorney who specializes in this area can help structure it correctly.

[ ] **Business Succession.** If you own a business, document your succession plans and coordinate with the appropriate advisors well before retirement.

[ ] **Multi-State Issues.** If you own property in more than one state or plan to relocate, consult with counsel on multi-state probate and domicile issues before they become a problem.

17
The Long Game

The initial enthusiasm that comes from beginning your financial transformation can be energizing. Those early stages often feel exciting because they're filled with the promise of change and the appeal of a future no longer tied to traditional work. But the journey ahead can be long. The middle stretches rarely feel as thrilling as the beginning. There will be periods when progress seems slow and goals feel far away. This is when consistency becomes a quiet test of commitment.

To stay on track, building a dependable rhythm matters more than motivation. Long-term financial progress functions much like a marathon where the early miles feel fast and hopeful but the real progress comes from the steady and deliberate pace held in the middle. The simple and repeated actions, the annual reviews, the contributions, and the small daily choices are what keep things moving forward even when motivation dips.

This chapter is a guide to the systems and behaviors that keep a plan alive over time. It's a practical look at the habits, tools, and mindset shifts that help you remain consistent long after the initial spark fades.

The Boring Middle

Investors often talk about the boring middle. This is the time period between setting up your accounts and actually retiring, and it can last for decades. During this time, it can look like not much is happening because you're simply contributing money while the market goes up and down and life looks largely the same.

Embracing this boredom is one of the most important things you can do. In investing, excitement usually equals risk while boredom tends to equal compounding. If your financial life feels boring, you're likely doing it right.

Think of it like driving up a very long hill on a road trip. At the beginning, your speedometer barely changes even though your foot is on the gas. You're moving forward but it doesn't feel dramatic or exciting. The scenery looks mostly the same and the top of the hill still feels far away. Your investment portfolio works the same way. In the early years, you're pressing the gas by saving and investing but your account balance doesn't surge upward right away. Compound interest is quietly building underneath the surface even if its power isn't visible yet. Then as you finally reach the crest of the hill your car naturally begins to accelerate with much less effort. In the same way, wealth starts to grow more rapidly once compounding has had enough time to build momentum.

The boring middle is simply the long climb up the hill. You're not stuck, you're not wasting time, and you're not failing. You're doing the steady work that makes the fast acceleration possible later.

Monthly Money Date

One of the most reliable ways to maintain momentum is to schedule regular financial check-ins. Just as someone pursuing fitness tracks workouts, tracking your finances turns abstract goals into visible progress.

The environment matters more than most expect. Doing this hunched over a messy kitchen counter is a recipe for dreading it. A quiet desk or a favorite coffee shop works better. Pairing the check-in with something enjoyable, a favorite coffee or a treat you don't usually have, helps train the brain to associate the activity with something positive rather than something stressful. And keep one rule front of mind. No judgment. If the numbers are bad, approach them like a scientist observing data rather than a judge delivering a sentence. Shame kills consistency. Curiosity keeps it alive.

Making the monthly check-in a non-negotiable appointment helps. Choosing a recurring day, like the first Sunday of each month, and putting it on the calendar removes the decision of whether to do it. During this thirty-minute session, your primary goal is to confirm trajectory.

A simple four-point agenda tends to work well. The first is a net worth check, tracking total assets minus liabilities. This single number cuts through the noise. Even if the market is down, seeing debt decrease reinforces forward movement. The second is a savings rate audit, calculating what percentage of gross income was saved that month. If you earned $10,000 and saved $2,000, your rate is 20%. Watching this number fluctuate keeps spending honest. The third is a leaks review, scanning credit card statements for recurring subscriptions that were forgotten or categories where spending crept up. The fourth is an allocation confirmation, verifying that automated transfers happened and that contributions went through. Automation is powerful but machines can fail, so take two minutes to confirm everything worked as intended.

Annual State of the Union

While the monthly check-in focuses on tactics, a separate annual review handles strategy. Picking a date that's easy to remember, like the day after your birthday, and blocking off two hours tends to work well.

The annual review covers a few key areas. The first is rebalancing. If stocks have grown too large relative to a target allocation, selling some of the winners and buying other assets like bonds restores the intended risk level. When selling assets to rebalance, the funds should remain inside the account and be reinvested into other holdings rather than withdrawn, since withdrawals may be subject to taxes and potential penalties.

Tax-loss harvesting is another area to review annually. Selling losing positions in a taxable account to offset gains may reduce your tax bill, but it should be done in coordination with a tax professional or financial planner to avoid unintended consequences.

An insurance audit should also be completed once a year. Life changes, and coverage often needs to change with it. Getting married, having a child, or buying a home may mean increasing your life insurance or homeowner's insurance coverage.

Finally, beneficiary designations on retirement accounts deserve a look. These should still match current wishes, especially after a divorce or a death in the family.

Red Folder Protocol

If something unexpected happened tomorrow, would a spouse or trusted person know how to access financial accounts? The Red Folder, introduced in the previous chapter, is the operating manual for your financial life. The protocol is to keep it current, accessible, and known to the right folks.

What goes inside is straightforward. A list of all financial institutions where accounts are held, along with login credentials or instructions on how to access them through a password manager. A contact list covering the CPA, financial advisor, estate attorney, and insurance agent. A letter of instruction explaining what you want done. Copies of the will, power of attorney, and any trust documents. You'll also need to tell your trusted contact where to find the folder.

Accountability Systems and Support

Motivation fades quickly when goals are carried alone. Pairing with a friend who shares similar financial goals, or a partner or spouse, transforms the journey from a private effort into shared support.

Sharing percentages and wins rather than dollar amounts keeps the conversation comfortable. Telling a peer you hit a 25% savings rate this month is a meaningful statement without requiring full financial disclosure.

A visual dashboard also helps. Numbers on a spreadsheet can feel dry, but a chart tells a story. Using a spreadsheet or financial tracking app to turn progress into a line graph makes the upward trend visible over time in a way that raw numbers don't.

And as covered earlier, a fee-only Certified Financial Planner can provide structure when personal discipline wanes. They serve as a paid accountability partner working on behalf of your future self.

Celebrating the Micro-Wins

Long-term goals lose their emotional pull when the finish line is more than a decade away. Creating micro-wins along the way maintains momentum. A micro-win might be paying off a credit card, reaching the first $100,000 invested, or negotiating a lower insurance rate. These moments deserve acknowledgment.

When a major milestone is reached, the 1% rule should be considered. Taking one percent of the gain and spending it guilt free keeps celebration proportionate. If $10,000 of debt is paid off, $100 toward a dinner, paid in cash, is a meaningful acknowledgment. Documenting the win, writing down the date and what was accomplished, creates a record that years later becomes proof of how far things have come.

Recovering from Setbacks

Even the most disciplined plans encounter setbacks. A job loss, a market crash, or a health issue will eventually interrupt momentum. The measure of success is how quickly recovery happens.

When something goes wrong, three steps tend to matter most. The first is to cut all discretionary spending immediately to limit damage. The second is acceptance. A low savings year is okay. It doesn't mean the plan failed. It just means life happened. Acknowledging it removes the shame that could otherwise trigger you to abandon the plan entirely. The third is restarting small. When ready to rebuild, starting with a 5% saving rate, rather than trying to immediately make up for lost time, re-establishes the habit first. The act of saving matters more than the amount.

An example helps illustrate this. Let's say you are three years into your plan when your home's air conditioning unit fails in July. The replacement costs roughly $6,000, equal to your entire planned Roth IRA contribution for the year. You may feel as though you've lost a year of progress. Still, you don't try to make up the full $6,000 by cutting everything else to the bone. You cancel an upcoming weekend trip to offset some of the cost, accept that your savings rate will drop from 25% to 10% for the year, and simply resume your automated monthly transfer of $500 the following month. By December, the HVAC expense is a memory. The habit is still intact.

Staying Consistent

The structure being built here is a financial home. Every month it holds, another brick gets added. It doesn't come together all at once. Most of the time it doesn't even feel like much is happening. There will be stretches where progress feels slow or where something in life pulls attention elsewhere. Those are the moments this system is built for. When motivation dips, the structure keeps things moving. When the next step isn't clear, it gives something simple and concrete to follow.

Over time, these routines start working in the background. The monthly check-ins keep things visible. The annual review keeps the direction right. The Red Folder makes sure the people who matter aren't left guessing. Accountability keeps things honest. And when something goes wrong, the reset approach gets things back on track without overreacting.

Stick with this long enough and the work starts to change. What used to take real effort starts to feel routine. You stop reacting to every market wobble or news headline because you've watched enough of them come and go. The plan stops being something you have to manage and starts running quietly in the background. That's the whole point. Not a flawless plan, but a system that keeps working through whatever life throws at you.

Chapter Seventeen Actions

Setup (Complete today)

[ ] **Schedule Your Money Date.** Open your calendar and set a recurring event for the first Sunday of the month or your preferred date.

[ ] **Define Your Monthly Agenda.** Add the four-point checklist, net worth, savings rate, leaks review, and allocation confirmation, into the description of your Money Date calendar event.

[ ] **Define Your Annual Agenda.** Add your State of the Union items (rebalancing, tax-loss harvesting with a professional, insurance audit, and beneficiary check) into the description of your annual event.

[ ] **Schedule the State of the Union.** Set a recurring annual event, such as the day after your birthday, for the deep-dive strategy session.

[ ] **Locate Your Documents.** Ensure your retirement vision and IPS are saved in the same folder for easy review. When motivation dips or a market headline creates the urge to act, pull them out and read them before making any decisions.

[ ] **Automate Savings.** Confirm or set up automatic transfers so money moves into your retirement and savings accounts within 24 hours of payday.

Legacy (Complete this week)

[ ] **Red Folder.** Get a physical binder or create a secure digital folder.

[ ] **Write the Letter.** Draft a simple letter of instruction for your spouse or heirs explaining where the money is and who to call.

[ ] **Populate the Folder.** Add your account list and access instructions, key contacts (CPA, financial advisor, estate attorney, and insurance agent), your letter of instruction, and copies or locations of your will, power of attorney, and trust documents.

[ ] **Tell One Trusted Person.** Let a trusted contact know the folder exists and where to find it.

Support (Complete this year)

[ ] **Find a Partner.** Identify one person you can talk to about money openly. Schedule a coffee date to discuss goals.

[ ] **Set Up the Dashboard.** Create a simple spreadsheet or download a tracking app that allows you to see your net worth as a visual chart.

[ ] **Set Accountability Rhythm.** Decide how often you'll check in with your partner, monthly or quarterly, and put those meetings on the calendar.

[ ] **Link Your Reset Protocol.** Save a one-page summary of your reset steps with your IPS or in your Red Folder so you know exactly what to do after a setback.

18
The Path Forward

You've come a long way to get here. You've taken a hard look at where you stand today, built a vision of your ideal retirement and know the strategies to realize it, as well as projected your readiness to see if you'll get where you want to go. Now we need to switch gears and look at what it takes to actually get you there. That's where execution begins. From here, progress depends on whether your daily decisions consistently support the future you've defined.

In personal finance, that's often where things begin to break down. The strategy may be sound and the path clear, but turning decisions into consistent action is often harder than expected. The same pattern appears anywhere long-term plans depend on sustained follow-through.

Over the years, I've worked with many organizations that invested significant resources into strategy development. The strategy was clearly defined, the milestones were established, and implementation plans were handed over to the organization for follow-through. From there, I moved on to the next strategic project as planned. Later, I often learned that the strategy defined in the prior project had never been fully implemented, not because it was flawed, but because implementation managers didn't ensure sustained focus.

This is a common issue, and it's backed by research. *Harvard Business Review* reported that companies realize only about 63% of the financial value their strategies promise, while other studies have cited failure rates of up to 90% for strategic initiatives in general. And the data points to follow-through as the primary driver. Plans are created, but not operationalized. Goals are set, but not tracked. Decisions are made, but not reinforced. While personal finance doesn't produce a single failure rate in the same way, a similar underlying pattern is well documented. Research consistently shows that many of us intend to save more, invest consistently, and follow long-term plans, yet often fail to follow through unless we have structure. So if your plan is going to work, you'll want to take on one additional role, one that puts structure around your strategy and makes sure it gets carried out.

In a company, that role often belongs to a project manager. They don't usually create the strategy. They put structure around it. They break it into steps, set deadlines, keep progress moving, and adjust when something slips. For your personal finances and retirement plan, that's a role you'll play. You're responsible for making sure the plan actually gets carried out, not just thought about. That means setting the timeline, tracking progress, and making adjustments when things don't go as expected. It also means following through on the details that are easy to ignore, like confirming savings are automated, reviewing accounts regularly, and making sure the decisions you've already made are actually put into action, whether by you or by someone acting on your behalf, such as your planner.

When I started applying the same project management discipline to my own finances, something clicked. I stopped treating my retirement plan like a document I'd revisit someday and started treating it like an active project with deadlines, milestones, and a schedule. The difference wasn't the strategy. The strategy was already there. The difference was the structure around it. And yes, I know it sounds like a stuffy approach that requires a project manager certification. It doesn't. The structure is straightforward. It comes down to three primary steps: set aside time, check progress, and consistently follow through. That's how you turn your plan from an idea into something that actually moves your financial life forward.

When Execution Breaks Down

We touched on this earlier, but it's important to revisit here because execution often falters in predictable ways driven by our behavior. The *present bias* we covered in Chapter 4 is one of the most persistent forces. As a reminder, it's simply a term for something we all experience, the tendency to prioritize what feels immediate over what matters in the long term. Even with a clear plan in place, short-term decisions can gradually pull you away from your long-term goals. The plan doesn't disappear. It just gets pushed aside, one small decision at a time.

I remember a stretch where I kept telling myself I'd increase my savings rate after the holidays. Then after the vacation. Then after a home repair. So even though the long-term plan was clear, the immediate always had a reason to come first. That's present bias doing exactly what it does. It doesn't feel like a choice to deprioritize the future. It feels like a reasonable response to what's right in front of you, but it's unreasonable when you look at it through a long-term lens.

Inertia is another major factor and it's often misunderstood. In simple terms, inertia means we tend to keep doing what we're already doing. If nothing has been set in motion, it's easy to do nothing at all. In finances, that can be a powerful force. If savings aren't automated, they usually don't increase. If accounts aren't reviewed, they often stay untouched. This is why some organizations now automatically enroll employees in retirement plans. Once the right action is already in motion, you're far more likely to stick with it.

Once I automated my savings, I stopped having to decide whether to save. The money moved before I ever saw it. What felt like discipline before became an automatic. That's the power of getting the right things in motion. You stop fighting yourself and the system just runs.

But inertia is only part of the problem. Even when you intend to act, this process still asks you to make a steady stream of decisions over time, and that creates a different kind of friction called decision fatigue. It builds quietly as choices accumulate. When enough piles up, the natural response is to delay or avoid. Reviews get postponed, adjustments get pushed out, and what starts as a small delay becomes a pattern. The plan doesn't fail all at once. It weakens gradually.

That becomes even harder when progress is difficult to see. In personal finance, results are often slow and hard to notice in the short term. Without visible feedback, it becomes harder to stay engaged. You don't feel the impact of consistent saving month to month, so it's easy to question whether the system is working at all.

Overconfidence adds another layer. Research shows that as we age, financial confidence tends to remain steady or even increase while actual decision-making ability declines. That gap can lead to mistakes, particularly when managing complexity. The issue is a natural mismatch between what we think we can handle and what we actually can.

Taken together, these forces create a consistent pattern. Execution breaks down not because the plan is unclear, but because it depends too heavily on ongoing attention, effort, and willpower. Gradually, the gap between intention and action widens.

How To Keep Execution on Track

These same forces show up in personal finance just as clearly as they do in organizations, which means you need a structure that works with human behavior instead of against it. Start by reducing friction. The fewer decisions you have to make in real time, the more consistent you'll be. For example, automating savings and simplifying account structures reduce the effort required to stay on track. When the right actions happen by default, progress continues without requiring constant attention. If saving requires a decision every month, it won't happen consistently. If it happens automatically, it will.

Pre-commitment is one of the most effective tools. Decisions made in advance are far more likely to be carried out. When you set your savings rate, schedule savings increases, and commit to recurring reviews, you remove the need to revisit those decisions later when distractions are higher. You're not relying on future discipline. You're relying on structure.

Visibility matters as well. When progress is tracked, it becomes real. Monitoring your net worth or savings rate creates feedback that reinforces behavior and gives you a clear signal that your actions are producing results. Without that feedback, even a well-functioning system can feel disconnected.

Cadence is what keeps everything aligned over time. You don't need constant attention, but you do need consistent attention. A monthly check-in, an annual review, and periodic adjustments are enough to keep your plan functioning. Execution doesn't rely on intensity alone. It depends on a consistent rhythm. It also helps to recognize what execution should feel like. In many cases, it will feel uneventful. Fewer decisions, fewer surprises, and less noise are signs that the system is working. Progress at this stage is steady, not dramatic.

With that in mind, the below launch protocol is designed to help you put these ideas into practice. Execution stays on track when the right actions are easier to repeat, easier to monitor, and easier to maintain over time. That kind of structure is built by putting the right routines in place early and reinforcing them consistently.

Launch Protocol

This 90-day structure isn't a new set of tasks. It's a way to sequence and reinforce the actions you've already defined throughout this book so the plan begins to function in real life, not just on paper. Think of it as your first test of whether your intentions can hold up as daily behavior.

The first 30 days are about getting the foundation right. The goal is to confirm that the core pieces are actually in motion, savings automated, vision finalized, and the first monthly review on the calendar. Small adjustments to expenses or income made early tend to compound in meaningful ways later.

Days 31 to 60 are about strengthening what's already running. The basics should feel more natural by this point. The work becomes about refining, reviewing, and making sure the investment approach and cash reserves are aligned with the plan.

Days 61 to 90 are where momentum builds. A first quarterly review gives a real read on progress. By the end of this phase, the plan should feel less like something you're managing and more like something that's running on its own.

By now, your plan shouldn't feel theoretical. It should feel operational, with structure, visibility, and momentum in place. From there, progress becomes a matter of consistency.

Into Execution

From here, your future will be shaped less by what you know and more by what you keep doing.

That's what makes this stage matter. A good intention only becomes a different life through concrete steps, like increasing your savings rate on schedule, keeping reviews on the calendar, and following the guardrails you've already set. Not through dramatic effort, and not by always getting everything right, but through actions that are steady enough to matter and repeated enough to change something.

Change rarely happens in a single moment. It happens when what you decide starts showing up consistently in how you live. Little by little, what once felt uncertain starts to feel familiar. The future you couldn't quite picture starts to take shape in your daily life. And over time, it shifts more than your finances. It changes how you relate to the future itself. Money stops being something that happens to you and starts being something you direct.

I've felt this shift in my own life, and it didn't arrive with fanfare. It shows up as fewer sleepless nights when the market dips. More confidence in the date you've chosen to step away from work. And a growing sense that the retirement you've envisioned and planned for isn't something distant anymore. It's something you're actively building. That's what tells you your work is doing its job.

And that's where this leads. A retirement on your own timeline, lived on your own terms, and built deliberately.

"Someone's sitting in the shade today because someone planted a tree a long time ago."

WARREN BUFFETT

Appendix A

Your Personal Investment Policy Statement (IPS)

This document is a commitment to myself. It defines how I will manage my portfolio and provides a steady guide when markets are volatile or emotions are running high. Before making any investment change, I will review this policy and confirm that the decision supports my long-term strategy.

1. Purpose and Goal

Mission: ____

Time Horizon: ________________

Primary Goal:
[ ] Long-term growth
[ ] Retirement income
[ ] Capital preservation
[ ] Legacy
[ ] Other: ______________________

Spending Rule: ____________________________________

2. Target Asset Allocation

This is the long-term mix I believe I can maintain even during major market declines.

Asset Class	Target	Role
U.S. / Global Equities	____%	Long term growth
Bonds	____%	Stability and income
Cash	____%	Liquidity / Reserve
Inflation Hedges such as TIPS or REITs	____%	Inflation protection

I will rebalance if a major asset class differs from target by more than ____ percentage points.

3. Investment Selection Rules

I will build this portfolio using the following rules:

Low cost: I will primarily use diversified index funds or ETFs and generally avoid funds with expense ratios above ____%.

Diversification: I will maintain exposure across major asset classes and, within equities, across both U.S. and international markets.

Simplicity: If I cannot explain what an investment does in one sentence, I will not own it.

Quality: For fixed income and cash reserves, I will favor high quality, liquid holdings.

4. Contributions, Withdrawals, and Taxes

I will contribute $_________ per month or _______% of income.

I will direct new contributions first to underweight asset classes.

When I need withdrawals, I will generally take them from cash, bond reserves, or overweight asset classes first.

I will minimize capital gains taxes by using contributions, dividends, and interest for rebalancing before selling appreciated holdings.

When taxable sales are necessary, I will consider tax impact and, where practical, sell the highest cost basis lots first.

I will avoid short-term capital gains unless there is a compelling reason.

5. Rebalancing and Maintenance

I will not trade based on headlines, forecasts, or market narratives.

Review date: __________________________

Rebalancing method: I will first use contributions and cash flows to rebalance. I will sell holdings only if needed after considering taxes and transaction costs.

Sell rule: When raising cash, I will generally sell from overweight asset classes first.

6. Behavioral Guardrails

I will not check my portfolio daily.

I recognize that market declines are a normal part of investing.

I will not change my strategy during a market panic.

I will only change this IPS after a meaningful life event, goal change, or planned review.

If I am losing sleep over market volatility, I will consider a more conservative allocation only after careful review, not in the middle of a decline.

7. Review and Accountability

I will review this IPS at least annually and after any major life event. Major changes may be considered after retirement, major income change, inheritance, health change, change in spending needs, or family or estate changes.

I will not change this plan in response to market headlines, short-term performance, or fear. Any changes to this IPS will be made only after careful review and because my goals, time horizon, or financial circumstances have meaningfully changed.

Appendix B

Recommended Reading and Tools

Here's a curated list of trusted, motivational, and tactical resources to support your journey toward retirement.

Books: Classics & Foundation

THE TOTAL MONEY MAKEOVER by Dave Ramsey — The ultimate baseline. A step-by-step plan to take control of your finances, eliminate debt, and build wealth through discipline and budgeting.

RICH DAD POOR DAD by Robert T. Kiyosaki — The book that changed the definition of an "asset" for millions. Essential reading for understanding why you must build a portfolio that puts money *in* your pocket, rather than taking it out.

THE MILLIONAIRE NEXT DOOR by Thomas J. Stanley and William D. Danko — The original data-backed study on how real millionaires behave. It shatters the myth that high income equals high wealth.

YOUR MONEY OR YOUR LIFE by Vicki Robin and Joe Dominguez — A classic guide to transforming your relationship with money.

THE SIMPLE PATH TO WEALTH by JL Collins — A straightforward, no-nonsense guide to investing and building long-term wealth using index funds. If you read only one investing book, make it this one.

I WILL TEACH YOU TO BE RICH by Ramit Sethi — A hands-on guide to automating your money, eliminating debt, and designing a "rich life" (which includes guilt-free spending on what you love).

Books: Mindset & Psychology

THE PSYCHOLOGY OF MONEY by Morgan Housel — A masterclass in how our emotions, ego, and pride influence our financial decisions. It teaches you how to *behave* with money, which is often more important than the math.

DIE WITH ZERO by Bill Perkins — A provocative read that encourages you to focus on life experiences and thoughtful spending, rather than just mindlessly accumulating until the end.

ATOMIC HABITS by James Clear — It teaches you how to build the small habits that make saving and investing automatic rather than a chore.

THE 4-HOUR WORKWEEK by Timothy Ferriss — While often seen as a business book, this is the bible of lifestyle design and mini-retirements.

Books: Strategy & Specific Audiences

THE AUTOMATIC MILLIONAIRE by David Bach — The definitive book on the Pay Yourself First principle. A quick read that reinforces the importance of automating your savings so you don't have to rely on willpower.

THE MONEY BOOK FOR THE YOUNG, FABULOUS & BROKE by Suze Orman — Aimed at younger adults but packed with timeless financial advice on credit, saving, investing, and student loans.

WOMEN & MONEY by Suze Orman — A guide to empowering women to take control of their finances, build confidence, and plan for the future.

THE ULTIMATE RETIREMENT GUIDE FOR 50+ by Suze Orman — Practical advice for those nearing retirement, including planning for healthcare, managing income streams, and navigating changing economic conditions.

QUIT LIKE A MILLIONAIRE by Kristy Shen and Bryce Leung — Perfect for those interested in alternate paths. It explores using geographic arbitrage to retire early.

Blogs & Websites

Mr. Money Mustache (mrmoneymustache.com) — The grandfather of the modern FIRE movement. Focuses on early retirement through stoicism, bike-riding, frugal living, and intentional spending.

The Mad Fientist (madfientist.com) — Excellent for the optimization phase. Features advanced strategies on tax optimization, Roth conversion ladders, and travel hacking.

Early Retirement Now (earlyretirementnow.com) — The deepest dive into the math of withdrawal rates on the internet. Essential reading for designing your retirement paycheck.

Our Next Life (ournextlife.com) — Thoughtful reflections and actionable advice on the psychological transition into post-retirement living.

Financial Samurai (financialsamurai.com) — A contrarian and aggressive look at wealth building, often focused on higher-income earners, real estate, and passive income streams.

Podcasts

ChooseFI — The encyclopedia of the financial independence movement. Interviews and crowdsourced insights on everything from geo-arbitrage to starting side hustles.

The Stacking Benjamins Show — A fun, magazine-style show that makes learning about personal finance, investing, and retirement headlines approachable and light-hearted.

Afford Anything — Hosted by Paula Pant with the tagline "You can afford anything, but not everything." Deeply explores the tradeoffs of smart money decisions.

The Retirement Answer Man — Hosted by Roger Whitney. This is specifically for those over 50. He focuses less on “how to get rich” and more on “how to rock retirement” without running out of money.

YouTube Channels

The Money Guy Show — Hosted by professional financial planners, they offer a very grounded, step-by-step "Financial Order of Operations" that is safe and effective.

Two Cents (PBS) — Great for quick, digestible explanations of complex financial terms and concepts.

Tools & Calculators

NewRetirement (Boldin) — A comprehensive planning tool that allows you to model tax brackets, Roth conversions, and healthcare costs over time.

FIRECalc / cFIREsim — Free stress test calculators. They run your numbers against every period in stock market history to see if your plan would have survived the Great Depression, the 1970s inflation, or the dot-com crash.

Empower (formerly Personal Capital) — Excellent for net-worth tracking and seeing all your investment accounts in one dashboard.

Index

www.ingramcontent.com/pod-product-compliance
Lightning Source LLC
LaVergne TN
LVHW022156200926
848481LV00006B/1758
* 9 7 9 8 9 9 4 4 2 3 5 1 6 *